THE
ANNE BOLEYN
BIBLE

THE
ANNE BOLEYN
BIBLE

MICKEY MAYHEW

PEN & SWORD
HISTORY

AN IMPRINT OF PEN & SWORD BOOKS LTD.
YORKSHIRE - PHILADELPHIA

First published in Great Britain in 2023 by
PEN AND SWORD HISTORY
An imprint of
Pen & Sword Books Ltd
Yorkshire – Philadelphia

ISBN 978 1 39908 372 0

A CIP catalogue record for this book is available from the British Library.

Typeset in Times New Roman 11.5/14 by
SJmagic DESIGN SERVICES, India.
Printed and bound in the UK by CPI Group (UK) Ltd.

Pen & Sword Books Limited incorporates the imprints of Atlas, Archaeology,
Aviation, Discovery, Family History, Fiction, History, Maritime, Military, Military
Classics, Politics, Select, Transport, True Crime, Air World, Frontline Publishing,
Leo Cooper, Remember When, Seaforth Publishing, The Praetorian Press,
Wharncliffe Local History, Wharncliffe Transport, Wharncliffe True Crime and
White Owl.

For a complete list of Pen & Sword titles please contact
PEN & SWORD BOOKS LIMITED
George House, Units 12 & 13, Beevor Street, Off Pontefract Road,
Barnsley, South Yorkshire, S71 1HN, England
E-mail: enquiries@pen-and-sword.co.uk
Website: www.pen-and-sword.co.uk

or

PEN AND SWORD BOOKS
1950 Lawrence Rd, Havertown, PA 19083, USA
E-mail: uspen-and-sword@casematepublishers.com
Website: www.penandswordbooks.com

Contents

Acknowledgements vi

Introduction.. viii

1   The ancestry of Anne Boleyn 1

2   From Blickling Hall to Hever Castle 9

3   A Norfolk girl in Belgium 12

4   Mary, or 'The Other Boleyn Girl' 27

5   Catching the eye of a king 31

6   The most important man in her life 37

7   Courtship, consummation, and the Papal Brexit 45

8   Patriarchal promises – The birth of Elizabeth Tudor 63

9   Miscarriages, misery and Mark Smeaton 76

10 The short journey to the scaffold 113

11 Erasing Anne 135

12 A daughter's silent pride – Anne Boleyn through the lens of
Elizabeth I 139

13 Anne Boleyn Bibles 142

14 Anne Boleyn at the movies, on TV, in song and on the stage 152

15 The Tudors 163

16 Looking to the future: '*SIX*' & Jodie Turner-Smith 167

17 Merchandising, marketing and schooling – Anne Boleyn and the
essence of English nostalgia 172

18 Fan Boleyn 178

19 Timeline, from 1501 (or thereabouts) to 2023 182

Bibliography 185

Filmography 192

Index 194

Acknowledgements

A book of this nature relies on the goodwill of a sizeable cast of individuals. I am eternally grateful to those who gave both their time and also their expertise, and especially to those who were keen to discover something new about Anne Boleyn (and her executioner) and who were not afraid to embrace new facts. I am particularly indebted to the staff at the British Library and also the libraries of several of my old alma maters, including the London School of Economics and London South Bank University (especially Dr Jenny Owen), and also Birkbeck. Besides that, those who helped me sift the usual and – it has to be said – by now overworked primary sources also deserve my deepest thanks.

For that oh-so indiscreet conversation with an Italian colleague at one of the above-mentioned bastions of learning, that ran roughly along the lines of '...well, of course you know we have the other thing as well...' this followed by a theatrical finger sliding across the throat in mimicry of a beheading, well, for that I am eternally grateful. To Catherine Tobin and Sue Parry, for advice on how Anne's story is taught in schools, I also extend my thanks. I applaud Caroline Angus, for her advice regarding Anne's involvement with Cromwell's Poor Law. Also, Sylvia Barbara Soberton, for advice on Anne's ladies-in-waiting; Alison Weir, for that hearty exchange on the matter of Elizabeth I's locket; Antonia Fraser; Margaret George; Retha Warnicke; Phillipa Vincent-Connolly (whose 'Timeless Falcon' Boleyn novels are well worth a look); for solidarity amongst disabled historians; the Prison de la Motte Castrale in St Omer; St Omer Cathedral; the various staff and guides at Blickling Hall; Father Victor and Father Danny, for showing me just what Jesus would really have meant to a 16th century Christian woman; and finally, the late, great Eric Ives. Meanwhile, to those who – albeit rather reluctantly – placed me more directly on the trail of the so-called Swordsman of Calais (the real one, not 'Jean Rombaud'), I am eternally indebted, as I am to the custodians of what remains of his so-called 'Sword of Calais'.

Acknowledgements

Finally, this book is dedicated to my mother, Rosemary Eileen Mayhew, for all her years of tireless support and devotion.

This book is crafted for the authentic Anne Boleyn fan. Whilst it is called 'The Anne Boleyn Bible', I am well aware I have not included every single book, nor indeed every single item of tat ever produced and bearing Anne's unmistakeable image. To have done so would have required almost a doubling of the page count. However, I believe I have made a very judicious choice of what was to be included, and also what I decided to leave out.

Introduction

Today there is a fast-growing Anne Boleyn cult. She appeals both to adolescents and to ageing romantics. Her story has a Wagnerian intensity of love, death and betrayal, shot through with a very un-Wagnerian sense of reckless fun, of daring sexiness. But there is a deeper reason for the growing obsession with her. The flowers (left anonymously on her grave each year on the anniversary of her death) acknowledge an unease; we love her story but feel guilty toward her.

Brenton, 2010, paragraph 2 of 14

There are few English queens – indeed, few women in history – whose biographies have been as contested as that of Anne Boleyn. Even to this day, almost nothing about Anne Boleyn is agreed upon by either historians or novelists, from facts such as the year of her birth (1501 or 1507/8), to more vexed questions about how to interpret her reign and her downfall.

Russo, 2020, p 1

Anne Boleyn, second wife of Henry VIII, King of England, was executed on the morning of 19 May 1536 on charges of treason and adultery, the latter charge also encompassing an allegation of incest. Said charges were almost certainly fabricated – for various reasons – although several prominent historians have raised their heads above the parapets and declared that they believe there was perhaps a kernel of truth to them; G. W. Bernard, for one, who made a case for Anne's guilt in his controversial book *Anne Boleyn – Fatal Attractions* (2011). However, the merest suggestion of any wrongdoing on Anne's part does, as ever, elicit a howl of protest from her many fans; it is not a topic undertaken by the thin-skinned, certainly. The various primary sources – basically all of the usual suspects, including the Letters and Papers of the Reign of Henry VIII, along with the Spanish Chronicle, etc – have been all but wrung dry in the frenetic search for fresh information. Verbal histories have, however, been for the most part ignored; basically, if it wasn't written down then it didn't happen. This has left the modern Tudor field of literary endeavors basically one big recycling machine. For this book, the approach was going to be a little different, but it would, in one sense, follow a pattern set by previous historians.

Namely, since Anne's execution, her story has become a palimpsest, constantly rewritten and reworked for subsequent generations, until all trace of the real woman, the fiery religious reformer, is lost, replaced by a six-fingered sex kitten with a sharpish tongue and a petulant pout. This work will, for one thing, attempt to anchor the radical religiosity of Anne Boleyn, a stance some Tudor historians claim has been amply covered, whilst others will declare quite suddenly that it hasn't been covered in any great detail after all. And then the recycling begins. Still, Anne remains a striking figure. Every other year, it seems, we are treated to another take on her life, on TV, on the big screen, or even onstage. Her life and 'crimes' appeal to a modern audience and also to those fascinated by the salacious, scandalous nature of the charges laid against her, even as older, 'wiser' heads frown at such fripperies; there is an enchantment for the forbidden, after all. David Starkey comments on that fascination with Anne Boleyn, saying that she 'had the gift of arousing strong feelings. People were never neutral: they either loved her or loathed her.' (Starkey, 2004, p257.) Nothing has changed on that score, for certain. Even when she was alive, people could barely agree on the spelling of her surname, let alone the more pertinent personal details; 'Boleyn' has been alternatively spelt in Tudor times as 'Bullen', 'Boleyne', 'Boullant', 'Boullan' and 'Bollegne', to name just a few.

Charges of alleged adultery aside, Anne was certainly party to the breakdown of Henry VIII's marriage to the devoutly Catholic Catherine of Aragon. In the ruthlessly patriarchal society of the Tudors, Catherine's failure to beget a male heir led Henry VIII to annul their marriage and then to seek a second wife, namely Catherine's lady-in-waiting, Anne Boleyn. This led to England's eventual break with Rome, when the Pope refused to grant Henry a divorce. Dovetailing neatly with this was the fact that Anne was an active promoter of reform against the abuses of the Catholic Church. In fact, she was an integral part of that initial Reformation. It was Anne who alerted Henry VIII to various banned texts that promoted the rule of a king within his own realm, without any jurisdiction from foreign powers, aka the Pope. Because the Reformation helped ease forth Henry VIII's break with Rome, the image of Anne as a reformer has become indelibly linked in some quarters with the resultant schism, and therefore with notions of 'Englishness', and with English independence from foreign rule. It was Brexit before Brexit, if you like.

This somewhat nationalistic mantle is further magnified by their daughter, Elizabeth I, who perfected the work set about by her mother when it came to the establishment of the new Protestant regime. When required, Elizabeth Tudor could clamp down on Catholics with as much brutality as her predecessor and half-sister 'Bloody Mary' Tudor had with Protestants. This further cements the idea that Anne Boleyn is an attractive figure because she, alongside the Tudor genre as a whole, represents a very specific, almost a nostalgic form of 'Englishness'. But although the topic might be seen as almost intrinsically 'English', she was actually 'fashioned' at the French court in her teenage years, and it was that very foreign allure which many historians have credited with igniting the initial interest of Henry VIII. As Alison Weir has remarked, Anne Boleyn is many things to many people, English to some and quite French to others. Nowadays, she doesn't even have to be white. Very soon, one imagines, she'll no longer be binary either.

Films, TV, historical works and popular fiction regarding Anne Boleyn have proliferated in recent years, due perhaps in no small part to the success of Showtime's *The Tudors* series (2007-2010), in which Natalie Dormer's fiery portrayal of Anne stole the show for the first two seasons and cemented an idea of the tempestuous Tudor queen for an entire generation. Tourists from across the world flock to see the site of Anne's imprisonment and execution at the Tower of London, or to pay homage at her childhood home of Hever Castle. Replica costumes of varying quality are sold online, and, among other weird and wonderful Boleyn paraphernalia available, the internet auction site eBay sells, among other things, rings that 'allegedly have been infused with the spiritual essence of Anne Boleyn.' (Weir, 2009, p335.)

In 2014 a mass media campaign was employed by London Underground which depicted the famous National Portrait Gallery image of Anne as an enticement to visit the Tower of London. Anne schemes in Phillipa Gregory's bestselling novel *The Other Boleyn Girl* (2001); she is the 'calculating concubine' in the Booker Prize winning *Wolf Hall* (2009), which later transferred to the stages of the West End and then to the small screen, woven into the sequel *Bring Up the Bodies* (2012). She was also the star of her own stage show, namely the Howard Brenton play *Anne Boleyn*, which was performed at the Globe Theatre several years ago. In 2021, Jodie Turner-Smith took the appeal to a whole new level when she became the first black actress to play the tempestuous Tudor queen. We can never, it seems, have enough Anne Boleyn.

1

The ancestry of Anne Boleyn

A hare darts across the Blicking Road and then enters the field over on the other side. Heedless of the admittedly rather negligible traffic, a little girl sets off in pursuit, despite the admonishments of her parents, who watch from the tongue of sandy gravel leading up to Blickling Hall, birthplace of Anne Boleyn. The hare, so the little girl will tell them, is – according to the author Norah Lofts, at least – actually Anne herself, reincarnated and free at last from the grasp of her ruthless husband, Henry VIII. It is, therefore, with something like a wail of disappointment that the child watches the hare quickly vanish into the long grass between a pair of rather bemused cows. Crestfallen, the little girl turns and waits patiently for her mother to escort her back across the road. Such incidents speak of the rather modest but nevertheless intrinsic hold that Anne has on this particular part of Norfolk. You have to look a little to find her, but when you do, you discover that Anne Boleyn runs through the county like water. For instance, 'In 1909, 1925 and 1938, Blickling Hall played host to a masque, written by Walter Nugent Monck, celebrating the life of Anne Boleyn and attended by the dowager Queen Mary, who was a patron of the pageant at Blickling.' (Grueninger & Morris, 2015, p24.) And as Tracy Borman explains, 'The first known reference to the Boleyns is found in the deed for a small plot of land close to Norwich in 1188.' (Borman, 2023, p5.)

As far back as 1844, when Selina Bunbury wrote *The Star of the Court or the Maid of Honour and Queen of England, Anne Boleyn*, Blickling Hall was considered the place of Anne's birth: 'More than three centuries ago the giant trees that still shadow the bright greensward of Blickling Park might have spread the broad shade of their leafy arms over the young and joyous head of the lovely daughter of that house, the fair and fascinating Anne Boleyn.' (Bunbury, 1844, p4.) And it is a bright and beautiful place, 'Circled by a wilderness of woodland sprinkled with myriad flowers such as bluebells, meadowsweet, loosestrife and marsh orchids, and swept by the eastern winds.' (Weir, 2011, p5.)

As to that rather reluctant hare, well, this author witnessed that particular 'incident' whilst attending the Anne Boleyn Festival in 2012; modest maybe, but Blicking Hall can certainly still boast the connection when it wants to. Even the rather more curious claim – namely that Anne's ghost returns every 19 May (the day of her execution), holding her severed head in her lap – has crowds gathered at the gates on that particular evening, hoping to catch a glimpse of the royal apparition. On such occasions, she is said to arrive by night in a spectral coach helmed by a headless horseman; her brother, George, perhaps? Visitors also claim to have glimpsed her wandering in the approximate spaces she inhabited in her former home (the present structure isn't the one Anne knew), perhaps searching for the rooms she once occupied as a child. When news of George's execution reached Blickling back in 1536 (days before Anne herself was beheaded), the phantom image of a headless man was soon seen being dragged around the lanes and fields by a troupe of four black stallions. As for their father, Thomas, well, for having apparently failed to intervene in the beheading of two of his children, his ghost is doomed to cross twelve bridges in the area before cockcrow (dawn), on a route that takes him from Blickling to nearby Aylsham, before passing through such places as Meyton, Oxhead and Wroxham. They do love their spooks in Norfolk!

So, Anne Boleyn was born in Blickling Hall c.1501, or else in Hever Castle in Kent c.1507 (or some date between the two). The debate still rages regarding the definitive answer, but the more probable is c.1501, due to the dating of a letter from Anne to her father, sent from the court of Margaret of Austria in 1513, from a position in the royal household that would have been daunting for a girl only seven or eight years of age. Thus, the present Blicking Hall in Norfolk – now built upon the remains of the old Boleyn manor house – lays that modest but insistent claim upon the pedigree of one of the most famous women in the world. However, Marie Louise Bruce makes a strong case for dating Anne's birth to 1507, and her birthplace, therefore, as Hever Castle, to which the family moved shortly beforehand, when she says '...no parish records were then kept, so Anne's birth was unrecorded, but the scholar, historian, and antiquary William Camden, in his *History of Queen Elizabeth*, published in 1615, sets it as 1507, a date which fits in with other clues we have and which is positively confirmed in *The Life of Jane Dormer, Duchess of Feria*. The Duchess, a friend of Queen Mary I of England, was born in 1538, and her biographer, Henry Clifford, was for many years a member of her household, so is a trustworthy source.' (Louise Bruce, 1972, p9.) Still, this is some several years after Anne was beheaded, when her tainted memory was still banished from the lips of the court and the public at large. The jury is still out on this one, I'm afraid.

Actual sketches of the original Boleyn version of Blickling Hall remain as elusive as does an accurate portrait of its most famous scion. The current structure is Jacobean and was built sometime during the 1620s, whilst the original structure was purchased by Anne's great-grandfather, Geoffrey Boleyn, in around 1452. The house as it stands today bears almost no resemblance to that original red-brick building, but certain parts, chunks and discreet whispers remain of the structure in which Anne was born, including the moat. The Boleyn family emblem, the bull, also graces Blickling Hall at various junctures; the Great Hall, meanwhile, houses two life-size wooden reliefs of both Anne and her daughter, Elizabeth I.

A short drive from Blicking Hall, down various idyllic country lanes and some startlingly flat landscape, lies the tiny village of Salle, not far from Reepham. The village church of St Peter and St Paul in Salle contains many brasses to the Boleyn family, dusty slabs paying homage to various of Anne's illustrious ancestors who once dwelt in this far-flung little hamlet. In fact, some of those illustrious ancestors actually helped build the church and owned large tracts of land in and around Salle. Sadly, nowadays the building seems almost in a state of ruin, a stale air of neglect slapping one about the face on pushing open the great front door. However, that self-same sense of abandonment is perfect for the historian seeking to peruse the Boleyn ancestry within at their leisure. Norah Lofts once encountered a sexton there, who told her:

> he had kept vigil on the night of 19 May, and had seen nothing except a great hare which seemed to come from nowhere – he was sure he'd shut the door behind him. It led him, he said, a fine chase, jumping over the pews, twisting and turning. Then he stubbed his toe on the base of the font and when he recovered his balance the hare had vanished. Everything about him, especially the dialect which I have spared you, proclaimed him to be a true Norfolk man; yet when I said, "Well, she was supposed to be a witch, you know," he asked blankly what that had got to do with it? I had the pleasure of telling him that a hare was one of the

shapes that a witch was supposed to be able to take at will, which is one reason why many Norfolk people would have to be very near starvation before they would eat hare meat. He had never heard *that* one, he said. So he had regarded his ghost-hunt as a failure, and had told his tale in all innocence. It left me wondering. (Lofts, 1979, pp184-185.)

Thus, the enthusiasm of that little girl this author witnessed is upheld, after all. Some have also wondered whether or not Anne is in fact secretly buried in this remote village church. Lofts herself muses on the fact. So, besides the hare, and now the possible secret burial – not to mention the witchcraft – this serves as a way of steeling you, the reader, against the veritable miasma of legends, myths and lies that surround the legacy of Anne Boleyn. But some of these tales might, in fact, be true; or at the very least unprovable either way. St Andrew's Church, meanwhile, adjacent to Blickling Hall, is almost sumptuous in comparison to that of St Peter and St Paul, and also contains several brasses to the Boleyns. Anne was probably baptised in this church.

Anne was likely the younger daughter of Thomas Boleyn and his wife, Elizabeth Howard. Elizabeth came from the wealthy, influential and affluent Howard family. Her brother was Thomas Howard, the third Duke of Norfolk, one of the most powerful and prominent noblemen at court, although on a personal basis he was somewhat repellent, and though married to Elizabeth Stafford, daughter of the disgraced Duke of Buckingham, he had countless mistresses. Several of these women were apparently garnered from the very lowest rungs of the household establishment, including a washerwoman (Elizabeth Holland) and several others, some of whom took considerable umbrage at having to doff their hat to their lover's wife. Indeed, on one occasion it was said that Elizabeth Stafford was set upon by several of these women, who proceeded to tie her up and then sit on her chest until she spat blood; very Prisoner Cell Block H.

Besides cropping up in the countless fictional works on Anne's life, Thomas Howard also appears onscreen several times: in *The Tudors*, he is portrayed in suavely scheming fashion by Canadian actor Henry Czerny; in *Wolf Hall*, aired some several years later, a more realistic take on the character is provided by Bernard Hill. Besides this 'illustrious' uncle, Anne could also include in her forebears 'an earl, the granddaughter of an earl, the daughter of one baron, the daughter of another, and an esquire and his wife.' (Ives, 2004, p4.) In fact, her mother could actually claim a line of descent that went all the way back to Edward I. However, Elizabeth Boleyn remains a highly elusive figure. There are no portraits of her and only the scantiest details of her life; that she served at court under several Tudor queens before her daughter ascended to the throne, for one thing; that she was also a part of her daughter's household. Aside from that, precious little is really known. Even '...the date of Elizabeth's marriage to Thomas Boleyn is not recorded. It has been estimated to have been as early as 1495 and it was certainly by 1499.' (Norton, 2013, p73.) On the whole, but unsurprisingly, given the patriarchal bent of the time, she is quite utterly eclipsed by her ambitious and accomplished husband.

It is believed that Anne's sister Mary – of *The Other Boleyn Girl* fame – was probably the elder sister, and that their brother George was either a little older or a little younger than Anne herself. Another brother, Thomas, apparently died in his teens (he is buried at Penshurst), whilst yet another sibling, Henry (buried in St Peter's Church at Hever), did not long survive infancy. According to the testimony of Thomas Boleyn, his wife was pregnant so frequently – almost yearly – that giving birth must have been, for the poor woman, rather like shelling peas. If the 1501 birthdate for Anne is indeed correct, then all of the surviving siblings were probably born at Blickling Hall and, as said, baptised at nearby St Andrew's Church. Infant mortality was dangerously high in Tudor times, so to boast five children surviving infancy and then to have four of them make it to their teens was something of an achievement. Thomas Boleyn was a diplomat of some considerable skill in the court of Henry VIII, the young King having ascended to the throne on the death of his father, Henry VII, in 1509. Thomas was the son of Sir William Boleyn, a man who served as sheriff of Kent, Norfolk and Suffolk, no less, whilst William's father, Geoffrey Boleyn, had served for a year as Lord Mayor of London. Thomas's mother, meanwhile, was Lady Margaret Butler, daughter of the 7th Earl of Ormond. The Ormond inheritance would resurface during Anne's youth, with an arranged marriage proposal almost seeing her spirited away from the King of England forever; the 'alternate history' avenues of thought are quite amusing on that score.

Thomas was present at countless pivotal moments in Tudor history, including the wedding of Henry VIII's elder brother, Arthur Tudor, to Catherine of Aragon. He was among those who escorted Margaret Tudor to Scotland to marry James IV, and he was knighted as part of Henry VIII's coronation celebrations. Flexibly linguistic, he was an adaptable asset to the new court as much as he had been steadfast in his service to Henry VIII's father. Not only could Thomas converse, but he was also physically adept at fitting into the new, masculine, young King's lifestyle, jousting against him on several occasions. Despite some suggestions, the Boleyns were most certainly not 'nobodies' who rose on prominence via the sexual favours of their womenfolk. Rather, via her father's ambition and verve, 'Anne Boleyn was born into a family that intended to consolidate its position by strong, not exactly disinterested, traditions of loyalty to the monarch.' (Fraser, 1993, p144.) Certainly, the presence of Thomas at the nuptials of Arthur Tudor and Catherine of Aragon, whose faltering wedding-night efforts would eventually become so important to Anne herself, meant that he was perhaps better informed than most in regard to Catherine's virginity and the fact that it was perhaps not quite the closed case she would later maintain. Any inside information Thomas may or may not have had on that score was probably discreetly filed away for future use, in the unlikely – although, as it turned out, rather prescient – fact that Arthur perished but Henry VII wanted to keep hold of the Spanish princess and marry her off to his other son instead.

So, the Boleyns were self-made but also well-connected – hence the Howard marriage – but it is doubtful they really dared dream that one of their daughters would one day sit on the throne of England itself, let alone the fact that her daughter would be deemed perhaps the greatest queen the country had ever seen. Certainly, in a powerfully patriarchal society, girls were deemed far less important than boys, hence there being no readily discernible date for the births of either Boleyn girl, although, having said that, we don't know quite when brother George was born either (the year 1504 is tentatively offered by historians).

The children appear to have been close, especially Anne and George. It takes only the smallest leap of the imagination to imagine them foreshadowing the footsteps of that little girl in 2012, haring across a road which was, in the early 1500s, barely a rutted track, and then bounding off into the fields beyond, perhaps with Thomas the Younger in tow. Calling her to caution, George might have addressed Anne as 'Nan', the shorthand for most Annes of the time. Certainly, George would have received a better education than either of his sisters, and to have been considered more important, but Thomas Boleyn was not shy about thrusting his daughters into the spotlight, and given his courtly connections, this was a task relatively easily accomplished. Long before she left England for a finessing of her education, Anne would have been taught to read and to write, and to compose her correspondence with that theatrical flourish of which the Tudors were so proud. She would know some history, and rather more religiosity in her infancy than most children know today by the time they finish their schooling altogether. As a boy, George would sidestep the more feminine convention of learning to embroider, a skill at which his sisters would soon become rather adept. He, like his sisters, would turn out to be something of an accomplished dancer. He would certainly have been coached in regard to courtly etiquette; all of the children would learn how to ride, and, quite possibly, how to hunt at a relatively early age. It is doubtful the children would have indulged in bloodsports whilst in Norfolk, but the possibility of them tearing up the Kent countryside in pursuit of some petrified creature is far more realistic (the Tudors were not known for their compassion where animals were concerned and considered hounding a deer or a fox to its death merely a good day's sport). On rainy days, the children would play cards, chess or some other game to pass the time.

At the time of Anne's birth, the family were Catholic, although that was soon to change. God – and Jesus – would have been a big part of Anne's life, in a way that nowadays would seem, perhaps, rather hard to fathom. Tudor society didn't necessarily revolve around religion; some people hardly went to church at all, but still it was a million miles removed from today's mostly irreligious culture. For Anne, God was not an abstract concept and nor was the Devil; they were almost living, breathing – albeit unseen – entities, one to be worshipped and the other to be avoided at all costs. Certainly, her future actions underlined how much her spiritual side meant to her.

However, the fact remains that we know precious little about Anne's life before her father decided to disengage her from the bosom of her family and send her to Europe. We can only speculate, finding her day-to-day life at times almost impossible to imagine; a world with no TV and no mobile phones, no cinemas and no shopping malls. If anything, the Boleyns, like the rest of the population at the time, were far more connected to the natural world than we are now, and probably spent their time far more productively than simply scrolling through the latest apps on their smartphones. Certainly, Anne and her siblings were sufficiently green to consider the move from Blickling Hall in Norfolk down to Hever Castle in Kent more an adventure than the wrench it might have been for their mother or the task it might have been to a more modern sensibility; that connection, at least for the children, was one quite easily broken. After all, their father's future lay at the court of Henry VIII, and that was far more accessible from Kent than it was from Norfolk.

2

From Blickling Hall to Hever Castle

Thomas Boleyn inherited Hever Castle from his father. Likewise, Sir William Boleyn inherited Hever Castle – formerly known as 'Hever Brocas' – from his father, Geoffrey Boleyn, who converted the property and made some major renovations in around 1462, making it more a manor house than the fortress that the word 'castle' suggests. (There has, in fact, been a dwelling on the site since 1270 or so, but the present structure was apparently licensed in 1383). Located in the village of Hever, not far from Edenbridge in Kent, Hever Castle is nowadays perhaps one of the premiere sites of pilgrimage for Anne's rather fervent fanbase.

Relatively intact from the time she first came to call it home, Hever Castle certainly exudes an almost fairy-tale fascination upon the visitor, nestled in a secluded dell in that verdant Kent countryside. Restoration work by the Astor family (the last owners before it was opened to the public) seems to have done little to blemish the 'authentic' feel of the place. Whereas at Blicking Hall one needs a certain dollop of imagination to imagine Anne and her siblings darting across fields near the family home, at Hever it almost seems possible to catch a glimpse of them from the corner of one's eye whilst squaring up the building for a panoramic shot on your iPhone. However, when the family arrived from Norfolk in around 1505, the place was swathed in forest, the impressive frontage almost spoilt by an abundance of boggy marsh. Originally – i.e. before the renovations – a moated, medieval castle, Thomas Boleyn further updated the building to resemble a more fashionable – albeit still moated – manor house. It is thought that the apartments the family occupied were situated on the west elevation, with the solar (in Tudor times, a solar was considered any room or sequence of rooms in which a given family lived and slept) containing three rooms, with the great chamber at the centre.

In the present day, Hever Castle's inner hall is chock-full of fabulous Tudor portraits dangling from some exquisite Italian walnut panelling, although when Anne lived there this area was actually the kitchens.

9

The present drawing room was used as a domestic office in Tudor times. Anne's bedroom is a delight to behold, although the provenance isn't quite certain, but it seems a sure bet to say that at least one – or indeed several – of the children occupied it at one time or another. The room designated 'King Henry VIII's Bedchamber' is a piece of period beauty, but again with a *slightly* doubtful derivation.

The Book of Hours room contains several prayer books that once belonged to Anne and in which one may see examples of her handwriting as well as her signature. The older item was possibly handed down to Anne by her mother and was originally fashioned in Bruges in around 1425, whilst the other was apparently created specifically for Anne in 1527. The older item bears the inscription 'The time will come', beneath a miniature of the Last Judgement. To punctuate the point, Anne has also drawn an astrolabe, to symbolise time. The latter book bears the rather touching line, 'Remember me when you do pray, that hope dothe lead from day to day.' Exactly when this was written by Anne is a little hard to say, but the timeframe is relatively tight. Kate McCaffrey, Hever Castle's Assistant Curator, has posed the theory that this book was inscribed between 1527 and 1529. Because Anne signed herself 'Anne Boleyn', it must have been inscribed before her father was elevated to Earl of Wiltshire/Ormond in 1529. Thereafter, Anne was styled 'Anne Rochford' and would almost certainly have signed herself thus. Remaining examples of her correspondence indeed show her to have been quite fastidious in regard to the use of titles she had been afforded; pious perhaps, but not quite following the humble example of Jesus Christ. Allowing for Anne's ego, we can be fairly certain that it was inscribed between 1527 and 1529, when she was caught up at the height of the King's passion. As to whom this quaint little rhyming couplet is dedicated, we do not know for sure. However, because of the dates between which the verse had to have been written, there is a possibility that it wasn't dedicated to a specific person at all, but that it was more of an imperative to any given reader to remember and pray for Anne when her life was endangered. This perhaps relates to the crisis of 1528 when Anne was taken gravely ill with the 'Sweating Sickness' at Hever, along with her father (Emmerson & *McCaffrey, Catherine and Anne: Queens, Rivals, Mothers,* Jigsaw (2023) pp67-68.) As ever, this cannot be proven, of course, but it would help to make sense of the apparent urgency of the message. Anne's signature is also present, although, in an act of the utmost historical vandalism, it has been cleaved asunder by the hand of a later binder, a person whom the great majority of Anne Boleyn aficionados would happily have had strung up from the nearest lamppost (or the nearest historical equivalent), given half the chance. Thankfully, the majority of the signature is still in situ. The book isn't in its original binding but looks instead to be housed in an early and rather plain replacement. The rhyming couplet is written opposite a depiction of the coronation of the Virgin; some sources say that Anne carried this book to her execution.

Hever Castle's Long Gallery is often reserved as a particular focal point for various exhibitions regarding Anne's life, ambitions and ancestry. In 2022 the castle hosted the 'Becoming Anne: Connections, Culture, Court' exhibition, which featured stunning original artwork of the interiors as Anne would have known them, courtesy of Castle Historian and Assistant Curator Dr Owen Emmerson. Of course, any self-respecting and sumptuous Tudor location also contains at least one gift shop, wherein Anne's image is slathered across everything from mugs and coasters to iPhone covers and cushions. Needless to say, Hever Castle does not disappoint on that score either.

As said, although less so than at Blickling Hall, it still requires an ample helping of imagination to imagine Anne's daily life at Hever Castle. Given that the place is ankle-deep in a beautiful, if somewhat treacly sort of English sentimentality, it can actually be quite difficult to envision the slightly more brutal existence the Boleyns must have enjoyed there some 500 years previously. Still, that hasn't stopped countless novels from imagining the young ingénue, chin on her fist as she gazes wistfully out from one of the windows into the near distance, wondering what her future might hold. There is clear evidence that the family came to consider Hever Castle 'home', despite owning several other properties. Dr Owen Emmerson explains, 'There are much grander and newer manors in the Boleyns' increasingly impressive portfolio of properties, so the Boleyns do not need to be at Hever: they want and choose to be here. Again and again later in the 1520s, we find the Boleyns at Hever. Thomas does much business from here, being a diligent steward to his lands and the nearby crown property of Penshurst, of which Thomas is appointed steward.' (Emmerson & Ridgway, 2021, p2.) As it stands, Anne probably spent some six or seven years at Hever Castle before her father decided that his clever little girl was destined for better things than simply lolling about on the various grassy knolls and exchanging vacuous pleasantries with the local poet/lothario.

Anne Boleyn was about to go abroad.

3

A Norfolk girl in Belgium

It was through various channels of influence as an ambassador to the Low Countries that Thomas Boleyn secured a place for Anne in the household of Margaret of Austria, daughter of the Holy Roman Emperor, Maximilian I. Initially, Thomas had been despatched to broker an alliance between Maximilian and the English against the French. Margaret negotiated the alliance on behalf of her father, and before long she and Thomas developed a good working relationship, which thus paved the way for his daughter's eventual removal from England and relocation under Margaret's care. Thomas Boleyn was either a sly opportunist or perhaps he was, in fact, simply excellent company for this most erudite of women.

At the time of Anne's arrival in Mechelen, Margaret was ruling the Netherlands on behalf of Maximilian, and her highly cultured court was seen, in part, as the essential finishing school for any girl wishing to win a place at the various European Renaissance courts. Without being too unkind, it was so sophisticated that it made the English court seem rather a provincial backwater by comparison.

As ever, we know nothing about Anne's departure from England and must fill in the gaps with a hearty dose of imagination. For starters, there is such a scant notion of the relationship with her mother that we cannot even decide whether Anne would have been heartbroken or indifferent at being parted from her. The parting would have been less alarming for one brought up in Anne's household, certainly, when many diplomats were able to secure places for their children in this way. Given the pace at which life moved in the sixteenth century, both Anne and her mother would have had some several months to get used to the idea. Anne was escorted to Mechelen court by one of Margaret's esquires, the Flemish nobleman Claude Bouton, and was one among eighteen young women then chosen to attend this foreign seat of culture and elegance.

Regardless of whether or not Anne missed her mother, it soon became apparent that Margaret would occupy the vacuum created by the relocating of this favourite daughter of the Boleyn household. In fact, via a letter she sent to Thomas Boleyn, it is apparent that Margaret quickly became all but enamoured of the precocious young Boleyn: 'I find her so well behaved and agreeable for her young age, that I am more obliged to you for sending her than you are to me [for receiving her].' (Starkey, 2004, p260.) It was only with some considerable reluctance that Margaret would eventually release Anne to attend the wedding of Henry VIII's sister Mary to the ageing Louis XII of France in 1514. Before that, Anne spent several happy years at Margaret's palace, located almost in the centre of the city. There, her education was furthered and refined, and her linguistic skills – particularly her French, in which she was tutored by the mononymously titled 'Symonnet' – developed to the point where she could happily converse in several different languages. However, her written French would take a little longer to master, as typified by this letter she sent to her father in 1514 (the original is currently held in Corpus Christi College, Cambridge):

> Sir, — I understand by your letter that you desire that I shall be a worthy woman when I come to the Court and you inform me that the Queen will take the trouble to converse with me, which rejoices me much to think of talking with a person so wise and worthy. This will make me have greater desire to continue to speak French well and also spell, especially because you have so enjoined it on me, and with my own hand I inform you that I will observe it the best I can.
>
> Sir, I beg you to excuse me if my letter is badly written, for I assure you that the orthography is from my own understanding alone, while the others were only written by my hand, and Semmonet tells me the letter but waits so that I may do it myself, for fear that it shall not be known unless I acquaint you, and I pray you that the light of [?] may not be allowed to drive away the will which you say you have to help me, for it seems to me that you are sure [??] you

can, if you please, make me a declaration of your word, and concerning me be certain that there shall be neither [??] nor ingratitude which might check or efface my affection, which is determined to [?] as much unless it shall please you to order me, and I promise you that my love is based on such great strength that it will never grow less, and I will make an end to my [?] after having commended myself right humbly to your good grace.

Written at
[? Veure] by Your very humble and
very obedient daughter, Anna de Boullan.'
(Sergeant, 1924, pp18-19.)

This author travelled to Mechelen in researching this book but was disappointed to find little trace of Thomas Boleyn's prodigy in any of the sunny courtyards and shadowed encloses of the palace of Margaret of Austria. However, the inner courtyard at least smacks somewhat of the dusty, cloistered walkways at Hampton Court Palace, although those expecting a gift shop dripping with Boleyn-related merchandise will be sorely disappointed. There is some conjecture – Tudor historians tend to use conjecture *a lot* – that Anne may have met Henry VIII whilst in Mechelen, during a post-victory visit against France, a visit wherein the King's great friend, Charles Brandon, Duke of Suffolk – better known to viewers of *The Tudors* as Henry Cavill – tried getting himself engaged to Margaret of Austria. If Anne did indeed cross paths with the King at this time, she made scant impression, and probably likewise; given the age gap then present, this comes as something of a mercy, really. Several decades later, Henry would be less discerning when it came to Catherine Howard, Anne's cousin and fifth wife of the tempestuous Tudor tyrant. Certainly, if Anne did meet Henry on this earlier occasion then she would have witnessed him in his prime; tall, well-muscled and simply oozing a charm yet to be soured by the pressures of patriarchy. When next she clapped eyes on him, his waistline would have expanded considerably, whilst his temper was doing its level best to catch up.

On leaving Mechelen, Anne became one of Mary Tudor's maids-of-honour, a position of some responsibility and social standing. Henry VIII's adored baby sister had, as said, recently married Louis XII of France, a man old enough to be her grandfather. When Mary was widowed (but not by smothering her aged husband, as a certain Showtime series suggested), Anne transferred to the service of the new French queen, Mary's young stepdaughter, Claude. Yet again, almost no details in regard to Anne's time in the French court are known, only that she would have avoided most of the famous licentiousness therein because Claude, notoriously shy and retiring, was pregnant by her husband, Francis I, for almost the entirety of her marriage, and thus spent much of her time sequestered away from the hustle and bustle of court life. Still, that hasn't stopped some historians from sneeringly suggesting that Anne nevertheless managed to pick up a few bedroom artifices whilst there, little talents she later deployed in keeping a horny Henry VIII sated but safely away from her precious 'maidenhead'. On this matter, it is perhaps more prudent to follow the lead set by G.W. Bernard when he says, 'we can do no more than speculate about whether Anne remained chaste or whether she enjoyed flings with courtiers: once more, that must be left to the imagination of historical novelists.' (Bernard, 2011, p10.)

Whatever else she may or may not have been getting up to, certainly Anne would have been aware of Marguerite d'Angoulême, sister of Francis I, although there is no evidence that she ever served her in any official capacity. Marguerite was 'an author, an intellectual, and a reformer of the Catholic church, whose personal religious beliefs certainly aligned with Anne's.' (Emmerson & McCaffrey, 2022, p73.) More than likely, in my humble opinion, Anne's religious beliefs were at this time probably still quite conservatively Catholic, and Marguerite – whether directly or indirectly – was among the first to kindle the flame of reform within the young girl. Marguerite was said to be 'so well instructed in the Lord, so well schooled in Holy Scripture, that she cannot be torn away from Christ.' (Knecht, 1996, p114.) She spent considerable time with Claude, often pacifying the poor girl whilst her husband was away 'courting' various provincial beauties. Given Claude's repeated pregnancies, coupled with her shy and retiring nature, Marguerite was left to perform many of the duties normally required of a queen consort. Therefore, it is via this relationship, perhaps more than any other that

Anne may have enjoyed whilst on the Continent, that we see how 'Anne Boleyn's religious preferences, like most other aspects of her character, seem to have been formed by her years in France.' (Starkey, 2004, p368.)

Marguerite may have become exceptionally close to Anne, or at least to have become something of a force to emulate; more likely the latter. In 1535, when Anne's star was starting to wane, she would write to Marguerite to say that her greatest wish, besides having a son, was to see and spend time with Marguerite again. Some authors have downplayed the relationship between the two women, whereas others have gone out of their way to emphasise it; lack of direct evidence tends to create such a dichotomy. However, if we are to understand Anne as something more than a one-dimensional vamp, then Marguerite d'Angoulême is, quite simply, key. To reiterate: Marguerite was a dedicated reformer, besides being learned and witty (one might almost apply those very same words to Anne herself). And so, whilst Claude suffered one confinement after another, her sister-in-law was busy inviting some of the most progressive religious thinkers of the time to frequent the various French palaces, where they would find a willing and protective patron in the form of the sister of the King of France.

Among the other notable names whom Anne might have rubbed shoulders with are none other than Leonardo da Vinci, who was presented to the court at Amboise in 1516 and who would have been rather an old man at the time; he died in 1519, aged sixty-seven. Besides being a painter and sculptor, da Vinci was also a scientist and an engineer. He was also homosexual, narrowly escaping conviction for sodomy in 1476 when he and several friends were involved in an 'incident' with a male prostitute. Quite what Anne made of the homoeroticism of many of his works, especially his Saint John the Baptist, remains unclear. The model for this particular masterpiece was said to have been 'Salai, a poor and delinquent boy with an intense angelic and androgynous beauty, whom Leonardo da Vinci met by chance in the streets of Milan in 1490: this "little devil" with the long curls remained his lover for a long time.' (Martel, 2019, p472.)

Like Marguerite, Anne would one day offer her patronage to various radical religious thinkers, although inviting them to the English court was quite another matter, given the schismatic see-sawing when Henry VIII began to tussle with Rome. On such occasions, Anne would even extend a helping hand to those men she may have met whilst at the French court, including one Clément Marot, the renowned French Renaissance poet. It seems almost unfathomable that someone as pointed and precocious as Anne would not have encountered these radical minds, possibly parrying with them on various points of doctrine and then coming away questioning her own Catholic faith. Basically, one might consider Marguerite an early evangelical (set on spreading the 'good news' of the gospels), encountering a young Anne Boleyn who, with her enquiring mind and her aptitude for learning, was a willing and ready receptacle for Reformist ideas. Eric Ives goes as far as to consider Anne 'infected' by the zeal for reform during this period.

When Thomas Boleyn went to stay with his daughter, around 1518 or so, he too would have been exposed to such Reformist ideas, if not aware of them already. Joanna Denny was adamant that he was smuggling Reformist texts into England for several years, and if this is so, then perhaps the credit for Anne's evangelist brand of reform is at least partially due to his parenting. Or perhaps the daughter 'converted' the father, and the entire idea of spreading the Reformation right the way up to the English throne came from Anne herself, whilst her father looked on aghast. Books were one thing, after all, but convincing the King of England into religious revolution quite another. Certainly, by the time Anne was toppled from the throne, her father was well known abroad as a patron of reform. Still, whoever caught the germ of religious genesis first, Thomas still had time to cut a swathe through the French court during his visit, invited in a freshly minted ambassadorial role to dine with Claude. He was also present as a representative of Henry VIII at the christening of the future Henry II, an event also attended by Marguerite d'Angoulême. One networked tirelessly at such events, deploying the usual airy Tudor platitudes from a quiver well-stocked with such commonplaces. Doubtless the two found that in Anne they had a veritable prodigy in common.

Another strong woman Anne may have met during her time in France was Louise of Savoy, the mother of Francis I. Having served as regent in 1515, her example of a woman wielding absolute authority would have been noted and nurtured by the young Boleyn, as would her passion for the political sphere. Louise of Savoy also cohabited with her husband and his mistress, as well as several of their illegitimate children. Such an unorthodox template may have braced Anne when she found herself in a similar situation with the King of England and his wife several years down the line. Charles Brandon, a notorious womaniser who was thus perhaps not the best judge of female authority, nevertheless wrote Louise a glowing reference in a despatch to Henry VIII, commenting that it was Louise 'who runs all'. There has also been some speculation that Anne was influenced by Renée of France, Claude's younger sister. However, she was little more than a toddler when Anne first arrived in Mechelen, which meant that by the time Anne was serving Claude, her younger sister was still just a small child. Therefore, any influence she may have had would have come purely by correspondence in later life. Renée was arrested as a heretic at one point but recanted.

Whether Anne attended the legendary Field of Cloth of Gold in June 1520 – that monumental exercise in empty rhetoric and timewasting tournaments that were passed off as a summit between England and France – is unclear. Some historians say that she probably was there, whilst others more wisely hedge their bets and add that well-worn Anne Boleyn caveat of 'perhaps she was there'. In his 2014 biography of Cardinal Wolsey, John Matusiak plumps for the former, with his description of Anne at the time as 'no longer a naïve newcomer to either the world of high politics or, for that matter, the seamier side of human affairs in general' is, sadly, something Anne's reputation has to contend with quite frequently. (Matusiak, 2014, pp191-192.) As G. W. Bernard alluded, you'll encounter a lot of this where Anne is concerned, especially in regard to her time in France.

Anne's time at the French court came to an end when her father summoned her back to England early in 1522 (some sources maintain it was towards the end of 1521). The reason for the recall was that Anne was to be betrothed to her Irish cousin, James Butler. The planned nuptials would settle a dispute between factions of Anne's family in regard to the titleship of the earldom of Ormond. James' father, Piers, coveted the earldom of Ormond, a title Thomas Boleyn also desired; his claim came via the fact that he was the son of the eldest daughter, Lady Margaret Butler. Lady Margaret's father had passed away in 1515. Apparently, Thomas relayed his concerns to Henry VIII via his brother-in-law, the Duke of Norfolk. Henry sought to resolve the situation by marrying Anne to James, hoping that her Ormond dowry might settle the matter. It seems that Henry wished to avoid the possibility of the thing evolving into civil war in Ireland, but somehow Thomas Boleyn talked him out of this particular avenue of resolution, possibly because he had grander ambitions for Anne and also because he still coveted the earldom for himself and not for James. The fact that the plan was dropped suggests that the wishes of the Boleyns held some considerable sway for the King. Mary Boleyn – by now a maid-of-honour to Catherine of Aragon – may also have had something to do with this. Now, Anne too was at court.

How high Thomas was aiming with regard to Anne at this stage remains unclear. Possibly she herself voiced the futility of pushing the cause of reform in a cold, isolated castle in Ireland. Either way, it seems astonishing that the wishes of Thomas Boleyn might have trumped the concern of a possible outbreak of mass violence, but they did. And perhaps he really was simply doing what his daughter suggested.

Either way, Anne's plans were crystallising fast, but they still lacked a particular focus. Her sister's budding relationship with the King would provide just the inspiration she needed. Anne was by now caught up in the first tumultuous waves of the Reformation then sweeping across Europe as an answer to the perceived endemic corruption in the Catholic Church. She had also returned to England disciplined in the French 'ways'; witty, stylish and adept at playing the courtly games of dalliance that were all the rage on the Continent. In England, such dalliances stuttered somewhat at the staider surroundings fostered by Catherine of Aragon. However, her standard of education, as advanced as it now doubtless was, still wouldn't have set her as far above her English contemporaries as some allege. In his book on Thomas More, Richard Marius for one says that 'the sixteenth century is the first after the classical age when we find fairly large numbers of educated women in all the European countries, in many respects a century of great queens and great female religious figures. In England alone, the list of accomplished women is long enough to show that More's views were part of a stream of thought and not merely a drop in the desert of feminine servitude.' (Marius, 1984, p223.) The precepts of the great humanist Erasmus, who advocated for the education of women so that they might command that great bulwark of Tudor Christianity, namely the home, had already been adopted by Catherine of Aragon in concern to her daughter Mary's education. Regardless, Anne was soon to set the tone for styles to come, at least, whilst apparently – according to contemporary commentators – making the most of her modest beauty to stand out from the crowd in a way calculated to catch the eye. Looks were but one arrow in her quiver – and quite possibly of her least concern – but she knew how best to deploy them in order to begin that slow, arduous climb toward the cause of reform.

But exactly what did this young woman look like, who was soon to take that austere English court by storm? Well, she was a brunette, chestnut-hued as a girl but darkening as she matured, and her best features were undoubtedly her eyes; big and brown – almost black, in fact – with long, 'wet-look' lashes. We are told countless times that she wielded them almost like weapons in that highly contrived game of courtly love. She wasn't particularly tall, almost girlish in build, with, in her own words, 'a little neck', but she held herself with some considerable style and poise. But, for all that we think we know about Anne Boleyn, so much – including most of those all-important physical details – remain largely elusive. We have no idea what her voice sounded like, for instance, or how she looked when she smiled. What were her teeth like? Were her breasts – her 'duckies', as Henry VIII called them – as pretty as he considered? What were her standards of personal hygiene? Also, what time did she get up in the morning and what time did she go to bed? What did she dream of? So many questions, and the lack of answers remains a timely reminder that we actually know very little about her.

There was certainly no mythical sixth finger, although some historians have nervously suggested that an extra fingernail might not have been entirely out of the question; no great wen (a boil or cyst) dangling from her neck either, although she apparently 'had a large Adam's apple, "like a man's".' (Borman, 2017, p143.) There has been some conjecture that the mythical sixth finger may have been a small extra thumb growing out of one of her existing thumbs; unlikely, but not implausible. If indeed Anne had an extra fingernail, well, this is sometimes known as an 'accessory nail', a condition quite uncomfortable and one unlikely to have been tolerated by someone of Anne's often fiery temperament. Still, in Tudor times at least, what could not be cured had to be endured, and perhaps it simply riled her the same way her future husband's ulcerated leg would one day aggravate him. Actually, 'accessory nail' is so rare as to be almost a medical phenomenon (it is more common on toenails), but that very rarity means that perhaps this feature, so specific a spot for her detractors to settle upon, really did exist after all. Yes, there just might be a kernel of truth to it; it's too exact a detail, basically. Yet, the rumour that she also had an extra breast would most surely not have escaped the attention of even the most demure and unaffected sideward glances. In fact, 'Despite being under the closest scrutiny during her life as consort and queen, none of the contemporary chroniclers of the time mentioned any abnormalities in Anne's appearance.' (Dunn, 2003, p59.) However, a defect as tiny as 'accessory nail' was one easily covered by those draping Tudor sleeves.

But while she was no ravishing beauty, Anne did have 'that indefinable quality known as sex appeal, which made men find her irresistibly attractive'. (Weir, 2008, p263.) A great deal of the anecdotes regarding Anne – at the various junctures of her meteoric rise to power – come courtesy of Eustace Chapuys, the imperial ambassador to England for Charles V, nephew of Catherine of Aragon. Chapuys was, perhaps quite understandably, not entirely complimentary about Anne. In fact, this might be something of an understatement, given the religious shifts England was then experiencing, coupled with the part Anne was soon to play in them, never mind the relationship between Chapuys' master and the woman Anne would soon usurp. Variously, Chapuys referred to Anne as 'the Concubine', 'the Grand Enemy' of the Catholic faith, 'more Lutheran than Luther himself' and a 'heretic', for 'whatever is contrary to the Catholic faith is heresy'. (Denny, 2005, pp54-55.) However, partly because of the length of his tenure – 1529 to 1545 – but also because he was a highly talented, competent, and industrious worker, his commentary upon Anne, biased as it is, remains for the most part invaluable. Still, Susan Bordo argues that the 'default' Anne Boleyn is entirely the creation of Chapuys: 'Anne is the creation of a many-centuries-long telephone game that turned politically motivated lies into inflammatory gossip and alchemised that gossip into "history".' (Robison, 2016, p80.) At the time he arrived in England, Chapuys was a little short of his fortieth birthday (either that, or he'd just passed that milestone), making him an ideal contemporary to the King. Through what appears to be sheer charm and professional persistence, Chapuys seems – at least as far as the historical eye discerns – to have sidestepped altogether the typical prejudices the English harboured towards a learned foreigner in their midst; quite simply, he won people over. As a humanist, he corresponded with Thomas More, another man who would prove to be no friend to Anne as time wore on. But more of More later.

So, we have some idea of what the English court made of her, but what did Anne herself think of the country she had departed almost a decade previously? Henry VIII had been on the throne for over ten years, but his marriage to his brother's widow had produced just the one child, and a girl, at that. In the intensely patriarchal Tudor society, it was almost unthinkable that a woman might ever ascend to the throne and wield power without a man to steady her hand. However, it would be a mistake to imagine that the Tudors – or Henry VIII in particular – considered women entirely unfit to govern, albeit with the caveat that he himself was alive but otherwise occupied. When he went off to war with France in 1513, for instance, Henry left Catherine of Aragon as regent in his absence; she would acquit herself well in warding off a sudden Scottish invasion. However, whilst a woman might adequately manage the throne of England for a measured stint, it was still preferable to have a man holding the reigns of power in the long-term. Henry cautioned that if a woman 'shall chance to rule, she cannot continue long without a husband, which by God's law must then be her governor and head, and so finally shall direct the realm'. (Guy, 2017, p8.)

Unfortunately, Henry had at that point no legitimate son, only a bastard borne by Bessie Blount, one of Catherine's maids-of-honour. Thus, whilst this boy – Henry Fitzroy – was showered with all the airs and titles conceivable, nothing could change the basic fact that he was the result of an adulterous liaison. Added to this, as Catherine aged, so did her chance of conceiving a boy dwindle away; by the time Anne arrived back in England, Catherine was in her late thirties. Thus, whilst conception was not out of the question, the timeframe to provide that male heir was contracting quickly. Did Thomas Boleyn scent a possible power vacuum where Catherine was concerned and begin deploying his daughters (for certain, Mary caught Henry's eye first) with a view to toppling her? Those who covet the crown of perpetual victimhood for Anne cleave to this theory, whilst those who wish to imbue her with a little more agency hold that perhaps she herself perceived this lack. Either way, the English court in 1522 coalesced around the King, whilst Catherine withdrew evermore into herself and her pained brand of Catholic piety. The court also coalesced around London. Whilst nowhere near the swollen behemoth of a city it is now, London was nevertheless expanding in the early 1520s at a dizzying rate, peppered with royal palaces and peasant hovels alike; the population may have been as high as some 60,000 inhabitants. Amongst those Tudor residences soon to be associated with Anne were Greenwich Palace, Hampton Court Palace (formerly the property of

Cardinal Wolsey), and Whitehall Palace (at this point known as York Place, besides being, again at this point, another Wolsey residence).

Access to the King was strictly regulated, but Henry was a popular monarch – at least, before he became cantankerous, bloated and schismatic – and not at all shy about showing himself to the general populace. In Tudor times, the country celebrated the presence – the mere idea – of the King, who had been placed in his exalted position by no less a personage than God himself. As such, it was fitting Henry should have an abundance of stately residences at his disposal, whilst the great majority of his subjects made do with fleapits of varying quality. Those palaces were large and luxurious, though by modern standards still woefully primitive. Sanitation was almost non-existent, whilst the notion of 'health and safety' would have left your average Tudor courtier doubled up with condescending delight. A thin but palpable sheen of opulence often barely covered a rather gritty and unpleasant underbelly – rather like Tudor society in general. Bodily hygiene was for the most part a mere curiosity, whilst male courtiers would often relieve themselves in any convenient corner, as long as one wasn't quite literally pissing on the king's moccasins. Besides hygiene issues, bodily discomforts abounded, and all lived with the ever-present possibility of a sudden and rather unpleasant death, be it from the countless Tudor maladies then circulating, or else simply falling foul of the King's temper. Such circumstances served to make people hardened and rather indifferent to the daily sufferings of others. Basically, life was short and brutal, and one simply had to make the best of it, leaving the line between the 'refined' royal court and the average Londoner somewhat difficult to discern: 'Polite society was almost as violent, almost as crowded and credulous, almost as brutal as the "lesser sort". Though a gentleman might hesitate to rob a plague-infested corpse of its riches, he eagerly plundered the estates of fallen ministers and luckless courtiers, and often he did not have the decency to wait until the victim was dead.' (Baldwin Smith, 2010, p79.)

Despite those aforementioned advances in the education of women, men of the Tudor era were still very much at the top of the pecking order. Women were seen as subservient, although at court they were treated with considerable respect. This code of honour was based on the Arthurian idea of chivalry, which Henry VIII set so much store by; that is, unless a woman happened to fail at fulfilling her primary task as a child bearer, in which case she was tossed aside like a dud battery. Women's sexual natures were considered best tamed through marriage, and always seen otherwise as somehow 'naughty' or 'tempting'. This partly explains the later widespread reviling of Anne Boleyn, whose 'explicit' sexuality was said by her Catholic detractors to have 'lured' the King away from the devastatingly devout Catherine of Aragon.

Childbirth was another peril women had to endure, but the experience gave them at least some agency over their own bodies; the birthing chamber was very much the domain of the midwife, and men were not permitted to enter. However, the life expectancy of your average Tudor infant was limited at best. The main reason for Catherine of Aragon's dismissal as Henry VIII's first wife was her inability to bear a male heir; a son called Henry lived only briefly, whilst several other children were stillborn. Her sole surviving child, Mary, was much beloved by her parents, but the fact remained that she was still 'just' a girl. In 1522 England was wondering when – and increasingly *if* – a male heir might ever materialise. Perhaps coloured by the zeal for reform, Thomas Boleyn played Anne like a ticking time-bomb, keeping her from James Butler, readying her to provide for the country if thus required. Anne, carrying within her that providential seed of reform, would have been obedient on the surface to the 'true' faith, whilst behind the scenes, books were exchanged, ideas discussed, and the likes of pivotal reformer Martin Luther quietly venerated. And perhaps the idea was all her own.

Already, London was beginning to change. Ostensibly a Catholic city – England was then still a Catholic country – London had the scent of religious upheaval in the proverbial nostrils, as word of the Reformation began wafting in from the Continent. However, for those who cocked an ear to this plea for church restructuring, the consequences could be brutal. Being burnt alive was considered a fit punishment for a heretic in Tudor England, with one's banned books often preceding the accused into the fire in a great show of righteous pomp and indignation. The aforementioned Thomas More was a great burner of both books and also innocent souls.

When Anne first rose to prominence at court, she was in no position to help these poor unfortunates, but as her influence ballooned, so too did her capacity to intervene as and when she could, although such measures were often employed with the utmost discretion; for the most part, the English were then still far more partial to their local church than to the idea of reform. The majority rejoiced in the burning of heretics and often took their children to witness the spectacle; sometimes the children were even allowed to carry the faggots used to fuel the fire. At that stage of the proceedings, all that could save the accused was to recant, whereupon they would be required to perform some public penance or other instead. Perhaps because of such violent responses to the cause, the Reformation was initially somewhat a piecemeal affair, and not accompanied by the great anti-Catholic orgies of violence often seen on the Continent. As Haigh explains: 'it took twenty years to get from the first real attack on Church jurisdiction in 1532 to the first Protestant church service in 1552.' (Haigh, 1993, p13.) In fact, what would be considered the Henrician Reformation to which Anne Boleyn was so integral would in fact be undone in subsequent years, before her daughter finally secured what might be termed a full Reformation in 1559.

For Londoners, Luther was a logical progression from the Lollards and their 'leader' John Wycliffe (1331-1384). In fact, one might almost call the Lollards 'Proto-Protestants'. Luther was a German priest and scholar who rebelled against the teachings of the Catholic Church, penning – and then pinning – his seminal *Ninety-five Theses* in 1517, thereby commencing what would soon come to be termed as Protestantism, the unbridled cry for reform that would be silenced no longer. However, 'Luther's ideas had only slight impact in England before Henry – for his own, decidedly un-Lutheran, reasons – turned against the pope.' (Haigh, 1993, p12.)

Regardless of the impact Luther made after posting his trailblazing work on a church door in Wittenberg (in Germany) on 31 October 1517 – where he was professor of moral theology at the town's university – such covert religious disobedience remained a dangerous game (the door, a veritable relic of reform, was burned by French troops in 1760). On the road to reform, Luther struggled with starving both body and spirit in serving God and often felt that Satan was close by and snapping at his heels. Life under Catholic doctrine was hardly a happy experience for him. When such thoughts overwhelmed, so we are told, he flung either his inkpot or some faeces in the direction of his diabolic, ethereal pursuer. Nowadays, aspects of Luther's work are seen as somewhat problematic; he was virulently antisemitic, for one thing, and it seems likely that many of his adherents aped his views. It was Chapuys who called Anne '...more Lutheran than Luther himself', a statement most would want to distance themselves from given the antisemitic angle, this despite historians relying so ardently on Chapuys' dispatches at other times. But more of Luther's antisemitism later. Meanwhile, it is somewhat erroneous to think the King would eventually dismiss the papacy for his own 'decidedly un-Lutheran' reasons. In fact, they would be someone else's reasons and not his at all, and actually quite influenced by the Lutheran doctrine. However, Henry was a man malleable enough to think that he was the author of his own destiny in that regard, whereas it would actually be Anne at the helm of that big, blustering Tudor juggernaut, either at her father's behest or under her own steam. But that was still some several years into the future.

In the meantime, in 1522, although Henry VIII sat steadily atop England's socially seething pecking order, it was actually Cardinal Thomas Wolsey, son of a humble Ipswich butcher, who really ran the show. Having studied theology at Oxford, it took little for this man of great ambition and even greater girth to climb to the position of royal chaplain to Henry VII. When he came to ascend the throne, Henry VIII's interest in jousting, women and wine gave Wolsey free rein to assume the mantle of power, concerning the new King only as and when necessary. In 1514 he became Henry's chief minister; a year later, he was Lord Chancellor. A decade or so after that, Wolsey was merely one among many who knew that Catherine of Aragon had run out of time to produce a male heir. It is doubtful, however, that he ever imagined the lengths to which his master would go in order to beget a son by his wife's new lady-in-waiting, Anne Boleyn. In the battle between Anne and Wolsey, only one of them would survive, but whilst Wolsey would be fighting mainly to preserve his own skin, for Anne it would be the future of religion in England for which she entered the fray.

4

Mary, or 'The Other Boleyn Girl'

Before Anne Boleyn, there was another Boleyn girl.

In the main, Mary Boleyn has sat quietly, uncomplainingly, in her sister's shadow. Were it not for the novel by Phillipa Gregory – and the subsequent onscreen adaptations – then most laymen would likely never have even heard of her. To this day, certain details remain obscure even to the expert. No one is sure where poor Mary was laid to rest, for instance, although some speculate that it might be in some concealed corner of Rochford Hall in Essex, a manor house inherited by Thomas Boleyn via his mother and given to Mary and her second husband, William Stafford. Others say she rests now at Hever Castle, again in some secluded and secret spot.

As a child, one imagines she also sat somewhat obscurely in her smarter sister's shadow, and that when Thomas Boleyn took them at twilight onto the eaves of Hever Castle and tried pointing out where God sat in the sky above, Anne engaged with her father whilst Mary sat applying plum juice to her cheeks in lieu of the rouge she was too young to own. This certain lack of initiative probably prevented Thomas from sending her for further fashioning in renowned European courts, despatched instead to wait on Mary Tudor, where she would soon be reunited with Anne. Probably the sisters giggled together at the thought of having to marry an old crab like Louis XII of France, although Anne likely had the sense to know when at last to stop laughing.

It was initially thought that Mary Boleyn remained in France – like Anne – after the 'tragically widowed' Mary Tudor returned to England and married Charles Brandon. During that time it has been suggested that Mary led an exuberant sex life whilst serving at the French court, eventually landing in the bed of the new French King himself; that he possibly christened her 'His English mare' has merely cemented the sneers. Even the papal nuncio called her (well after the 'fact') 'a very great and infamous whore'. (Weir, 2007, p134.) Soon, Mary's burgeoning reputation was apparently enough for Thomas Boleyn to pluck her from the French court, escorting her back to Hever Castle under a cloud of disgrace. However, more recent research suggests that Mary in fact returned to England along with the widowed Mary Tudor, and that the sum total of time she actually spent in France was a little less than a year. Obviously, this is still time enough for her to have enjoyed the attentions of the French King and countless others besides, although she would have needed a sexual appetite bordering on nymphomania to sleep with enough men to earn the sobriquet Alison Weir recently gave her, purloined from the aforementioned papal nuncio; her biography of Mary is entitled *Mary Boleyn – 'The Great and Infamous Whore'* after all.

It wasn't long after her introduction to the English court – as a maid-of-honour to Catherine of Aragon – that Mary managed to inveigle herself into Henry VIII's bedroom, shortly after his liaison with Bessie Blount. Further dismissing the 'whore' tag, several historians have speculated that the deeply pious Catherine was unlikely to have taken a 'notorious' woman like Mary into her service, although she may have had no choice. If Henry liked the look of Mary Boleyn, then that was exactly where she would be best situated to hop into his bed, when the time came. The fact that Henry seemed continually to pluck his amours from the ranks of his wife's waiting women suggests a certain sadistic bent on his part, given that word of the liaisons was always likely to drift back to her. It was a habit he would refine for most of his subsequent marriages.

How long the affair with Mary lasted – several years is the best guess – and how intense it actually become has been open to speculation for centuries. However, it must be pointed out that 'the notion of history as a critical analysis of observable and verifiable events in the past is a product of the modern age.' (Aslan, 2014, p30.) Returning to Mary's relationship with the King, well, certainly it was passionate enough that rumours persist to the effect that the two children she bore her first husband, William Carey, were actually Henry's. Mary's new position certainly won her family considerable favour, despite serving to make William Carey perhaps the biggest cuckold in the country.

Anne had returned to England when Mary was at the peak of her 'popularity', but the sisters remained as relatively distant as ever. Whether

Mary ever furnished Anne with the carnal details of what to expect from the King when she later became his obsession is not impossible; several of the 'racier' Tudor novels readily regale the reader with such scenes. One of the only recorded instances of Mary and Anne appearing together at court concerned the Shrove Tuesday pageant 'The Chateau Vert', performed at York Place. Various courtly women played the part of various 'virtues'; Anne was 'Perseverance' (although several historians have contested this), and this author wouldn't be the first to comment on the irony of that particular naming, whilst Mary was 'Kindness'; again, I wouldn't be the first to raise an eyebrow at that specific irony. The pageant was actually Anne's first recorded appearance at court since her return from France, and Showtime's *The Tudors* uses it – in the third episode of the first season – as the ideal springboard for which to introduce Henry to Anne (Mary herself is oddly absent from the event in that version). The part of 'Constancy', meanwhile, was taken by Jane Parker, daughter of Henry Parker, 10th Baron Morley. Several years later she would marry George Boleyn, in what would turn out to be one of the unhappiest arranged Tudor marriages on record. That, however, is a tale for another chapter.

Several years after Mary married him, William Carey perished from the 'Sweating Sickness', that scourge of the Tudor population, in the summer of 1528. He left his wife and their two children with a considerable amount of debt. By then, Anne's star was in the ascendancy and she used her influence to have Mary's children placed in her wardship. Given her straitened circumstances, Mary was probably more grateful than distraught at the prospect of being separated from her offspring. Still, Mary was witness to Anne's climb to the throne, accompanying her in 1532 when she and Henry visited France, Mary taking part in the masque with which they entertained Francis I.

By 1534 Anne was Queen of England, and Mary had fallen in love with, and then married, a 'lowly' soldier called William Stafford. His lack of social standing caused such a schism within the ranks of the Boleyn family that Mary was all but kicked out of court. Later, she and Anne reconciled somewhat, after a penniless Mary was forced to come grovelling for money. From that point on, Mary's life drifts into tantalising obscurity. Where she was and what she thought when her sister was so spectacularly toppled, we do not know; perhaps she mourned the loss of her brother George more than she did that of ambitious Anne. Either way, she died in July 1543, at which point Henry VIII had just married his sixth wife, Catherine Parr. As previously stated, even the whereabouts of poor Mary's body remain a mystery. But in closing, we must again praise Phillipa Gregory for making her the star of her 2001 novel. Only after that point do the various books about Mary really begin to proliferate.

Perhaps a more dignified epitaph for Mary Boleyn might be that she wasn't so much 'The Other Boleyn Girl' as quite simply, in her own right, '*Another* Boleyn Girl'.

5

Catching the eye of a king

After the collapse of the Butler proposal, Anne formed a romantic attachment to Henry Percy, the son of the Earl of Northumberland. This was around the time that Mary Boleyn became Henry VIII's mistress. How much Anne's relationship with Percy actually progressed is open to some debate, but some believe it went as far as the star-crossed lovers actually breaking with protocol and arranging their own marriage. Of course, the various novels often suggest it went further than that, but then, the point of fiction regarding Anne Boleyn is often as much concerned with titillating as it is with entertaining. Percy was certainly a catch, but Anne's Reformist agenda would have flowered less as his wife than they would as the Queen of England. Perhaps she was simply waylaid by love or had yet to realise how far ambition might really take her. Anne was certainly in something of a position to foment her romantic desires. She was now also one of Catherine of Aragon's ladies-in-waiting, trading on her French fashions and her Continental education to make herself the centre of any social gathering. Added to that, she was also an accomplished musician and a talented, if sometimes showy, dancer.

However, behind the scenes things soon began to disintegrate. Her relationship with Henry Percy was dissolved by the intervention of Cardinal Wolsey, with Percy pledged to marry Mary Talbot, a daughter of the 4th Earl of Shrewsbury; for all her finesse, Anne was still 'just' a woman with little real influence. In fact, Wolsey was actually doing Anne a favour, although neither of them realised it at the time. Some historians have suggested that a more pertinent reason for Wolsey wrenching Anne away from her sweetheart might have been because the King already had his eye on her, but the chronologies don't concur. This is the scenario offered in the 1969 movie *Anne of the Thousand Days*, but there is too great a disparity in the dates regarding Anne's liaison with Percy and the first documented evidence of the King's interest for it to be anything other than highly speculative. Some say Anne caught

Henry VIII's attention as early as 1524 (which is unlikely) and others as late as 1526 (almost certainly); either way, he soon dropped Mary Boleyn and began courting her sister, although Anne initially refused his advances and may only have accepted them when she realised how much they might help bridge the way to reform.

1526 is the year upon which most historians agree Henry first declared his affection for Anne. 'On Shrove Tuesday, Henry VIII appeared in the tiltyard at Greenwich in a magnificent jousting outfit of cloth of gold and silver embroidered in gold with the words *Declare je nos* – 'Declare I dare not' – which was surmounted by a man's heart engulfed in flames. There can be little doubt that the object of his new passion was Anne Boleyn.' (Weir, 2011, pp164-165.) Some among the Boleyns doubtless saw a glittering opportunity opening up before them if Henry's affections could be recaptured and then leashed on a more permanent basis by their clever Anne, who herself, meanwhile, harboured more spiritually advantageous ideas.

How much of her subsequent courtship was thus encouraged by her family, and how much was down to her own initiative has not been, and, unless essential new documents are unearthed, probably never will be satisfactorily discerned.

Perhaps Anne allowed Henry's courtship because she – or her father – sensed the patriarchal power vacuum created by Catherine of Aragon's failure to provide a son for England, with Anne considering it her nationalistic duty to step into the breach and offer up her womb for the masculine good. In tandem with this (this author's particular hypothesis), Anne – and perhaps again her father – also sensed a golden opportunity to push forward the Reformation in a way they had hitherto never even envisaged. After all, who better to steer the King of England in such a radical direction than the woman he would soon profess to love? To wit, 'To play for high stakes with any hope of winning called for self-confidence, steady nerves, and subtlety. Anne had all three.' (Bagley, 1962, p60.) Perhaps Thomas Boleyn really did deploy his cherished daughter toward the King after all, and quite with her consent, but not for profit, as is so often surmised, but perhaps because she really was the walking equivalent of a religious dirty bomb, primed to go off all over this cosy little Catholic country.

Initially, Anne was dismissed from court following the cessation of her relationship with Henry Percy. Most likely she went down to Hever

Castle to cool her heels, lick her wounds and also to begin nursing rather an un-Christian grudge against Wolsey, even though, as said, he'd probably done her an unwitting favour. Over time, however, Anne compartmentalised her personal feelings about Wolsey, refusing to allow them to cloud her judgement when it came to promoting the cause of reform. But that was still some way in the future. In the present, Percy duly married Shrewsbury's daughter Mary and tried to forget all about the witty, erudite girl from Norfolk with the flashing black eyes and the disconcertingly girlish laugh; Anne, meanwhile, settled into a routine of enforced Kentish domesticity. Whilst there, she may have rekindled her friendship with the poet Thomas Wyatt. This tall and athletic composer and lyric poet was a relative local, hailing from Allington, near Maidstone. Besides that, his father had assisted Thomas Boleyn as constable for Norwich Castle. Thomas Wyatt entered Henry VIII's service around 1515 or so, marrying Elizabeth Brooke in 1520, although the marriage was another example of a Tudor arrangement gone sourly awry. When the King made Wyatt an ambassador, he and Elizabeth effectively went their separate ways. At some point, Wyatt seems to have fallen for Anne hook, line and sinker. His later poem which mentions 'Brunet' is a clear reference to the woman then causing England to convulse:

...since I did refrain
Her that did set our country in a roar
The unfeigned cheer of Phyllis hath the place
That Brunet had...

The 'Phyllis' referred to is Wyatt's later mistress, Elizabeth Darell, who turned up in season two of *The Tudors*, played by Krystin Pellerin.

For centuries – quite literally – historians have been tying themselves in knots trying to find allusions to Anne in various other of Wyatt's works, and then speculating that this meant they were at some point lovers – this before she became Henry VIII's second wife. Still, the general consensus seems to be that they weren't, and that Wyatt was merely one among many pursuing Anne during the 1520s. That is, until she caught the King's eye, at which point all competition discreetly fled in the opposite direction.

That Wyatt was publicly interested in Anne was apparently conveyed to the King via a bowls game during which both men boasted of the jewels they wore, pieces which they maintained came courtesy of Anne; Henry was apparently aghast when he recognised the jewel Wyatt was sporting. Wyatt knew then that the game was up – there was no competing with the King of England – despite also using one of Anne's ribbons to measure distances between the bowls. In the end, Wyatt conceded to Henry, at least in regard to the size of his particular trinket. Behind the scenes, he would harbour an unrequited passion for Anne Boleyn for some several years, although quite how bright his ardour burned remains a matter of some contention:

> Whoso list to hunt, I know where is an hind,
>   But as for me, hélas, I may no more.
> The vain travail hath wearied me so sore,
> I am of them that farthest cometh behind.
> Yet may I by no means my wearied mind
> Draw from the deer, but as she fleeth afore
> Fainting I follow. I leave off therefore,
> Sithens in a net I seek to hold the wind.
> Who list her hunt, I put him out of doubt,
> As well as I may spend his time in vain.
> And graven with diamonds in letters plain
> There is written, her fair neck round about:
> *Noli me tangere*, for Caesar's I am,
> And wild for to hold, though I seem tame.

At some point, Anne abandoned Wyatt's lyrical flirtations and returned to court, resuming her role as one of Catherine's ladies-in-waiting. By now, there seemed little doubt but that the King was quite taken with her, even if Anne herself was already playing him like the proverbial fiddle and thinking three steps ahead in terms of what she might achieve if only she pandered to his grossly oversized ego. Nothing stayed secret in the Tudor court for long, and doubtless word soon leaked back to Catherine that her husband was engaging in another of his 'idle flirtations'. At what point she realised that this latest amour was a far meatier prospect than the likes of Bessie Blount and Mary Boleyn may only be guessed at, but to her credit Catherine continued to carry herself with her signature sangfroid. Eventually, however, Henry broke the news that he considered their marriage to be invalid on the basis that she was his brother's widow, and such a union was, in fact, a sin, at which point Catherine's redoubtable composure is said to have all but evaporated. Meanwhile, Anne left court again, this time with Henry's undoubted affection accompanying her down to Hever Castle in the form of countless love letters and other plaintive pleas; 'besotted' doesn't quite cover it, although less kinder tongues have gone as far as to call it 'stalking'. Whether this was a tactical withdrawal on Anne's part, designed to keep Henry keen, or whether the ardor of his advances in fact quite horrified her has never been satisfactorily ascertained, and unless her lost replies to his letters resurface, doubtless never will.

Anne was at Hever Castle for a year or so, during which time the King continued to bombard her with various missives, this from a man who apparently loathed letter-writing. Perhaps she showed them to her paternal grandmother, Lady Margaret Butler, who was by this stage suffering from some sort of mental illness and appears to have been confined to Hever Castle on a permanent basis. Quite possibly she was becoming senile – she was in her early seventies at the time – and Anne may have confided the contents of the King's letters, safe in the knowledge that any advice the old woman offered could be construed as gibberish if repeated to the wrong person. These letters were apparently later stolen by Cardinal Lorenzo Campeggio when he came to judge on the King's marriage to Catherine. They are now held in the Vatican. What happened to Anne's original replies remains unclear, but possibly Henry had them destroyed around the time Anne was executed. Of course, if ever they were to turn up …

Finally, for whatever reason – the pursuit of power or more likely the desire to spread the Reformation – in the middle of 1527, Anne acceded to her beau's propositions and sent Henry the gift of a jewel, upon which was depicted a woman clinging to a boat in rough seas; she, Anne, was the damsel in distress and Henry was the steady boat. Either that, or the boat represented their courtship and Henry was the diamond affixed to the bow of the ship, doing ... something to steer the way to an eventual marriage (personally, this author plumbs for the former interpretation).

The Tudors were great aficionados of this sort of allegorical messaging; even a straightforward missive scribbled in the pages of one of Anne's Book of Hours (this one is held at the British Library) had to be lyrical at the very least. Whilst Henry had said fairly straightforwardly, 'If you remember my love in your prayers as strongly as I adore you,

I shall hardly be forgotten, for I am yours,' Anne returned the feeling with, 'By daily proof you shall me find To be to you both loving and kind.' Henry's message was doodled beneath a depiction of the flayed Jesus Christ, supposedly an allegory for his lovesick pangs of longing. Anne's, meanwhile, underscored an image of the Archangel Gabriel informing the Virgin Mary that she was to have a son sent from God (The Annunciation). Of course, what she wanted in return – reform – she cannily kept to herself.

When she eventually returned to court, the three of them – Henry, Anne and Catherine – began to cohabit under the same roof in a sort of bizarre, uneasy ménage à trois. Various anecdotes trickle down over the years in regard to this particular period, some of which have the ring of truth and others which don't. For instance, that Anne and Catherine once played a game of cards in which Anne kept turning up the king, leading Catherine to comment on her rival's desire to have said monarch or nothing at all. Or that Catherine continued to embroider Henry's shirts and that Anne flew into a veritable rage when she found out. This one is a more widely circulated titbit, and apparently more authentic a nugget of 'gossip' than the aforementioned card game. The countless movies and TV series concerning this Tudor triumvirate all offer their own juicy little scenes, often with a fiery but demure Anne being put firmly in her place by a regal but visibly concerned Catherine. Certainly, most of Catherine's ladies-in-waiting would at this stage have sided with their mistress, even though they knew she was in serious trouble on the childbearing front. One among them was a quiet, unassuming girl from Wiltshire called Jane Seymour...

6

The most important man in her life

'To Jesus Christ I commend my soul; Lord Jesu receive
my soul.'
Anne Boleyn, on the scaffold at the Tower of London,
19 May, 1536

The most important man in her life? No, we're not talking about Thomas
or George Boleyn here. Or even her future husband, Henry VIII. Without
a doubt, the most important man in Anne's life was Jesus. His was the last
name on her lips when she faced the Swordsman of Calais, and she wasn't
just paying lip service either. Modern minds can barely comprehend the
religiosity of the Tudors at the best of times, let alone what they felt upon
the very precipice of death. It can be difficult for the layman to really
immerse themselves with conviction into an epoch in which Jesus was
perhaps the most important person in the lives of the populace. Certainly,
for Anne it was always Jesus. The French poet Nicolas Bourbon, whom
Anne's efforts helped pluck from a French prison to the English court,
said, '...the spirit of Jesus which enflames you wholly with his fire.' He
was not wrong. Her brother knew it too, translating various texts for
her and often engaging in fiery religious disputes with dinner guests, a
privilege sometimes denied Anne herself, because of her closer proximity
to the centre of power. In fact, such was George Boleyn's reputation for
this sort of Reformist rhetoric that Chapuys often pled ill-health rather
than suffer an evening of such discourse.

The man whom the Tudors knew as Jesus remains not entirely
dissimilar from the one still worshipped today: the slightly effete, doe-
eyed victim of Rome and of his Jewish brethren. Such an image was
initially considered idolatrous when first the Reformation surfaced,
but it was one that quickly regained popular currency. It was in fact
during the Renaissance (beginning in the 14th century) '...that people
began creating more realistic-looking (and sometimes gory) crucifixes,

which are crosses showing the crucified Christ. Seven centuries later, overfamiliarity with the image of the cross has sometimes bred contempt, or at least indifference.' (Talbot, 1998, p189-190.) Brought up a Catholic, depictions of Jesus were commonplace to Anne, and were far enough removed from the many saints invoked for money in the corrupt Catholic charge to be free from the stink of scandal as she found herself gripped by reform.

When Anne was born, England was unquestionably Catholic; the smell of schism was on the horizon, but it was still some several decades away. However, regardless of the creed, the fact remained that the lives of the populace were steeped in religion, though the workings of it remained as lofty and unreachable as the monarch himself. Church services were conducted in Latin and thus impenetrable to most of those attending; at least, to the uneducated classes, which in Tudor times constituted the greater part of society. Anne could read Latin but making sense of a church service would have taken some several years to master, and even then, the texts deployed were often deemed impenetrable to even the devotedly devout.

The fact that such services were therefore seen as the intellectual province solely of the priests who performed them would become an immense source of frustration and inequity once the dissatisfaction of the layperson was stirred into action by the protagonists of Reformation. When she became Queen of England, Anne would leave the vernacular Bible in her apartments for her ladies to read and to gain – paraphrasing Natalie Dormer's Anne in *The Tudors* – 'spiritual nourishment'. However, the truth is that even English priests sometimes had rather a slippery grip on what they were preaching. There was no formal groundwork for the vocation, with much of what aspirants learned being picked up at school and then supplemented by offering assistance at the parish altar. Even those who made it as far as university found little concrete guidance in the syllabus, and physical recourse to Rome was offered only to the richest (naturally). Thus, with these priests either cherry-picking the words of Jesus as they saw fit, or else misunderstanding them entirely, there was no way for the layperson to whom they were preaching to put such sermons into any constructive context. But despite the relative ignorance of the general populace in this regard, there was still a great demand for religious tracts of all kinds, particularly meditations on the Passion of Christ. In fact, 'Everyone lived within a system of moral laws derived from the Old and New Testament prescripts and enforced by Church teaching and Church courts.' (Haigh, 1993, p285.)

The maintenance and upkeep of their local churches was of paramount importance to the populace. Records suggest that St Andrew's Church at Blickling was fiercely maintained by the Boleyns, both during the time when Anne was in residence and after, when the core family relocated to Kent. For the Tudors, churches were 'community centres, where people met God and their neighbours to mark seasons of the year and stages of life, to be reminded of duties and ask forgiveness of sins, to seek safety in this world and salvation in the next.' (Haigh, 1993, p294.) For Anne as a child, English Catholicism presented no problem at all; rather, it became problematic on the Continent and then those oppositional ideas seeped back toward England. People like Anne, who moved from England to the Continent and then back again were ideal vessels through which to import the message of change pioneered by Luther and his like. But when Anne was touched with reform, it didn't stop her from being a Catholic. Therefore, she probably wasn't 'more Lutheran than Luther himself', as Chapuys sneered, though she owed Luther a great deal, even if she didn't adhere to all he suggested. Doubtless, her views were massaged somewhat by Philipp Melanchthon's refinement of Luther's rather tempestuous tenets.

Had Anne lived, so Claire Ridgway has suggested, then it is more than likely that she would have become what is considered a Protestant, but at the time of her execution in 1536 she was still much more a Catholic (as was most of England; reform was still a very London and Southeast-centric affair). As Haigh explains, those in the midst of the Reformation had no idea that it would be a fairly linear process of turning England from a Catholic country into a Protestant one. Historians may see this in hindsight, but in the midst of the storm, as Anne herself was, there was no such guarantee, and perhaps she herself didn't actually want it, either. What she wanted was reform and not revolution, but the Pandora's Box, once forced open, was too tumultuous for such distinctions. Some have considered her a Christian humanist, which basically means that Anne believed that human freedom and individual conscience, as well as rational enquiry, were all part of the Christian spiritual journey. Erasmus, possibly the premiere Christian humanist, even dedicated a translation to her father and commended Anne within the text. Like Anne, Erasmus was a Catholic committed to reform. He died the same year that she did, and like Anne – had he lived – then he too might have become a Protestant. But Erasmus counted among his friends two men who would pay the ultimate price for opposing (among other things) Anne's ascent to the throne – Thomas More and Bishop Fisher. Really, Anne's religious beliefs were something of a potpourri, aligning with those of Marguerite d'Angoulême: 'For all her interest in Lefevre and Luther, [she] never broke with the Roman church. Her faith has been described as neither Catholic nor Lutheran, but as a strange personal mixture derived from a variety of sources, including Lutheranism.' (Knecht, 1996, p161). Anne almost certainly emulated such a stance.

That Anne found comfort in the Scriptures is almost certain, discovering, as did countless others, that Jesus entered the world to save sinners and not to condemn them. To Anne and her fellow Reformers, 'the secondary aids of Catholic practice, the images, penances, and pilgrimages, were distractions, at best irrelevant and at worst idolatrous.' (Haigh, 1993, p58.) As said, images of Jesus himself escaped this initial scourging of tradition. Although as late as 1536 Anne still endorsed sermons that made a case for some of these ceremonies, her almoner was not just her mouthpiece but had a mind of his own and possibly she conceded on those aspects of his preachings as long as he thrust in the metaphorical dagger exactly where she wanted it; more on this particular episode later.

For Anne, salvation was to be sought simply in Jesus himself and not in the plethora of saints conjured up by the Catholic Church. Luther knew this and espoused it fervently: 'Another text from Paul lit up for him: Romans 13.1, "Let everyone obey the superior powers, for there is no authority except from God". This has been described as the most important text of the Reformation.' (MacCulloch, 2009, pp614-615.) Anne had a particular passion for Paul's epistles from the New Testament. However, as in the case of her aforementioned almoner, she struggled with some Reformist tenets even while she embraced others wholeheartedly. The concept of justification by faith alone, a key tenet of Lutheran doctrine, Anne found problematic: 'The just shall live by faith.' (St Paul to the Romans, Chapter 1, Verse 17.) On that basis, Anne was not quite the Protestant martyr that one of her chaplains, William Latymer, or the martyrologist John Foxe maintained. Neither, as we shall see, was she quite prepared to question the miracle of the altar. It seems she had yet to take the leap of faith that would allow history to consider her a true Protestant. She was, therefore, much more Catholic when she died. As for justification by faith alone, Collinson explains:

> Luther would teach that we are saved by another righteousness, Christ's righteousness. Only faith, itself a gift from God, can take hold of this righteousness. Hence justification by faith alone, *sola fide*. This is something that happens all at once, *auf einmal*, not bit by bit, *stucklich*. It is like a marriage. Christ, the bridegroom, takes as His bride a wretched and depraved prostitute and at once she acquires His riches and He her wretchedness. The sinner does not cease to be a sinner, but is no longer seen to be a sinner. He is at one and the same time a sinner and justified: *simul justus ac peccator.*' (Collinson, 2005, p48.)

Thus, good works are not performed for the selfish motive of achieving salvation, but simply because performing good works is the right thing to do; the kind thing to do. Some historians have struggled to reconcile this with the ambitious and occasionally – for want of a nicer phrase – 'gobby' Anne, but her entire purpose was to capture a position of extreme power and use it for reform; she didn't often have time for simple niceties.

Despite her distaste for the more overt examples of idolatry, Anne still observed certain key dates in the Catholic faith, including Maundy Thursday (The Thursday before Easter), wherein the Last Supper is commemorated, when Jesus ate with his disciples for the last time and then washed their feet for them. During her time as Queen of England, Anne and – one presumes – Henry performed the Maundy Thursday ritual, washing the feet of as many poor people as years they were old, whilst purses of Maundy money (alms) would also be given to these humble supplicants. Anne's generosity in regard to the Maundy purse has been well documented, but usually in the context of pitting her against her apparently more parsimonious predecessor. However, given that one of the main driving concerns for Jesus was with the poor, Anne is to be applauded, and perhaps the rather unflattering comparison can be upheld. Eric Ives stumbles somewhat when he points out that Anne was more likely to help the poor if they were Reformist in nature. True Christian charity would in fact have extended to all supplicants, and her generosity in that regard would have baffled both 'sides' of the schism.

During her incarceration in the Tower of London, Anne still received communion, revering the bodily presence of Jesus in the consecrated bread and wine. Before communion, mass would be observed, although as far as mass was concerned, Luther maintained that 'the main purpose of the mass itself was to strengthen the faith of the individual communicant. He could see in the Scriptures no reason for regarding it as a "good work" from which other persons might benefit. To regard it in any sense as a sacrifice merely derogated from the all-sufficiency of Christ's unique sacrifice on the Cross.' (Dickens, 1965, p62.) Anne herself subscribed to the notion that the various religious ceremonies were more as an aid to memory than an actual manifestation of what we might consider the supernatural. Historians have used this time in the Tower to suggest Anne was much more moderate than some might suppose. However, it must be remembered that she was facing death in May 1536; a weakening of resolve, a harkening back to older forms of worship – to childhood – may have been a comfort, more than the idea that she was casually renouncing her Reformist ideals. Aids to memory were a great comfort at such a time. In fact, the uncertainties may have been some several months in the gestation: 'When Tristram Revell, early in 1536, tried to dedicate to the Queen his English translation of Lambert's own *Farrago Rerum Theologicarum*, which denied the sacrifice of the mass, Anne refused the request.' (Ives, 2004, p283.) Whilst Ives rejects the notion that Anne spurned this work because of her 'precarious position' in 1536, this author advocates it. I believe that self-preservation for the greater cause of Reform was uppermost in her mind at the time, meaning a tactful distance needed to be observed from certain 'heretical' tracts; unless her temper – given vent via one of her almoner John Skip's sermons, that is – overcame her.

That Anne was probably – like Luther – antisemitic seems likely, although the contradiction in holding such views when Jesus was himself a Jew would likely have been an incongruity quite lost on her, as indeed it was to the majority of the populace. For those living in Tudor times, the primary Jewish opponents of Christianity would have been, as Aslan explains, '...the spiritual heirs of the Pharisees – the rabbinate – [who] became the primary Jewish opponents of the new Christian movement, and so it is natural that the gospels would have made them appear as Jesus's chief enemies.' (Aslan, 2014, p255.) This would likely have been the view that Anne and her contemporaries held in regard to the

Jews. Part of Luther's stance came from his failure to convert various Jews to Christianity, which quickly ballooned to the point where he was calling for their houses to be burned and their books to be mashed into pulp. Luther's stance regarding the Jews changed in 1536, the year Anne was executed, so it's likely she was never the rabid anti-Semite he became. Had she lived, the unpleasant truth of what today we might consider near-Nazi ideology may have left some aspects of the whole Anne Boleyn cult rather hard to swallow. Likewise, she would have had little time for the notion that her beloved Bible was actually something cobbled together in Rome decades after the fact, and that the hero of the piece was actually a rabble-rousing Jew with decidedly radical Jewish nationalist inclinations. This man bore little resemblance to the doe-eyed, peace-loving Christ she knew, moulded thus by Paul after his encounter with Jesus on the Road to Damascus. But although she may not have realised it, Anne and her Reformist contemporaries actually had more in common with that radical Jewish nationalist than they realised. After all, were they not all rallying against religious corruption, be it in Rome or Jerusalem, looking to save the souls of simple folk in villages like Salle and Blickling, Nazareth and Bethlehem?

Clearly, Anne's religiosity doesn't titillate as much as the scandals that surround her. In that sense, she shares much in common with another female religious pioneer who was refashioned into a prostitute and a figure of scandal, namely Mary Magdalene. Of course, even to suggest the comparison to Anne herself would have been the gravest of insults. In 591, Pope Gregory I conflated Mary Magdalene with Mary of Bethany and also the 'sinful woman' who washed the feet of Jesus, a mishmash from which was born the prostitute Mary Magdalene of popular culture. This was the Mary Magdalene with whom Anne was acquainted as a child. However, in 1517, as Luther made his bold move, the French Reformer and humanist Jacques Lefèvre d'Étaples published *De Maria Magdalena et triduo Christi disceptatio* ('Disputation on Mary Magdalene and the Three Days of Christ'), in which he railed against the aforementioned conflation of Mary Magdalene, Mary of Bethany, and the 'sinful woman'. A flurry of books and pamphlets were hastily published in response, most of which opposed the argument. Anne doubtless read both the assertion and the responses; such books were readily available at the French court (over a decade later, her brother presented her with an illuminated manuscript of one of d'Étaples' works). To them, the idea of Mary Magdalene as anything other than a prostitute would have been challenging, to say the least; still, as a Reformist text, they were obliged to consider it. However, it wasn't until 1969 that Pope Paul VI did away with the erroneous identification of Mary Magdalene as a prostitute, and in 2016 Pope Francis took the biggest step yet to rehabilitate her image by declaring a major feast day in her honour on 22 June. His 2016 decree put the woman who first proclaimed Jesus' resurrection on a par with the liturgical celebrations of the male apostles: 'By doing this, he established the absolute equality of Mary Magdalene to the apostles, something that has never been done before and is also a point of no return' for women in the church, said Lucetta Scarrafia, editor of the Vatican-published *Women Church World* monthly magazine.' (Bernstein & Scharf, 2019, paragraph 4 & 5 of 22.) Now, Mary Magdalene is referred to as 'Apostle of the apostles'.

Anne's star has followed a similar trajectory, from scandal to sublimity, culminating – for now, at least – with Hayley Nolan's 2019 book *Anne Boleyn – 500 years of lies*. And as Mary Magdalene went from supposed streetwalker to being recognised as 'Apostle of the apostles', so at last we begin to gain a greater understanding of Anne Boleyn, the religious Reformer, without whose intervention it is entirely possible the Reformation itself might have bypassed – or at least merely dented – England itself.

7

Courtship, consummation, and the Papal Brexit

Inevitably, word of Henry's relationship with Anne soon spread beyond court circles, along with the declaration of his intention to divorce Catherine of Aragon on the basis that their marriage was invalid, basically because Leviticus – in the Old Testament – declared the marriage of a brother to his dead brother's widow to be sinful: 'If a man marries his brother's wife, it is an act of impurity.' However, Anne refused to become Henry's sexual partner until he had obtained his divorce (recently, however, it has been postulated that Henry himself may have instigated the sexual ban, in a concerted effort to keep the liaison as 'legitimate' as possible). Quite possibly there was kissing, and perhaps even some mild heavy petting, but certainly no sex, despite what some of the films and TV shows suggest. Their son – when he arrived – would be no bastard, like Bessie Blount's boy. No, Anne would give the King a legitimate son, one begat in lawful matrimony. Therefore, neither of them would succumb to the temptation of sex before marriage. Anne abhorred the idea of finding herself cast off, like her sister or the aforementioned Bessie, raising a feted but ultimately ineffectual child of dubious origin. However, if it was actually Anne's decision to keep the King at arm's length, the move had rather a surprising effect; 'Denial and frustration had an explosive impact on him. They fired his ardour. He threw his boundless energy and will-power into obtaining that which he had been told he could not have.' (Tremlett, 2010, p260.) But this does not mean 'having' in the carnal sense. Henry simply wanted Anne for himself, and once that promise was secured, well, the sex could wait until things were legalised.

Of course, Anne's enemies were quite willing to believe that she and Henry were 'at it' at almost every available opportunity. Sadly, for them, 'Her virginity was confirmed by the Imperial Ambassador to Rome when, perhaps regretfully, he observed: 'There is no positive proof of adultery, none having yet been produced here at Rome but, on the contrary, several letters proving the opposite.' (Denny, 2008, pp44-45.) However, one thing guaranteed to dampen desire for both parties was a health scare. When the Sweating Sickness broke out in 1528, the notoriously hypochondriac Henry fled London, whilst Anne retreated to Hever Castle. Likewise, those who could also afford to flee to less populated areas promptly did so. In fact, one might almost think of this as the Tudor equivalent of a COVID-19 lockdown. Anne caught the disease but recovered, although her brother-in-law William Carey perished. Catherine of Aragon has been castigated by several historians for her ostensible attitude to Anne's struggle with a disease that makes COVID-19 seem like a mere trifling sniffle.

When all had sufficiently recovered their wits, the Pope was petitioned for a divorce for Henry and Catherine, but Rome had been sacked by Catherine's nephew, the ample-jawed Charles V, Holy Roman Emperor, leaving the Pope (Clement) almost hamstrung in his efforts. Charles for one would certainly not look kindly on his aunt being shoved aside in favour of a jumped-up nobody from Norfolk. It is worth noting, however, that Charles and Catherine were never particularly close, and their filial relationship has been somewhat overstated. For him, it was perhaps more a matter of principle rather than anything involving an aunt he barely knew. Regardless, Cardinal Wolsey was given almost carte blanche to tackle what was now being called 'The King's Great Matter', along with Cardinal Campeggio, England's last 'cardinal protector'. Campeggio's entire mission was, in fact, a delaying tactic on the Pope's part. For starters, it took Campeggio, with his nagging gout, a considerable amount of time to make it to England. (When he arrives in *The Tudors*, it takes him a certain amount of time just to enter a room, never mind a country.)

It wasn't until the summer of 1529 that the legatine court was convened at Blackfriars. Various highly unedifying testimony flew back and forth amidst the duration of said court, much of it centred around whether Catherine really had lost her virginity to Arthur Tudor on or shortly after their wedding night. Never mind that a dispensation had previously been issued by Pope Julius II in Rome, neatly sidestepping that passage from Leviticus. Now, however, the King of England was taking issue with that dispensation and arguing that the Old Testament passage was the proper way to proceed after all, thereby casting aspersions on the authority and wisdom of several popes in the process. It was during said proceedings at Blackfriars that Catherine dramatically appealed to the King's conscience (good luck with that, girl) by falling to her knees before him and then letting rip with a masterpiece of emotionally charged eloquence:

Sir, I beseech you for all the loves that hath been between us, and for the love of God, let me have justice and right, take of me some pity and compassion, for I am a poor woman and a stranger born out of your dominion, I have here no assured friend, and much less indifferent counsel: I flee to you as to the head of justice within this realm. Alas! Sir, wherein have I offended you, or what occasion of displeasure have I designed against your will and pleasure? Intending (as I perceive) to put me from you, I take God and all the world to witness, that I have been to you a true and humble wife, ever conformable to your will and pleasure, that never said or did anything to the contrary thereof, being always well pleased and contented with all things wherein ye had any delight or dalliance, whether it were in little or much, I never grudged in word or countenance, or showed a visage or spark of discontentation. I loved all those whom ye loved only for your sake, whether I had cause or no; and whether they were my friends or my enemies. This twenty years I have been your true wife or more, and by me ye have had divers children, although it hath pleased God to call them out of this world, which hath been no default in me.

And when ye had me at the first, I take God to be my judge, I was a true maid without touch of man; and whether it be true or no, I put it to your conscience. If there be any just cause by the law that ye can allege against me, either of dishonesty or any other impediment to banish and put me from you, I am well content to depart, to my great shame and dishonour; and if there be none, then here I most lowly beseech you let me remain in my former estate, and received justice at your princely hand.

During said speech, Henry twice tried to pull her to her feet, but this was Catherine's moment, and she was having none of it. Anne Boleyn might have shone in the odd pageant or two, but when it came to the big stakes, Catherine of Aragon was a consummate performer on the international stage. When she was done, she swished out of the building, never to set foot in it again, this despite the summons from the court crier wafting along in her wake. The proceedings were eventually adjourned by Campeggio, who declared that he would reconvene the court in October. As a result, Cardinal Wolsey, the man who effectively ran the country, was disgraced and eventually arrested for his inability to procure the desired divorce; rumours of a plot percolating around Catherine and a plan via the Pope to *order* Henry to submit and return to his wife sealed Wolsey's fate.

Whether Anne took any satisfaction from ruining the man who had once thwarted her passion for Henry Percy will never be discerned; some say she was on the verge of badgering Henry in rather an un-Christian fashion to have the prelate's head removed. As it was, 'She exposed his duplicity, talking of the years that had been wasted while he pretended to act on their behalf with Rome. All the time he had been their enemy, fooling Henry and wasting their chances of marriage. She spoke so eloquently that he grew very emotional and even began to cry. She said she could not go on as her youth was passing.' (Denny, 2005, p165.) However, circumstances soon meant that Anne wouldn't be reaching for her jar of skin-preserving cold cream just yet; Wolsey died on his way to London before he could be tried and executed, at the end of 1530. Thus, a major stumbling block to the divorce was removed and marriage for Anne and Henry glimmered tantalisingly on the horizon. Henry Percy had been tasked with arresting Wolsey, a move even the most ardent Anne apologist has trouble framing as anything other than a perfectly placed piece of karmic scheming.

With Wolsey out of the way, Anne's hold on Henry increased. Among the spoils secured in the wake of the prelate's fall was York Place, the contents of which Henry and Anne inspected personally (on 24 October 1529, with Anne's mother acting as a chaperone). In Hilary Mantel's *Wolf Hall*, Anne pores over an inventory of the contents with all the tact of a half-heartedly bereaved relative at the solicitor's reading of a particularly bounteous will. Her father also took advantage of Wolsey's fall to hammer home his new position of prominence, staging a masque for the French ambassador in which Wolsey was literally dragged down to Hell by a quartet of devils. The play was later put on for the King. But Anne wasn't entirely prone to trampling over Wolsey's memory. When, several years later, his illegitimate son, Thomas Winter, petitioned the King for financial assistance, it was Anne who came to his aid and promised to do what she could for him.

Wolsey's demise left Anne almost free from suspicion as she began introducing Henry to various Reformist texts smuggled in from the Continent. Traditionally, Anne has been given sole responsibility for igniting the King's rather wobbly Reformist tendencies; more recently, several authors have suggested that his dissatisfaction with Catholicism predates Anne's appearance. However, that idea seems simply too convenient for that to be true. No, he tasked Wolsey with getting his divorce because at that point he still believed firmly in the Pope's ability to pass judgement; it was Anne who started to sway him away from a dependence upon Popish infallibility. Any doubts harboured before that were embryonic at best.

Among these treacherous tracts to which she introduced Henry were William Tyndale's *The Obedience of a Christian Man*, alongside *A Supplication for the Beggars* by Simon Fish; Fish had previously been exiled from England by Wolsey, while Tyndale was in exile in Antwerp. *A Supplication for the Beggars* amplified the cries of the poor, from whose hands all of the alms of England had been plucked by greedy prelates. In return, all the priesthood did was pray for the souls hovering in Purgatory, marking up the number of paid masses needed to 'save' these poor, lost creatures, the better to extract money from distraught relatives. Anne's copy of *The Obedience of a Christian Man* had been confiscated by the Dean of the Chapel Royal, but Anne undermined him by going straight to the King, who then commanded the book to be returned.

Tyndale was a pivotal figure in the Reformation, providing the first translation of the Bible into English – also the first to be mass produced and then disseminated – although he would suffer for his beliefs, strangled at the stake and then burned in 1536, several months after Anne herself was executed. Regardless, Tyndale's translation remained in constant demand despite efforts to suppress it. Anne herself possessed a copy, with 'Anna Regina Angliae' decorating the gilt edges; doubtless she perused the Lutheran preambles at her leisure. Regarding *The*

Obedience of a Christian Man, 'Apparently, he [Henry] thoroughly enjoyed it, exclaiming: "thys booke ys for me and all kynges to rede".' (Warnicke, 1989, p113.) The book laid out quite clearly the idea that the king of any given country was also head of that country's church, and not the Pope – in fact, the Pope had arrogantly arrogated the authority of Christ. The text also offered a staunch defence of Luther.

Tyndale's books were burnt in large quantities whenever they were seized; sometimes the odd heretic would be thrown in along with them, simply to stoke the fire. Nevertheless, their seditious message began seeping slowly but surely into the fibre of English society. Simon Fish widely distributed Tyndale's works, alongside penning the aforementioned *Supplication*. He was branded a heretic by the Catholic Church for his troubles but managed to avoid a possible burning when he was struck down with the bubonic plague. For Henry VIII, however, the theological poison was in the wound; these tracts, once consumed, were not easily forgotten, and he had ample time to discuss them with Fish before his death, after pardoning him and allowing Fish to return to England. This royal pardon was personally engineered by Anne, who had seen for herself the profit in introducing Henry to the ideas that Fish set out, wherein he declared that the authority of the Pope in England effectively made a mockery – a puppet – of England's ruler. Henry lapped it all up and Anne was delighted. Now, she and the King were firmly on the same page and he became even more besotted with his erudite fiancée. In fact, she became his only safe conduit by which he could discuss these ideas. Whether or not Anne had at this point schooled herself into evincing any genuine feeling for him we will never know, but, as a tool for furthering the Reformation, Henry was now quite possibly her most cherished possession – better than any expensive bauble or jewel.

Early in 1531, Bishop John Fisher of Rochester was poisoned by person or persons unknown. Bishop Fisher was a staunch supporter of Catherine of Aragon in her battle to hang onto her husband and prevent her marriage from being annulled. Alongside Thomas More, Bishop Fisher viewed with increasing horror the idea that Henry VIII's rapidly expanding ego should allow him to go so far as to declare himself head of the Church in England, effectively cutting the entire country off from the succour of Catholicism. The wily Fisher would, however, soon manage to get Henry to agree to the caveat 'As far as the law of God allows', but as time progressed it would become increasingly an impotent proviso. Bishop Fisher was, therefore, viewed with some antagonism by the Boleyn faction, especially as Anne's influence over Henry increased. What Anne wanted Anne got, after all, unless it happened to be a speedy divorce for her gullible sweetheart. As it was, the years immediately following Wolsey's downfall turned out to be almost wasted in terms of bringing this to fruition. Little wonder that Anne erupted on occasion and lamented the happily married life she might have been living elsewhere, providing sons for a doting husband, sons which were, in her rather guileful words, 'the greatest consolation a woman can know.' Perhaps. In the end, it would take a statesman of Thomas Cromwell's canny mettle to finally break the deadlock where the King's first marriage was concerned. But this narrative isn't ready to revolve around that notorious character just yet.

After having appeared in Catherine's defence at the Blackfriars court, Bishop Fisher was driven to further, somewhat dangerous extremes, apparently conspiring to have England invaded so that Henry might be overthrown, at which point the religious life of the country might be quickly rectified. These plans came to nothing, however, and someone, it seems, got wind of his intentions. A cook – Richard Roose (or Rouse) – was persuaded to insert some sort of noxious substance to the porridge or broth that Bishop Fisher and his household were due to consume; this, as said, was in early 1531. It may have been common ratsbane – ratsbane, also known as white arsenic, was frequently used during Tudor times – but it may have been something more 'exotic', like henbane. Henbane, sometimes called 'stinking nightshade', is a highly toxic plant with psychoactive qualities, to which, rather bizarrely, pigs are apparently quite immune. Symptoms of henbane poisoning include a dry mouth, convulsions, vomiting, blurred vision and delirium. Then again, it may have been a sprinkling of wolfsbane which spoiled Bishop Fisher's dinner party. Wolfsbane is so toxic that the ancient Romans actually used it as a method of execution. Symptoms of wolfsbane poisoning include convulsions, nausea and vomiting, alongside confusion and also mania. Either way, when the meal was consumed, several of Fisher's servants died, whilst several of his guests were quite sick. Bishop Fisher himself survived. One has only to peruse contemporary accounts of the man – 'skeletal' – to imagine how parsimonious he might be where his appetite was concerned, a dietary choice that doubtless saved his life. Richard Roose was soon apprehended and interrogated in the Tower of London, whereupon he stated that he had thought the substance mixed with the meal was simply a laxative and that the whole thing was therefore meant as some sort of a scatological prank.

However, this tale didn't wash terribly well with his accusers. The crime of poisoning was so feared in Tudor times that the appalling punishment of being boiled alive – usually in oil – had been passed as a deterrent. In fact, such was the fear of being done away with by poisoning that tasters for various dishes and delicacies were regularly employed by royalty to sample the food before passing it to their betters. In accordance with the law, and having been found guilty of the crime of poisoning, Richard Roose was thus boiled to death on 5 April 1531 at Smithfield. Initially swathed in chains attached to a hoist mechanism, he was then winched up and outwards, before being lowered into a heated cauldron. A merciful death meant that the victim was lowered in head-first, but if the executioner had been ordered to prolong the agony then a victim was lowered in feet-first – *very slowly* – and even pulled out several times so that they might suffer still longer. There is no record as to which particular way Richard Roose met his fate.

The brains behind the attempt on Bishop Fisher's life were never brought to book, if indeed there were any; perhaps it really was just a scatological prank gone awry. Or perhaps Roose was an ardent supporter of Henry VIII's divorce and sought to hasten matters in a culinary manner by despatching Bishop Fisher; or perhaps he really was paid by the Boleyns to remove Bishop Fisher from the table, quite literally. Perhaps one particular person from the aforementioned family had a direct hand in it: 'Whether or not she [Anne Boleyn] was guilty can, of course, never be proved. That she was quite capable of it, though, is strongly suggested by a message she sent to Fisher in October 1531. She advised him meaningfully not to attend parliament in case he should have a repetition of the sickness he had previously suffered.' (Louise Bruce, 1972, p178.)

Anne apologists maintain that such slurs simply will not be countenanced, but in the context of the crimes – and the times – it is not altogether out of the question. It must be remembered, however unpalatable the facts may be, that this was the same woman who would whisper malicious nothings into Henry VIII's ear until Thomas More lost his head, and who threatened to box the ears of Catherine's daughter Mary 'like the bastard she was' if she didn't kowtow to Anne's newly enhanced status. That Anne had previously at least desired the downfall of Cardinal Wolsey has already been illustrated, but there now attaches to her such a cult of panegyric that it seems doubtful such accusations of attempting to do away with Bishop Fisher will seriously stick. You can't allow the possibility of poisoning to spoil the veneer of a good, tragic historical heroine, after all.

As it was, the tables were soon turned when Anne found herself on the receiving end of a rather nasty – and overly prophetic – death threat, wherein she was depicted losing her head in a doodle made in an old book of prophesies. She was also apparently hounded out of a house on the Strand – the home of Sir William Skeffington – by a mob some several thousand strong, bent on wreaking revenge for the wronged Catherine of Aragon. Anne barely escaped with her life, taking a barge along the Thames in order to flee the horde. And that was just the tip of the iceberg. 'Reports came in to the authorities of people who were saying that Anne Boleyn was a whore who should be burned at Smithfield.' (Ridley, 2002, p24.)

In defiance of these and other detractors, Anne would briefly employ the motto '*Ainsi sera, groigne qui groigne*' ('Grumble all you like, this is how it's going to be'). Later, around the time of her coronation, she would adopt the more conciliatory 'The Most Happy' (or 'The Moost Happi', to give it that peculiarly particular Tudor spelling). When granted her own coat of arms, they would feature both her Butler and Howard heraldry, whilst for her queenly badge she would fly a white falcon, lifted from her Butler forebears. However, unable to resist a dig even at her most triumphant, this falcon would sometimes be seen pecking at a pomegranate, which was Catherine of Aragon's emblem. Perhaps Anne so loathed the corruption of Catholicism that some of that rancour simply spilled over in regard to her attitude to Catherine, dribbling all the way down to the pettiness of falcons pecking pomegranates. Needless to say, word of such slights did little to endear her to the general populace, although for the most part, Londoners – the odd lynch mob aside – were either indifferent, mildly curious or just momentarily riled. Anne has fans aplenty nowadays, but during her climb towards queenship she won few plaudits from the general public. For all her work in promoting the Reformation and exposing corruption in the Catholic Church, the rather unpalatable fact remains that she was still a willing partner in the breakup of someone's marriage. And to give Anne her 'feisty' due, she was as much to blame as Henry. Time to stop excusing her and allow her to grow up, rather than forever regarding her as some sort of giant adult baby, pushed and prodded this way and that one minute, but sassy and go-getting when it suits the narrative.

Eventually, Henry VIII simply abandoned poor Catherine. In what soon became his signature brand of callousness, he rode out one day from Windsor Castle with Anne and courtier Sir Nicholas Carew (a cousin of Anne's), leaving Catherine behind, without word of where he was going, so that she might move there and thus greet him when eventually he arrived. Apparently, the royal couple often reconvened in such a fashion. Word was soon sent to Catherine that she and her household should move themselves to The More in Hertfordshire for the foreseeable future. Thus, Anne finally secured the exile of her rival, although as a vague balm for Catherine, her entire household were permitted to go with her. Whether a certain Jane Seymour was among them seems unlikely (she was at court by Christmas 1533 but may have shared a brief portion of the exile); quiet, unassuming Jane, who doubtless bore witness to some of the distress her mistress bore at being parted from her husband. At the time, however, there was no indication that Catherine and Henry would never actually see each other again. Thus, in her unknowing exile, Catherine continued to enjoy all of the trappings of queendom, although as time progressed her visitors dwindled, as courtiers hedged their bets and cleaved to Anne instead. Soon, Catherine would find herself moved to another establishment, and then another, in an early echo of the itinerant life Mary Queen of Scots would lead whilst imprisoned in England by Anne's daughter, Elizabeth, some several decades later. As these moves mounted, so was Catherine's household whittled away, whilst visits from her daughter Mary were forbidden. The breakup of the royal marriage was to have almost as devastating an effect on Mary as it did her mother, bitterness mounting as she watched the woman who had usurped her mother climb to the very peak of English royalty. As his paranoia grew, Henry sought to keep Catherine and her daughter apart, mainly because he feared they might together plot an invasion to overthrow him and put

Catherine back on the throne, whilst at the same time meting out some good old-fashioned Spanish justice to Anne Boleyn.

Back in London, events continued to unfurl in ways beneficial to the Boleyns. When William Warham, Archbishop of Canterbury, died, the family were able – over a number of months – to manoeuvre their own family chaplain, Thomas Cranmer, into the much-coveted position. (During her brief reign, Anne would elevate many more evangelical bishops into positions of leverage and power.) Born in Nottinghamshire in 1489, Cranmer was a Cambridge graduate exposed to Lutheran ideas around the time Henry VIII first began obsessing about Anne. Cranmer became a Doctor of Divinity in 1526. Several years later, having grabbed Anne's attention and then the King's recommendation, he oversaw a plan to canvas the opinion of academic theologians throughout Europe, an enterprise of which Henry also heartily approved. Cranmer would share digs with George Boleyn whilst they furthered the plan to dismantle Henry's marital problems. On becoming resident ambassador at the court of Charles V, Cranmer witnessed for himself the slow but inexorable spread of Reformation on the Continent. More cautious than either Anne or Thomas Cromwell, he was nevertheless determined to see change, albeit at a rather more sedate pace.

It was during his tenure as ambassador that Cranmer was informed of the fact that he was now Archbishop of Canterbury. However, his hallowed new position brought with it considerable risks; he had previously married a German woman who bore him three children. Considering that the English clergy were supposed to be celibate, such a move meant that Cranmer was at one point (supposedly) forced to smuggle her into the country in a packing crate. However, what he perhaps lacked in his own matrimonial matters, Cranmer more than made up for in helping facilitate Henry's divorce from Catherine. In fact, 'Once he had accepted the royal supremacy he struck out manfully against the papacy, while at the same time his mind was full of schemes for liturgical reform of which the King would not have approved. However, Cranmer kept these to himself and Henry had no cause to complain of the devotion of his archbishop.' (Moorman, 1973, p170.) But whereas Henry wouldn't listen to these 'schemes for liturgical reform', Anne most certainly did.

Cranmer wasn't the only rising Reformist star orbiting Henry VIII's court at that time. The aforementioned Thomas Cromwell was fast making a name for himself, despite relatively obscure origins in Putney, where he was born in around 1485. Now, Cromwell was a widower, one who had also lost two daughters shortly thereafter, possibly due to an outbreak of the Sweating Sickness, this in 1529. After an early career in legal circles, he found himself a position in the household of Cardinal Wolsey, surviving his master's spectacular fall from grace several years later. The revenge he exacted on those he believed caused Wolsey's downfall takes up almost the entirety of the first two books in Hilary Mantel's Booker-winning triptych. Before that, in a precursor of his later Reformist role, he oversaw the dissolution of several monasteries on Wolsey's behalf, the funds appropriated for the schools and colleges Wolsey wished to open.

After Wolsey's demise, Cromwell rose like a phoenix from the ashes, securing firstly a place in Parliament, and then on Henry VIII's privy council. He became master of the King's jewels in 1532, and in 1534 was appointed Henry VIII's principal secretary and chief minister; by 1535, he could add the title of viceregent to his impressive tally. As an initially discreet Reformist highlighting clerical corruption, Cromwell endorsed the idea that the King alone was responsible for the spiritual welfare of his subjects; meaning that Henry would therefore also be able to settle his marital affairs under his own steam. With Cranmer rather a quiet figure and Anne rather a lofty one, Cromwell '...was therefore the driving force behind the Reformation in the 1530s. He used his influence over episcopal appointments to ensure that Reformers were preferred; he made London the centre of a major preaching campaign during the period of the attack on images; and he intervened in the mayoral elections in London in 1535-7 in order to support candidates with Protestant leanings. Above all he orchestrated mass circulation of the English Bible.' (Guy, 1990, pp181-182.)

We cannot know at what point Cromwell was 'infected' with the zeal for reform. As late as 1518 or so he was heading an embassy petitioning the-then Pope Leo X for the reinstatement of indulgences, a practice he would later abhor. He returned to England in May 1519. Apparently, Erasmus' New Testament (second edition) was his travel reading, which made him question his career choices. Luther's works were also widely available when Cromwell travelled, and he later told Cranmer that it was the overall reading experience undertaken during the Rome embassy that made him realise where he stood on religion. Prior to that, he seemingly had no opinion either way. It was the duty of Reformers to spread the good news, and so perhaps Anne helped cement Cromwell to 'the cause'. It is an appealing, empowering picture, albeit one painted almost entirely in the colours of conjecture. But the evidence seems to be that she would have been preaching to the converted; they were already singing from the same gospel hymn sheet. Boleyn, Cranmer, Cromwell; now all of the pieces were in place, the Reformist troika assembled. 'Revolutions acquire a momentum that is hard to stop. In the England of the 1530s religious revolution was pushed forward by Henry's new queen, Anne Boleyn, by Cromwell, and by the new archbishop whom events had required, Thomas Cranmer.' (Collinson, 2005, p111.)

Initially, Cromwell and Anne, sharing a Reformist passion, worked in tandem, but that would change. They both had Henry's favour, but Cromwell's position was infinitely more insecure, this despite the fact that Anne's hold on Henry would come to depend almost entirely on her ability to produce the son she'd promised. The English clergy, meanwhile, raised a spirited defence against the King's rupture with Rome, but backed down in the face of possible parliamentary reprisals. Prominent among those who then left the court in a veritable 'holy huff' was Thomas More, then Lord High Chancellor. Knighted in 1521, appointed Speaker of the House of Commons in 1523, and then Lord Chancellor in 1530, this lawyer/author/devout Catholic is now venerated by said church as 'Saint Thomas More', basically for daring to stick his head above the parapets and saying 'No' where Anne Boleyn was concerned.

As the Reformers grew in power at the English court, so did More watch his own power against them begin slowly dwindling away to nothing. Until the advent of Henry VIII's divorce from Catherine of Aragon, the King had in fact enjoyed a close companionship – one might almost dare call it a fully-fledged friendship – with More. Together, they ventured onto the roof of Hampton Court Palace to talk about the constellations, and Henry even visited More at his family home in Chelsea and begged him to take a permanent place at court, something More always declined; the backbiters, the 'superficialites' and the professional social climbers weren't to his tastes, by all accounts. In his own words, More was under no illusions whatsoever that while Henry *appeared* to favour him, he would have his head off his shoulders in a moment if it might secure him a castle in a foreign land. Ever the idealist, More famously wrote *Utopia*, in which he imagined a perfect future society existing on a remote island, free from all forms of corruption. But despite his erudite demeanour, he was a vehement opponent of the Reformation. Of Luther, More said that he allowed nothing in his mouth but 'privies, shit and dung'. In the TV adaptation of *Wolf Hall/Bring Up the Bodies*, Anton Lesser's More goes as far as to declare that Luther's mouth is '...the anus of the world.' Doubtless More would also have adhered to the slur that Luther's mother was a bathhouse maid who enjoyed a night of passion with no less a personage than Satan himself. Likewise, More undoubtedly relished the news that Luther, when in hiding, suffered terribly from constipation.

On becoming Lord High Chancellor of England, Thomas More used his authority to burn many heretics at the stake. He burned books as well as heretics, whereas his predecessor, Cardinal Wolsey, had been more content to turn the occasional blind eye to the former and settled simply for toasting the latter if and when necessary. More's ire, however, would even scald those who imported the heretical texts of Luther and his ilk, regardless of whether those involved adhered to the doctrine of such contraband or not.

Wolsey had always thought a more fitting way for England to combat Luther's heresies was to have the King compose a response, which was published in 1521. For this, Henry was created 'Defender of the Faith', an irony – given what was to come – that has provided historians with fodder for enough wry remarks to fill a phonebook. But by the early 1530s England was fast becoming a secret haven for heretics, and Henry was besotted with a woman doing all she could to aid and abet them. Before Thomas More, when a heretic proved particularly bothersome, as in the case of 'Little Bilney', Wolsey would still press for a public recantation rather than a burning, although in the end Bilney recanted his recantation and was thus burned for his obdurate heresy, by which time Wolsey was long gone and Thomas More was proving himself a merciless prosecutor.

But still the heretics trickled unceasingly into England. The same year Bilney was burned, Thomas Boleyn 'told the Papal Nuncio that England "care neither for pope or popes". Henry was "both pope and emperor" in his own kingdom'. (Hattersley, 2018, p12.) Thus, whilst the Lutheran purges progressed, many were disgraced but left alive, a sure sign of which way the wind was starting to blow as far as Anne's influence was concerned. Regarding these ameliorated punishments, public penance was meant to signify repentance from sin on the part of the accused, but for the most part – as Anne rose to prominence – it was simply an exercise in humiliating heretics rather than beating them senseless or something. In the early 1530s it was not uncommon to see men or women sitting backwards on horseback, guided through the city streets, with paper hats on their heads emblazoned with the words 'For crimes against the King's proclamations'. Sometimes their clothes were festooned with pages from Tyndale's translation of the Bible. They were then forced to burn copies of said book, before being secured in the pillory (the stocks) and then publicly ridiculed by the kind and considerate Tudor public. Still, it was better than being burnt.

It is rumoured that Thomas More tortured heretics in a concealed dungeon in the bowels of his Chelsea home, either on the rack or by some other means, and that he kept them there in chains for weeks at a time, without proper recourse to the letter of the law. He also regularly wore a hair shirt (as did Catherine of Aragon, as her fertility waned and she sought divine intervention) but there is no evidence that Anne ever considered such self-mortifying means. Such things smacked far too much of the venerations that she – as a Reformer – abhorred. Historians partial to More have downplayed or even denied these aspects of his life, but medieval mud sticks, and the accusations remain a stain on his reputation. The play and the film *A Man for all Seasons* (a movie the Vatican insists is one of the greatest cinematic masterpieces of all time) sidesteps these slightly less salubrious sides to More, instead focusing on him as the man who opposed the tyranny of Henry VIII as he tore England away from Rome in order to marry his concubine. This scenario makes Thomas More the perfect Catholic martyr, which is exactly what he became when his friendship with the King dissolved and he found himself in opposition to Henry's wishes. Truly, the bravery – or the stubbornness – he showed in defying Henry VIII is nothing sort of astonishing. Initially, he returned to his Chelsea home and kept his head down, until he was required to sign the newly inscribed Act of Succession, as well as the Oath of Succession, the former of which confirmed the rights of Anne's offspring to inherit the crown, whilst excluding Henry's first daughter, Mary. The latter oath, meanwhile, made it law to recognise Anne as Henry's queen, besides reinforcing the point about the legitimacy of their children to take the throne. Refusing to violate his conscience, More was taken to the Tower of London, where he would shortly join Bishop Fisher, who was already festering away in a dank corner of that forbidding edifice. Like More, Bishop Fisher had shown a singular contempt for everything that the various oaths and acts occasioned.

Elizabeth Barton would prove, in her own way, almost as contentious a problem as both Thomas More and Bishop Fisher combined. A domestic servant from Kent – she would later come to be called 'The Nun of Kent' – Barton was seized by illness whilst still in her teens. Upon her recovery – which she maintained had been guaranteed by no less a personage than the Virgin Mary – she claimed to be a receptacle for divine prophesies, winning plaudits from the aforementioned More and Fisher, among others. Such receptiveness for the readily miraculous shows the spirituality – or, some might think, the gullibility – of the Tudors, so eager to believe the holy utterances of this Biblical ingenue. But believe they did, packing her off to a nunnery in Canterbury where she might prophesise in peace. However, despite Tudor credulity where the self-appointed messengers of Christ were concerned, Archbishop Warham studied Barton's prophesies and also her wider declarations, before setting up a commission to verify their authenticity, alongside checking that she wasn't a rampant heretic on the sly. Barton passed both tests with flying colours. Before the break with Rome, even the King had an audience or two with her.

But all that changed once it became clear that he intended to cast aside Catherine of Aragon and marry Anne. From that point on, Elizabeth Barton became one of the most vocal critics of the new relationship; or, perhaps more pertinently, she became the perfect puppet for those in power who opposed the situation. From her base at the Benedictine St Sepulchre' Priory in Canterbury, a safe enough distance – or so she thought – from the court, she stated with some confidence that if Henry remarried then he would be dead within months. One source maintains that she even said as much to his face, although quite how she managed to wiggle her way out of any immediate punishment remains unclear. She may also have confronted Henry – and possibly Anne – when he passed through Canterbury in 1532.

By then, Barton was apparently too popular with the public to discredit directly – she numbered several of the aristocracy among her supporters – a caution that seems almost astonishing given that, several years down the line, Henry VIII would make history by having his wife beheaded, regardless of how the public perceived it. Apparently, he was at this point still in possession of at least some of his faculties. Besides that, perhaps even he had realised that Anne was never going to be as popular a queen as Elizabeth Barton was a prophet.

Covertly, agents from the court retaliated by spreading the rumour that Barton was a rampant nymphomaniac, engaged in sexual relations with practically every monk at her priory. Besides that, they also suggested that she was perhaps mad rather than miraculous. Eventually, her luck ran out and in 1533 she was arrested. She was interrogated by Cromwell and various others and forced to admit that her miracles were a sham. Given that Cromwell's technique of wringing forth a confession 'allegedly' involved winding a length of knotted cord around the accused's head and then pulling it fast over their eyes, such confessions need to be taken with an entire packet of salt, rather than just a pinch; just ask Mark Smeaton, more of whom later. There was word of an inconclusive trial for Elizabeth, but in the end, Cromwell enacted a bill of attainder, which allowed for the accused to be judged guilty and then punished without recourse to a trial; the Tudors, for the most part, tended not to bother with such formalities when they really wanted to get rid of someone. It remains rather a miracle itself that Anne herself ever had the chance to stand trial, but then she was the Queen of England.

Barton and several of her associates were also made to perform some public penance for their crimes. In November 1533 they were paraded atop a scaffold at St Paul's Cross (site of the Old St Paul's Cathedral) and made to publicly renounce their utterances. After that, they were carted off – quite literally – to the Tower of London. Barton was then attainted for treason. Rather quaintly, being 'attainted' in Tudor times meant that a sort of 'moral stain' descended upon the accused, alongside the earthier problem of having one's goods, lands and titles confiscated by the crown. Ironically, Anne herself would fall victim to this peculiar legality when she herself fell from grace. For Barton, such legal slurs meant that she was now considered a false prophet, one spoke in a wheel of conspiracy designed to demean Henry VIII and foil his plan to marry Anne. She wasn't executed until 1534, when she was hanged at Tyburn (modern-day Marble Arch, at the top of London's Oxford Street) along with five of her supporters. Among them was Edward Bocking, the Benedictine monk who had guided Barton's career for several years, whilst also offering his services as her confessor. Bocking had also compiled a list of her prophecies to be disseminated to the public in manuscript form. After their hanging, the bodies were beheaded. Barton was buried in Greyfriars Church, but not before her head was impaled on a spike atop London Bridge. And as Anne Boleyn was the first Queen of England ever to be executed, Barton was the first – indeed the only – woman to have her decapitated cranium disgraced in so public a fashion.

The fallout from Barton's disgrace pulled in several others associated with her. Archbishop Warham's former chaplain, Henry Gold, was also executed for his complicity in the affair. In the television adaptation of Hilary Mantel's *Wolf Hall*, Barton was played with unnerving relish by Aimee-Ffion Edwards, a performance that came almost as an antidote to Claire Foy's grasping, petulant Anne.

8

Patriarchal promises – The birth of Elizabeth Tudor

In 1532 Henry ennobled Anne, making her Marquess of Pembroke. This raised her within the ranks of the aristocracy to the point where she might accompany him on an imminent visit to Calais and not be considered therein as some sort of upstart chambermaid punching well above her weight. At least that was the theory. The main thrust of the visit involved a rendezvous with Francis I, to seek his support for their forthcoming nuptials. The ennobling ceremony took place at Windsor Castle, with Henry personally partaking in the proceedings. Anne wore ermine trimmed with velvet, a material indication of her newly minted status if ever there was one. She was accompanied by her cousin, the Countess of Derby, as well as the Countess of Rutland; her uncle, the Duke of Norfolk, was also present. She knelt before the King as the patent was read out to her by Stephen Gardiner, the new Bishop of Winchester (since the death of Cardinal Wolsey). Henry then crowned her with a gold coronet and draped a crimson velvet mantle about her shoulders. A sumptuous banquet followed the ceremony, during which Anne was given a brief pause to enjoy her success thus far. The platform by which she would push forth her plans for reform had surged forward a stage, but it would not be fully secure until she was actually Queen of England. Accompanying the ennobling, she also received lands worth over £1,000 a year. Other members of her family had already benefitted from the King's bounty: her father, now Viscount Rochford, was ennobled as the Earl of Wiltshire and also Earl of Ormond (in 1529); George Boleyn was styled Viscount Rochford, whilst his wife Jane became Lady Rochford.

However, 1532 wasn't a time of total triumph. A blast from the past blindsided Anne when Henry Percy's wife announced that her husband's earlier betrothal to Anne therefore invalidated her own marriage; thus, she was basically inferring that the King had no claim to Anne, because she was already affianced to someone else. It was well known that the Percy marriage was a particularly unhappy one, giving this attempt on the part of Mary Talbot to free herself from so odious a union a certain whiff of suspicion. Several years later, when Anne was awaiting her execution, Henry Percy wrote to Cromwell and assured him that there had never been any betrothal between himself and the Queen. Clearly, then, in 1536, there was a sense very much of a man trying desperately to cover his tracks, considering that almost every man with any vaguely amorous connection with Anne was then either imprisoned or dead. In conclusion, it is best to wheel out that tried and trusted Tudor trope, in regard to the possibility of Anne in fact being legally betrothed to Henry Percy – we shall likely never know. As it was, Mary Talbot's 1532 gambit filtered all the way down to Anne's uncle, the Duke of Norfolk, and then to Anne herself. One can imagine the colour quite blanching from her face as she heard the news. An inquiry was ordered, but Henry Percy denied it, as indeed he would in 1536.

The voyage to Calais took place on 11 October 1532, with the sweethearts setting off at dawn from Dover on *The Swallow*, accompanied by an ample retinue of nobles; anything to make sure Anne's passage appeared as grand as possible. However, both before and during said visit, she was still effectively snubbed by various members of the French nobility because of her 'dubious' position and pedigree; so much for the Marquess of Pembroke. Marguerite d'Angoulême was among those whom Anne hoped might be there to greet her, but instead Francis I came alone. Friendships only went so far, given that he was negotiating a marriage for his son, Henry, to the Pope's niece, Catherine de Medici, future mother-in-law of Mary Queen of Scots.

. However, Anne was at least spared some of the snidey public remarks she experienced whenever she set foot on the streets of London; the French were far more used to the idea of a royal mistress, after all, although the ample English residency in Calais were apparently still less than impressed. The abundance of English faces on French soil – in Calais – will achieve greater significance when this narrative reaches the story of the man who beheaded Anne Boleyn. The last bit of England left in France, Calais was a town filled with traders, merchants and diplomats, a heady mix of mainly English but with a fair percentage French. More than anything, it was a garrison, and resultantly never the most relaxed of places. Back in 1532, lavish entertainments were still thrown for the visit, including bear-baiting and bull-baiting events, as well as several banquets. Stuffing your face until you threw up and then watching an innocent animal suffer was pretty much your Tudor staple of a good night out. Whilst Henry and Francis renewed their rather antagonistic bromance, Anne had time to catch up with Gregorio Casali, one of the key diplomats residing in Rome, a man who had spent the best part of five years negotiating on behalf of the English King in order to obtain that pesky divorce. Actually, to say that Anne 'caught up' with Casali is being too kind. Still smarting from her French snubbing, she rounded on him for failing to bring forth said divorce in a suitable timeframe. Precisely, 'A Captain Thouard passed on reports (albeit at second or third hand) that Casali had been "ill-treated by the Lady for not managing her affair better, for she had hoped to be married in the middle of September". He believed that Henry had intended to marry Anne in Calais, but for some reason the ceremony had been delayed, "to the advantage of the Emperor". One can only speculate what wrath the newly promoted Anne might have vented on an agent who had let her down.' (Fletcher, 2013, pp178-179.)

After cooling her heels – and her temper – in Calais for several more days, Anne managed to secure a private audience with the French King, after performing at a costumed masque where she quite literally shimmied and vogued around the hall along with a troop of her ladies, eight of them in all. At a prearranged signal from Henry, Anne loosened the bands holding her mask in place as she was dancing with Francis himself; Henry then whipped off the mask, much to the delight of his fellow monarch. To modern eyes this all comes across as rather camp and contrived, but the Tudors couldn't get enough of this sort of theatrical tomfoolery. Anne and Francis then retired to some discreet corner where he doubtless congratulated her on her lofty ambition now almost realised.

As it was, Henry and Anne were married on 25 January 1533 in a small ceremony in London, at Whitehall Palace. An earlier 'secret' ceremony was conducted on 14 November 1532, shortly after returning from Calais (perhaps at Dover Castle; others suggest Eltham Palace).

The 1532 date tallies better with regard to the birth of their daughter, Elizabeth, as a point at which they might have enjoyed their wedding night, with the child conceived some several weeks later. However, the 'officially recognised' date for the wedding remained 25 January 1533. Regardless, whatever went down in either Dover Castle or Eltham Palace at the end of 1532 left the couple sufficiently secure in the foreknowledge of their 'sanctioned' nuptials to abandon caution and finally to sleep together. However, it is also possible that it was whilst waiting out a storm in Calais that Anne and Henry first made love, and when Elizabeth was conceived.

The first subsequent signs of pregnancy manifested, for Anne, in the casual overconfidence that she was carrying the boy the Tudor patriarchy required. Now, all that remained was for her to be crowned and to provide where Catherine of Aragon clearly couldn't. With a son in the cradle, her plans for the Reformation could continue apace, and perhaps Henry wouldn't bother her to provide a spare for another few years.

Unfortunately, things would pan out rather differently. Back in England, Anne's position nevertheless became somewhat more secure, allowing her to act quite openly as the queen-in-waiting she so clearly was, receiving foreign diplomats and granting petitions to those who came seeking royal favour and patronage (and succour from persecution). But contrary to Anne's wishes, the vast majority of the English public remained firmly behind Catherine of Aragon, and still considered her to be the rightful Queen of England. They also considered her daughter Mary to be Henry's rightful heir, and not any 'bastard' born of the Boleyn woman. Clearly, many of them had more confidence in the idea of female rule than the King himself. Or Anne, for that matter.

Either way, it soon became clear that England's new queen-in-waiting was expecting. Anne, never one to pass up an opportunity to crow about her fecundity, couldn't resist dropping a few choice titbits to those around her: 'On February 22, coming out of her chamber into a crowded hall, she met Sir Thomas Wyatt. The news bubbled out of her. "Three days ago," she told him, "I had an inestimable wild desire to eat apples. I have never liked them before. The King says it is a sign that I must be with child. I tell him no. I cannot be!" At this she laughed out loud and ran back into her chamber, leaving the assembly agog with curiosity.' (Louise Bruce, 1972, p213.) One cannot fault her confidence, but knowing the outcome as we do, there is almost an overbearing desire to petition her to be just that little bit more circumspect. Certainly, Anne seems not have taken to heed any of the experience her predecessor had suffered in attempting to provide England with a male heir. But then, she wouldn't be Anne Boleyn if she cocked too much of an ear to what Catherine of Aragon had experienced.

One hopes Anne was at least tactful in not taking revenge on those who had maligned her during her rise to power. Sir Henry Guildford, for one, escaped her rather un-Christian wrath by dying several months earlier. Anne had threatened to strip him of his office when she became queen; Sir Henry responded by resigning and thus depriving her of the chance to exercise her spite, despite the King pleading with him not to pay heed to 'the words of women'. Several weeks after the announcement of her apple cravings, 'On Holy Saturday, 12 April, the Queen of England processing in regal finery at Court to the Vigil Mass of Easter was Anne Boleyn. On Easter Day Prior George Browne, Cromwell's landlord at Austin Friars, used his festal sermon or liturgical bidding of the bedes to pray for Anne as Queen, at which a large section of the congregation marched out in protest, provoking Henry to fury and prohibition of any such further demonstrations in the City.' (MacCulloch, 2019, pp218-220.) Anne might have just made her first public appearance as Queen of England but, clearly, the public still weren't having it.

Meanwhile, Cranmer '...humbly petitioned to be allowed to hold a court of enquiry into the King's "great cause of matrimony". The result of this enquiry, to no one's surprise, was a solemn archiepiscopal pronouncement that the King's first marriage was null and void, his second good and lawful.' (Plowden, 2010, p11.) Needless to say, this was done without approval from the Pope, egging on yet another stage of the break between England and the Papacy. As a result, poor Catherine was informed that she was no longer a queen at all, and to henceforth style herself 'Dowager Princess of Wales'. Possibly Anne crowed at the implementation of such a demotion, but even at this juncture, those historians with an almost pathological preference for her misread the situation; 'We all know how it feels to go into a relationship where the ex is still lurking in the background. We would not be human if we did not want them to just disappear!' (Ridgway, 2012, p143.) The trouble with this statement is that Catherine wasn't simply 'the ex'; she remained, as far as most of Europe was concerned – not to mention Prior George Browne's congregation – Henry's legal wife and the rightful Queen of

England. Catherine hadn't consented to the divorce, never mind the dubious legality of the thing. Nor was she 'lurking in the background', but rather had been quite literally prised from the court and shoved into an undignified exile. Let me repeat: *there was no consent whatsoever.* However, the fact that she didn't have her head lopped off means that her plight will always play second fiddle to that of Anne. Meanwhile, Catherine might have been banished, but she was still with spirit enough to deny that demotion for all she was worth, and, quite literally, to rip the paper to shreds where she scored through her newly minted relegation with a tightly gripped quill pen.

Soon, Parliament declared that Henry was now Supreme Head of the Church of England, sealing forever the split from Rome (bar the spirited and rather vicious later attempt by Catherine's daughter Mary to reverse the process, one smouldering Protestant at a time). Besides elevating the King to near-omnipotent status, the whole thing also amounted to a colossal triumph for Anne and her family, regardless of the fact that to most (this particular epithet coined by one Margaret Ellis of Suffolk) she was simply the 'goggle-eyed whore'.

Whilst all of the elaborate and rather lengthy coronation theatricals were rehearsed, Anne could perhaps take a little comfort and mirth in the company of her fool, Jane (sometimes called 'Jane Foole' or just 'Jane the Fool'). One of the less palatable facts about the Tudors is their propensity for corralling people with autism or mental illness – alongside various physical disabilities – into being their 'fools' or court jesters. Poor Jane was – presumably on Anne's execution – passed with some relish into the service of Catherine's daughter, never a woman known for compassion for her fellow man – or mentally ill woman – at the best of times. However, this may be something of a disservice to Mary, as records indicate that Jane was well cared for – at least in a material sense – while in Mary's service. From there, Jane managed to wind up serving Henry's last wife, Catherine Parr. In the BBC adaptation of *Wolf Hall/Bring Up the Bodies*, Jane is portrayed by Sarah Bennett. In 1535 Henry VIII's own fool, Will Somers, would flee the King's wrath when he dared joke about Anne and her daughter, even daring to call Elizabeth a bastard. Somers took shelter at the home of Sir Nicholas Carew, who was by then in the process of switching allegiance from Anne to the incoming Jane Seymour.

Anne was crowned Queen of England on 1 June 1533. By this time, she was visibly pregnant; radiant, even. Beforehand, commencing on Saturday, 31 May, she took part in a lengthy procession from the Tower of London – where she had stayed for several nights previously – and through the City to Westminster Abbey, where the actual ceremony took place. The route took in Tower Hill, before moving up onto Fenchurch Street. From there, it emerged onto Gracechurch Street and then made a right, towards what is today the entrance to Leadenhall Market. The procession then veered towards Cornhill and then Cheapside, before coming to the original St Paul's Cathedral. It then moved down Fleet Street and out of the City of London, towards Westminster.

Despite all the pomp, pageantry and effort that went into the parade, which had also included a magnificent river procession, the public's reaction was unenthusiastic. Of course, we have Chapuys to thank for this observation, but it isn't entirely impossible as there are no records of wild jubilation to counter his typically biased despatches. There were various stopping-off points during the land procession where Anne was invited to watch some little spectacle or other, put on especially by the residents of London. It was an exercise in royal bootlicking on a city-wide scale, with allegories aplenty, many emphasising Anne's fertility. No pressure there then. At Fenchurch Street she was regaled with a tableau which made great show of her links with France, including a group of children dressed as merchants, who greeted her speaking both English and French. At the corner of Fenchurch and Gracechurch Streets she was dazzled/intimidated by a tableau designed by no less a person than Tudor portraitist extraordinaire Hans Holbein. A series of Latin verses were held aloft by actors dressed as various gods and muses:

> Anna comes, the most famous woman in all the world,
> Anna comes, the shining incarnation of chastity,
> In snow white litter, just like the goddesses,
> Anna the queen is here, the preservation of your future.

As she sat in that litter of white satin dripping with cloth of gold, with these words dangling before her, her nerves must have been as taut as the string on a bow. Of course, Anne had already made that leap of faith which enabled her to promise Henry that she would give him a son;

to present a girl, after all this trouble, was quite unthinkable. As said, Chapuys considered the whole procession a 'cold, meagre affair', but his biased reportage was bound to be somewhat sour. The truth undoubtedly lies somewhere in the middle, for the unpalatable fact remained that the public still considered Catherine of Aragon the King's lawfully wedded wife. Besides this, she had a popular personal affinity with the common people, who, in return, saw themselves as offering shelter and succour to this Spanish princess, living so very far from her native land.

As mentioned, from the corner of Fenchurch and Gracechurch Streets, the procession turned right, up to the present entrance to Leadenhall Market. There, a large backdrop consisting of a castle draped by clouds had been erected to greet Anne, the fluffy plumes adorned with reclining angels and cherubs. In the very midst of the clouds, atop a green knoll, sat the figure of Saint Anne, the mother of the Virgin Mary. She was flanked by several of her illustrious descendants, including, of course, the man for whom Anne had endured to come this far, namely Jesus himself. Again, the message of the tableau was all about fecundity and providing the country with a male heir.

From Leadenhall, the procession moved across Gracechurch Street and along to Cornhill, where another tableau awaited Anne at the site of a conduit used to bring the spring waters down from the hills beyond London. Here, Anne was waylaid by figures representing the Three Graces, namely 'Glad Heart', 'Stable Honour', and 'Continual Success'. The procession then travelled to Cheapside, which was, in Tudor times, one of London's main shopping thoroughfares. (Today, little side streets bearing names like 'Honey Lane' and 'Milk Street' give an indication of some of the wares then on offer.)

Anne's cortege passed by buildings draped in cloth of gold and of velvet, with the various livery companies arrayed down one side of the street, whilst on the other a generous spread of London's citizenry gazed on in vaguely morbid curiosity. The procession paused as it passed Honey Lane, with Anne treated to more Latin speeches, punctuated by a few lighter musical performances. The procession then eased along past the church of St Mary le Bow, where she was presented with a gold purse full of money. It was bad form to peer inside and count the contents, so Anne quickly passed it to one of her ladies.

The procession then approached the original St Paul's Cathedral, where Anne was confronted with the spectacle of an empty throne.

Below, three gaily clad women held up a sign that said, 'Come my love, thou shalt be crowned'. The crowds, meanwhile, threw wafers bearing the message, 'Queen Anne, when thou shalt bear a new son of the King's blood, there shall be a golden world unto thy people.' Never let it be said that the Tudors didn't know how to labour a point. The mood was lightened somewhat by the spectacle of some several hundred children reading Latin poems. At the conclusion, Anne apparently responded with a joyous 'Amen', although whether this was in appreciation or perhaps simply an exclamation of fatigued relief that the whole thing was over remains unclear. From St Paul's, as said, the procession then moved off down Fleet Street and out of the City of London, before veering off towards Westminster.

As for the actual crowning itself, Anne wore robes of purple velvet trimmed with ermine. She arrived at Westminster Abbey under a gold canopy borne along by the Lords Warden of the Cinque Ports. As the ceremony proceeded, she prostrated herself before the high altar, before receiving the crown of St Edward. At this point, she was sat in St Edward's Chair, arranged in cloth of gold, the favoured piece of furniture on which all monarchs of England were crowned and anointed. The chair stood on a dais, itself positioned on a raised platform carpeted in red. She was then anointed by the Archbishops of Canterbury and York. Previously, the crown of St Edward, the prized piece of monarchical headwear, had only ever been used to crown a reigning ruler. One likes to imagine that at this pivotal moment Anne and Cranmer exchanged a wry, knowing and rather triumphant glance, as he passed her the rod and the sceptre. The King was present, albeit hidden from the proceedings behind a lattice-work screen, from where he could observe incognito. Anne's hair was free-flowing and by all accounts trickled all the way down to her waist.

The crown of St Edward was soon exchanged for a lighter model, after which Anne took the sacrament and then made the habitual offering at the shrine of the saint. She was then given a brief respite from these rather gruelling proceedings, taking some light refreshment before presiding over a sumptuous banquet at Westminster Hall. Several years later, her allegedly adulterous harem of lovers would find themselves being tried for treason within those self-same hallowed walls. However, in 1533, in the wake of the coronation, those walls, now hung with arras, had merely to observe the like of Charles Brandon, Duke of Suffolk, capering around on his horse in his role as high steward, along with Lord William Howard, deputising for the Duke of Norfolk. Anne herself was seated at a long marble table, on a marble chair mounted on a dais, under the customary cloth of estate. Only Cranmer shared this place with her, although the Dowager Countess of Oxford and the Countess of Worcester stood beside Anne, wielding a cloth by which they might conceal her if she wanted to spit 'or do otherwise' (quite what 'do otherwise' entailed is perhaps best left to the imagination). A further two gentlewomen were seated at Anne's feet, beneath the table, although for what practical purpose again seems unclear. Perhaps they were there to help Anne covertly consume a staggering total of eighty-two different dishes spread over three courses. This culinary ordeal came to a conclusion at six o'clock in the evening, following the closing ceremonies, after which it seems little short of miraculous that the new Queen didn't need to be carried bodily to her apartments.

More feasts occurred in the days that followed, along with jousts and other entertainments. The patriarchal pressure on Anne had now reached boiling point. The King and his courtiers had feted her, and even the citizenry of London had doffed their hats to her – or not, if Chapuys is to be believed – and now it was her turn to deliver the boy child she had promised. Henry would accept nothing less. But despite her crowning glories, most of the country continued to abhor her. A Lancashire priest, one voice among many, boldly asserted that Catherine was still the rightful Queen of England, before adding, 'Who the devil made Nan Boleyn, that whore, queen, for I will never take her for queen!'

To the modern reader, the strictly matriarchal world of Tudor childbirth seems more than a little odd. But before lifting the curtain on this one province where women reigned supreme, it is perhaps worth noting that whilst Anne's first pregnancy was initially quite benign, she suffered somewhat in her third trimester. In fact, her travails were such that the King was almost hoping she would miscarry, and thus put an end to her pains. Knowing and 'loving' Henry VIII as we do, it is hard to credit him with so compassionate a plea, but it seems there was at some point apparently a genuine risk to Anne's life.

Typical third trimester troubles include shortness of breath, urinary incontinence, haemorrhoids, and trouble sleeping. However, more life-threatening complications include preeclampsia, as well as placenta previa and placenta abruption. Preeclampsia can be fatal for both mother and child, but given the relatively primitive state of Tudor medicine, it seems unlikely Anne would have been successfully diagnosed and then treated, although the condition had been recognised for over a thousand years. With placenta previa, the placenta attaches lower in the uterus and may then block the cervix; with placenta abruption, possible heavy bleeding and shock can kill both mother and child, whereas with placenta previa the bleeding may not be as serious and the pregnancy may then continue unimpeded until natural delivery.

Given the veil of secrecy that surrounded the Tudor birthing chamber, we will likely never know for sure what occurred, but given that Anne seems to have been troubled during the entire summer of 1533, it may be that her problems were a simple accumulation of the more common third trimester problems, coupled with the weight of patriarchal expectations weighing so heavily on her shoulders. Certainly, despite Henry's concerns, no medical emergency was reported. They spent most of that summer at Windsor Castle, stewing in a pot of anticipation, excitement and thinly veiled trepidation.

In August 1533, a bedchamber was made ready for Anne at Greenwich Palace. To be more accurate, the place provided was little more than an elaborately decorated torture chamber. Light and fresh air were provided by one small, modestly veiled window, but those wily Tudor midwives considered even this concession a risk to the expectant mother's health and wellbeing. The tapestries decorating the birthing chamber were to depict only the gentlest and most beatific scenes – no gurning warriors or roaring animals, basically. Anything of that sort was apparently prone to prompting morbid fantasies in the mother's mind, which might then 'infect' her mind, the negative thoughts then transmitting to the child and causing it – at this late stage, even – to emerge malformed.

On 26 August, after a special mass at the Chapel Royal, Anne and her ladies retired to the queen's great chamber, the outermost room of Anne's vast suite. There, they drank a little wine and enjoyed some spices, before Anne's lord chamberlain put a stop to this rather tepid scene of revelry, praying that God would give the Queen a safe delivery. Anne then moved to her bedchamber, with only her ladies in attendance. At this point, the door was closed on the men and whatever happened inside the bedchamber became a concern for the women only. On 7 September, after almost ten days or so in confinement, Anne went into labour. However, instead of producing the anticipated son she instead delivered a redheaded girl, later christened Elizabeth. Apparently, the birth was relatively straightforward; if it wasn't, well, as said, the midwives kept their counsel, because no tales of mishaps have trickled forth from that sacred matronly sanctum. However, the blatantly obvious fact remained that the sex of the child was considered rather a major misstep.

The majority of films and TV dramas put great store in this particular point in the story, with Anne distraught upon learning that she had failed to make good on her heady patriarchal promise. Again, if indeed she sobbed and wondered what might become of her, well, the midwives and ladies present kept quiet about it. Certainly, Henry's face when informed of the fact that his great patriarchal gamble had gone so spectacularly awry must have been *the* classic 'Kodak moment' of the Tudor age.

Soured by Anne's failure to make good on her promise to deliver a son, he nevertheless declared that, as they were both still young, boys would surely follow. Quite how he came to this conclusion remains unclear, unless he fully intended to subject Anne to multiple pregnancies until she 'came good'. Meanwhile, 'The Catholic world guffawed and perceived evidence of divine judgement.' (Baldwin Smith, 1969, p61.) The various jousts and pageants that would have accompanied the birth of a boy were discreetly cancelled – the all-encompassing Tudor patriarchy at work – and the odd document or two were rather shoddily amended from 'Prince' to 'Princess'.

Some stir has been made of the fact that Henry failed to attend the child's christening, but as Retha Warnicke explains, 'His absence was dictated by religious protocol, of course, and not by his disappointment that she was a daughter rather than the son he had been expecting.' (Warnicke, 2000, pxiii.) Certainly, the child was soon given her own establishment at Hatfield House, with the recently demoted Mary Tudor, daughter of Catherine, now forced to wait on her as part of the newly created household. Or was she? More recently, it has been suggested Mary was simply forced to reside in the same establishment as her half-sister but wasn't actually required to demean her status by changing any Tudor nappies. Meanwhile, Anne struggled with this enforced separation from her newborn, although removing a royal baby from court was practically the norm. She visited Elizabeth as often as she could and eventually succeeded in having her moved to Eltham Palace, just outside London. Pretty soon, the child was spending ever-increasing amounts of time at the court with her mother, propped up against a cushion in order to give her a little regal bearing. Anne was never less than a doting, devoted mother, at least when protocol permitted.

A battle of wits soon ensued between Anne and Mary over Mary's recognition of Anne's new status as Queen of England. Among Anne's more contentious – and therefore hotly contested – missives at this time involved her instructions that if Mary did not toe the line then her 'ears should be boxed like the bastard she was'. Another occasion has Anne declaring that she '...wished that all Spaniards were at the bottom of the sea.' Small wonder that in Spain the term 'Anna Bolena' remains a name used to signify an untrustworthy, sexually unscrupulous woman.

Yet another well-worn anecdote has Anne and Mary hearing Mass together at Eltham Palace. Mary apparently threw her wicked stepmother a curtsey as she left, the later report of which filled Anne with delight – at last, the tempestuous stepdaughter brought to heel! Only she wasn't, because when Mary responded to Anne's gratefully worded missive, she declared herself quite agog that Anne had had the temerity to sign herself as 'The Queen', given that she was 'so very far from this place/exalted station.' This led to more heated language on Anne's part, although Mary apparently gave as good as she got. As a result of these fiery relations, it was even suggested that Anne and/or members of her family intended to poison both Mary and her mother. And of course, the person or persons responsible for poisoning poor Bishop Fisher had never been brought to book...

9

Miscarriages, misery and
Mark Smeaton

Anne miscarried or suffered some sort of phantom pregnancy in 1534. One minute it was rumoured that she was expecting and then quite suddenly all trace or mention of the promised prince promptly vanished. Possibly, the same thing later happened in early-to-mid 1535, but more likely the records simply mixed up that year with the previous one; we cannot blame the royal court for neglecting to keep a precise tally of the failure of Anne's pledged fertility. But the fact of the matter was that, slowly but surely, her stock was falling: 'No longer the witty audacious woman confident of her powers, she appeared tamed, even servile, following her husband about "like a dog its master", aware that even those who had once befriended her were deserting her in her decline, that foreign envoys were turning their backs on her.' (Hibbert, 1992, p15.)

Anne must have realised how foolhardy it had been to gamble on the capricious lottery of childbirth. Even the prototype coin minted in anticipation of the 1534 pregnancy must have come to seem like a cruel taunt. Often referred to as 'The Moost Happi' coin, it is considered the only surviving contemporary portrait of Anne, although the nose has been rather brutally battered off by hand or hands unknown. Either that, or the simple matter of casual handling over time has rubbed it away, given that the forehead is also smoothed down, leaving Anne looking as though some latter-day Boleyn sympathiser decided to give her a shot of Botox or something. The sculptor Lucy Churchill has completed an excellent reconstruction of the coin, which can be viewed on her website. Unfortunately, to the modern eye, even a restored coin from 1534 gives little real idea of Anne's appearance, bearing too much of a resemblance to the vaguely cartoonish – Holbein aside – portraits that the Tudors set so much stock by. The real Anne was, however, quick to realise that aping the coin's motto was the key to keeping hold of her husband whilst she tried desperately to conceive and then carry a baby to full-term.

Either Margaret ('Madge') or Mary Shelton, first cousins of the Queen, stepped into the breach at this point to become Henry's mistress. In *The Tudors*, the liaison is instigated by none other than Anne herself, as a way of keeping a controlling hand on Henry's extramarital affairs, whereas in real life it seems the thing happened more by chance than by any design on Anne's part. Yet again, it was simply a case of the King helping himself to the walking confectionery box that comprised his wife's ladies-in-waiting. Precise details about the Shelton sisters are hard to come by; several historians have suggested they may even have been one person, with misspelt names and poor records leading to two disparate identities. Either way, *The Tudors* opts for 'Madge' rather than Mary as the mistress of this particular period. 'Madge' would apparently get into hot water with Anne, not for bedding the King but for doodling in her prayer book. Coming from Anne, who had scribbled all over her own holy tomes when courting Henry, this was a bit rich.

'Madge' had in fact arrived on the scene in the wake of Henry's fling (or idle dalliance) with an unnamed lady who caused some considerable stir in the Boleyn household by befriending Catherine's daughter and promising to advance her cause come what may. This mystery woman is unlikely to have been 'Madge' or Mary, given that they were family, although it is not entirely out of the question; families fall out, after all. Some historians have speculated that perhaps the mystery woman was Jane Seymour putting in an early appearance – the character profiles match to some extent, given that Jane would later put great stock in befriending Mary – but most maintain that the identity of this particular amour remains enigmatic. Given this uncertainty, *The Tudors* decided to create an entirely new character, 'Lady Eleanor Luke', out of this mysterious mistress, although the plotline then mirrors reality, with Anne threatened enough to contrive to have her rival removed from court, although in reality she used her sister-in-law Lady Rochford to help usurp the cuckoo in the royal nest, rather than her brother. Concerning George Boleyn; he married Jane Parker around 1524, receiving the manor of Grimston in Norfolk as a wedding present from the King. If you believe the fictional accounts then the marriage was a less than happy arrangement; if you subscribe to the various TV shows and movies, then it was downright abusive. There were no children from the union, which suggests that George may have been homosexual, or possibly that problems with conception weren't limited – within the Boleyn family – strictly to his sister.

Although Anne and Jane would fall out in spectacular style several years later, initially they were sufficiently allied for Anne to contrive an argument between her sister-in-law and the King's mysterious new mistress. However, this rather cack-handed scheme was quickly uncovered, and it was Lady Rochford who instead found herself being sent packing from the centre of power. This rather lamentable backfiring of Anne's plan may, it has been suggested, have been what caused Lady Rochford to begin nursing such a grievance towards her sister-in-law; and if the marriage was as unhappy as rumoured, then George's delight at being temporarily freed from his termagant of a wife may have merely rubbed salt in poor Jane's wounds. Certainly, matters worsened when she found herself a place amidst a teeming demonstration of women marching for the rights of Catherine's daughter. Along with several others, Jane was tossed into the Tower of London for her intransigence. It was her first visit, but it wouldn't be her last.

Meanwhile, Anne's steadying hand on her husband's virility continued to weaken. 'Henry had reprimanded her, reminding her that she owed her position entirely to him, and that he was regretting the indulgence which he had hitherto shown her.' (Loades, 2017, pp56-57.) Then, at the end of 1534, an incident occurred at a banquet at which the Admiral of France was present. He and Anne were conversing, when suddenly she noticed that Henry had yet to return with the guest Anne had despatched him to summon, so that they too might make the Admiral's acquaintance. Those black eyes scoured the room and soon settled upon the sight of the King idly flirting with a rather attractive young woman, the task of guiding the guest to Anne's table quite forgotten. Anne burst out laughing at the sight, but it was the mirth of the disconcerted, and the Admiral found her demeanour tasteless.

Still, 1534 was not without its consolations. Anne acquired a lapdog called Purkoy – possibly a toy spaniel – the name derived from the French 'pourquoi' (why?). But although Henry no longer trotted diligently behind her, Anne had, in Purkoy at least, one faithful companion to keep her company as she struggled to reassert herself. However, Purkoy's star was not long in the ascendant; he died from 'a fall' at the end of the year, a blow broken to Anne by the King himself. The circumstances of the little dog's death are so mysterious – how does a dog die of 'a fall' anyway? – that it has led to several fictional works blaming Purkoy's death either on Jane Seymour (the chronology is slightly askew there, but it may well have been the 'unnamed lady' with whom Henry dallied before 'Madge') or else one of the many other courtiers disgruntled at Anne's lofty position. Unfortunately, Anne didn't do well with pets overall; several years previously one of her greyhounds had savaged a farmer's cow, the compensation for which came out of the King's privy purse. Meanwhile, another snarling animal was brought to heel when Anne fell out with her uncle, the Duke of Norfolk. Pertinently, she was said to have used words against him as '...one would not use to address a dog'. In response, he called her 'The great whore' (or, less flatteringly, but, as Robert Hutchinson points out, far more likely, knowing Norfolk, 'The big fuck').

All of this domestic drama took place against an increasingly fraught political backdrop. The final break with Rome occurred in 1534, when the Act of Supremacy recognised Henry VIII as sole head of the English Church. Excommunication – meaning your soul would be disbarred from entering Heaven – had been threatened several times in the leadup to this event, but it wouldn't be until 1538 that Henry was formally expelled from the Catholic Church (Luther had been excommunicated back in 1520, tossing the proclamation onto the fire upon receiving it). On learning of Henry's marriage to Anne, the automatic Catholic response had been to declare it invalid, and to issue the aforementioned threat of excommunication. However, in 1534 it remained just that: a threat.

To all intents and purposes, England was still very much a Catholic country; form and doctrine endured, but the major difference was that divine judgement was now issued by the King's temper rather than the Pope's procrastination. For Anne, regret at Henry's increasing irascibility was doubtless tinged with hope; the biggest blow to a corrupt regime had come to pass and there was time aplenty – or so she thought – to ease through the remaining changes and perhaps reconcile with a suitably chastised Rome. To reiterate, she wanted reform, not an entirely new religion that would sweep the old one aside in some sort of revolutionary movement. Never one for false modesty, she was, however, quick to remind Henry that he was 'more bound to her than man can be to woman, for she extricated him from sin.'

Henry himself, meanwhile, '...however slowly and unwillingly he had achieved his supremacy, once he had it, found he rather liked it; it appealed to his self-importance as a king and to his self-image as a concerned Christian. What had been designed as a weapon to gain a new queen and implemented to protect the new marriage became an essential attribute of kingship.' (Haigh, 1993, p121.) C. S. L. Davies argues that, 'the divorce from Catherine of Aragon was necessary for the national interest; it is much harder to do so (though in other respects Catherine is the more sympathetic figure) in the case of Anne Boleyn. In this sense Henry's actions came close to what contemporaries understood by tyranny: "all things pertaining to the state of [the] realm to hang only upon [the ruler's] will and fantasy". So much power – alongside the ability to dismiss his longstanding wife – caused Luther to bluntly dismiss the English Reformation as "What Squire Harry wills".' (Davies, 1976, pp236-237.) Regardless, the Catholic default setting resolutely maintained that Henry's marriage to Catherine remained true and valid. But when Catherine eventually died, the shift would actually have far from liberating repercussions for her 'less sympathetic' successor.

Soon, a further bout of executions was required to bring the public to heel in regard to the burgeoning Reformist regime. The Carthusian monks of the London Charterhouse at Smithfield were opposed to Henry VIII's religious rewiring, spurred on by the obstinacy shown by Rome. These simple, pious men simply could not countenance that the Pope no longer had any authority in England and that they were no longer to invoke his name even in their prayers. Worse still, that name was to be expunged from all service books, on Cromwell's express orders. One by one, the various religious houses were being shut down, their occupants either imprisoned or fleeing the country.

There was resistance to these dissolutions, and several times Cromwell's enforcers came off worse than the holy men they were evicting, but for the most part the suppressions went ahead unimpeded. Several of the Carthusian monks were sent to their deaths in May 1535, their half-starved bodies hauled unceremoniously through the streets of London to Tyburn. There, they suffered the full horrors of a traitor's death, hung, drawn and quartered for the benefit of a baying crowd. Sadly, 'In the sixteenth century violent and painful death was too much of a commonplace to be regarded with the same revulsion as it is today.' (Plowden, 2010, p22.) It was a slow, agonising and humiliating end, a theatre of sadism that leaves a bad taste in the mouth of those who prefer to see Anne Boleyn in her entirety rather than simply a cherry-picked portrait of unadulterated panegyric. Doubtless, given how frequently we are reminded what a strong and forceful woman she was, she must have fought to spare these men and yet somehow they still ended up dead. And they were just the first.

Bishop Fisher was next. His confinement in the Tower of London had already crippled his health and worn his cadaverous body down to the bones, so losing his head was by then likely something of a mercy. Pope Paul III created him a cardinal in the hope of a more humane confinement, at the very least, but to no avail. Henry replied with characteristic bluster that the new cardinal's hat could stay where it was; he would soon send Fisher's head to Rome to join it. Bishop Fisher – or Cardinal Fisher, even – was tried in Westminster Hall before a jury which counted Thomas Boleyn amongst their number. He was charged with treason, denying that Henry VIII was now head of the English Church; this statement had been tricked out of him by the unscrupulous Richard Rich. Found guilty, Fisher was initially sentenced to be hung, drawn and quartered, before the King commuted the sentence to a more merciful – and speedier – beheading. Possibly Henry feared an uprising of public sympathy, given that the feast day of Saint John the Baptist, Fisher's patronal namesake, was imminent. It seems likely that the King was fast grasping the fact that his public image was crystalising into something rather unwholesome, given that Saint John the Baptist had been executed by Herod Antipas partly for challenging Herod's marriage to his brother's divorcee, Herodias. Antipas was not the sort of monarch one wanted to be held up against in comparison, given that he was also responsible for returning Jesus to Pontius Pilate, after Pilate had initially handed the captive Christ over to Antipas because Jesus had stirred more 'dissent' in his region than in Pilate's. For Henry, such similarities would be particularly bad PR for someone already in the process of pissing off the entirety of Catholic Europe.

In the end, Fisher was beheaded on Tower Hill on 22 June 1535; the feast day of Saint John the Baptist was 24 June. The execution gave Fisher the chance to comport himself with serenity and dignity in the face of such state-sponsored brutality. The scene works particularly well in season two of *The Tudors*, with Irish actor Bosco Hogan playing Bishop Fisher, whose time in the Tower has indeed left him so frail that he ascends the scaffold by metaphorically crowd-surfing the goodwill of the gathered spectators. Their cheers soothe his frayed nerves as he steadies himself on the executioner's block. In real life, Fisher's corpse was left naked on the scaffold for several hours before it was impaled on a pike and slung into a makeshift grave in All Hallows' Barking, just shy of the Tower of London. Several weeks later, it was reinterred in St Peter ad Vincula, the church located within the grounds of the Tower, minus the head, which was stuck on a pole on London Bridge. However, given that the head apparently seemed to prosper rather than to rot, it was hurriedly taken down and then tossed into the Thames. The vacant spot upon the tip of the pole would soon taken up by the severed head of Thomas More.

Like Bishop Fisher, Thomas More suffered terrible privations in the Tower of London. The various petty humiliations were payback for multiple 'affronts' to the new regime, which included not attending Anne's coronation in 1533. When he eventually went to trial, More was confronted by even more Boleyns than poor Bishop Fisher had had to contend with; not only Anne's father but also her brother, as well as the Duke of Norfolk. Further dubious testimony by Richard Rich helped usher in the inevitable guilty verdict, with the best version of the trial – in televisual terms – coming with a bravura performance from Anton Lesser as More in *Wolf Hall* (2015). Like Bishop Fisher, More was sentenced to be hung, drawn and quartered, but again the sentence was commuted to the more merciful beheading, although not apparently because of any saint days threatening to further dent the lustre of Henry VIII's rapidly mouldering public image.

The execution took place on Tower Hill on 6 July 1535. After More's severed head replaced that of Bishop Fisher on London Bridge, it was rescued by his daughter, Margaret. Now, both he and Bishop Fisher are Catholic saints/martyrs, their exalted titles adorning countless schools and churches across England. Thus, two good men had died so that Henry VIII might manage his own divorce, and so that Anne Boleyn might become Queen and promote her Reformist project. A great deal more blood would be spilled before the thing was done, least of all Anne's itself.

Whilst doing her best to bear a son, Anne still had time for the causes closest to her Reformist heart. When she and Henry went on progress in the summer of 1535, there were ample pauses at various religious houses, wherein Anne bore witness to some of the corruption she knew existed within the Catholic Church. The abuse of indulgences was of particular import, something she and Cromwell agreed upon when he set about levying sanctions on the monasteries ahead of the progress. Previously, in 1533, for instance, he had also investigated Thetford Abbey under Anne's instruction.

Clearly, when Anne and Cromwell pooled their Reformist resources, they were an effective and formidable team, even though he often had one eye on profit and merely the other on the Reformist agenda. Still, without them complementing each other as they did, the Reformation in England would look rather different. They were trailblazers, in fact, and they both knew it. As for those monasteries, well, the very notion of a monastical house was anathema to the Reformist belief. Reformists believed salvation was free to those who believed in it and then placed their faith in Jesus, whereas Catholic doctrine maintained that it was the church that bestowed this gift, and such practices were best observed in religious houses.

As for the abuse of indulgences, this was something that Anne was determined to abolish. An indulgence was basically the diminution of temporal punishment due to sin, with the guilt forgiven. In order to garner for oneself an indulgence, the penitent must perform an act of goodness or charity; or, more likely, they might pay for their indulgence, hence the charming little ditty attributed to the Dominican friar Johann Tetzel, 'When a penny in the coffer rings, a soul from Purgatory springs.' (An alternative version reads, 'As soon as the gold in the casket rings, the rescued soul to heaven springs.') Luther was particularly scornful of the practice, maintaining that deliverance was free for all, and that no labours – especially not in fiscal terms – were required to obtain it. In fact, as Collinson explains, the practice was pretty much the galvanising point for Luther, perceiving as he did that indulgences were being sold simply to settle the debts of a German archbishop, as well as funding a major rebuilding project for St Peter's in Rome.

Besides the misuse of indulgences, the 1535 progress also cast a condemning eye upon the practice of fake holy relics, in particular 'The Blood of Hailes', a vial displayed at Hailes Abbey in Gloucestershire.

This vessel supposedly contained droplets of the blood of Jesus, collected perhaps by a diligent disciple while the poor man hung suspended on the cross. In reality, the fluid was found to be a sort of resin, although it was initially thought to be the blood of a duck, regularly renewed; bad news for any waterfowl native to the area. This 'relic' remained on display until several years after Anne's execution, although some say her intervention caused a brief removal in 1535, before it was restored.

The fact that she did not succeed in having this ingenious fake decisively confiscated does nothing to blemish an otherwise exemplary record. Even under pressure, Anne was an ardent Reformist, stamping out corruption wherever she could. She was also a veritable mother hen to those whose religious beliefs marked them out as heretics, acting as patron and benefactress to countless students with Reformist leanings, both at Oxford and at Cambridge. A William Barker was one such beneficiary, whilst Nicholas Heath, a future Archbishop of York, was another. Such assistance involved a great deal more than a one-off handout. Sometimes, Anne would see that the student in question was provided with enough financial assistance to fund the entirety of their studies.

She was also charitable to those whose main concern was less with education and more with simply staying alive, using a sub-almoner to patrol various parishes and make a list of the poor who might be in need of some monetary assistance; those of a Reformist bent often took priority. Sometimes Cromwell assisted her in such endeavours. At other times, they would bat back and forth between them the rumours they had heard of corrupt clergy and misused monasteries, before despatching men to seek out and further investigate such matters. Increasingly, she and Cromwell would act to close these places altogether. But they were not unmerciful in their approach; if a monastery passed their inspection and was found to be 'uncontaminated' then it might survive. Likewise, some venues were able to buy/bribe their way out of suppression, although there is no suggestion Anne was ever involved in these transactions, some of which seem to have been entirely kosher, whilst others have the distinct whiff of a backhander.

The disagreeable fact persists, however, that many people turned out of the monasteries had nowhere to go and lived the remainder of their lives at barely subsistence level. Apparently, Anne's Christian charity did not extend to them. Certainly, she encountered difficulties when

Right: St Peter and St Paul church in Salle; many of Anne's Boleyn forebears are buried here. (Author's own)

Below: Blickling Hall; the original building is long gone, but Anne was born here nevertheless. (Oscarporras/Shutterstock)

Above: Hever Castle in Kent; Anne's childhood home and a virtual mecca for her many fans. (Alexandra Reinwald/ Shutterstock)

Left: Margaret of Austria; perhaps the first powerful ruler to recognise Anne's potential. (Conrat Meit, Public domain, via Wikimedia Commons)

Above: Mechelen Palace; Anne spent several of her formative years here. (Author's own)

Below left: Queen Claude of France; almost perpetually pregnant, life in her service was far from thrilling. (Public domain, via Wikimedia Commons)

Below right: Louse of Savoy; another strong female ruler whom Anne would take as a role model. (School of Jean Clouet, Public domain, via Wikimedia Commons)

Left: Marguerite d'Angoulême; she, more than any other matriarchal monarch, influenced Anne into embracing the concept of Reform. (Clouet, Public domain, via Wikimedia)

Below: Luther pins his 95 Theses in Germany; one day, Anne's detractors would consider her '… more Lutheran than Luther himself.' (Ferdinand Pauwels, Public domain, via Wikimedia Commons)

Above left: A young Catherine of Aragon; by the time Anne arrived back in England, this Spanish queen's glory days were well behind her. (Michael Sittow, Public domain, via Wikimedia Commons)

Above right: Henry VIII; filling out somewhat, but when Anne first met him still a man of considerable power and physical presence. (Public Domain, via Flickr)

Right: Mary Boleyn; Anne's sister has in recent years emerged as a 'historical celebrity' in her own right. (Public domain, via Wikimedia Commons).

Left: Thomas Wyatt; historians have obsessed for centuries over whether he and Anne enjoyed a fling, or even something more serious. (CC BY SA 4.0, via Wikimedia Commons)

Below: Anne Boleyn didn't have six fingers; however, an 'accessory nail' feature on one of her hands remains a feasible option. (Xray Computer/ Shutterstock)

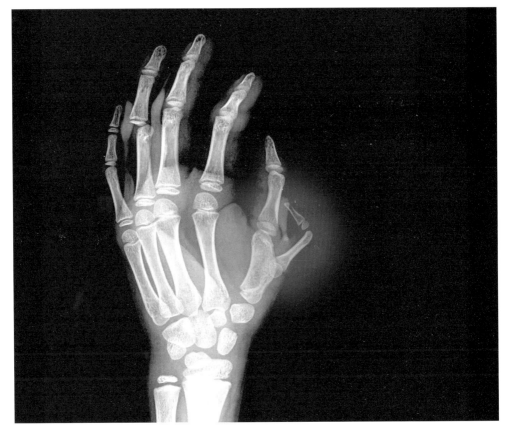

Right: Anne Boleyn's iconic 'B' necklace has become a pop culture icon. (Author's own)

Below: Cardinal Wolsey lost his position because he couldn't get Henry VIII a divorce; he lost his life shortly thereafter. (John Pettie, Public domain, via Wikimedia Commons)

Thomas Cranmer managed to annul the King's marriage to Catherine of Aragon; he was Anne's quiet compatriot in the pursuit of Reform. (Gerlach Flicke, Public domain, via Wikimedia Commons)

Thomas Cromwell; together with Anne and Cranmer, Cromwell completed a Tudor triumvate of Reformist power and influence. (Public domain, via Wikimedia Commons)

Above: Greenwich Palace; Anne gave birth here in 1533 and was arrested here, some several years later. (Public domain, via Wikimedia Commons)

Right: Jane Seymour; she toppled Anne using a fast-tracked portfolio of the techniques Anne herself may have used and has been reviled for it ever since. (Public domain, via Wikimedia Commons).

Above: The Tower of London; Anne proceeded from here for her coronation in 1533 and came back in disgrace in 1536. (Pisaphotography/ Shutterstock)

Left: A somewhat woefully stylised painting of Anne at her lowest ebb; accused of multiple counts of adultery, including incest with her own brother, her world at this point was all but disintegrating. (Édouard Cibot, Public domain, via Wikimedia Commons)

HERE LIETH S. THOMAS BVLLEN
KNIGHT OF THE ORDER OF THE GRTER
ERLE OF WILSCHER AND ERLE OF ORM
VNDE WICHE DECESSED THE 12
DAI OF MARCHE IN THE IERE
OF OVR LORDE 1538

Above: Thomas Boleyn's tomb; his reputation has been as ravaged over the centuries as have those of his daughters, but in truth he was merely an ardent Reformist combatting Catholic corruption. (Author's own)

Right: A young Elizabeth Tudor; she was Anne's greatest gift to England. (Luminarium.org, Public domain, via Wikimedia Commons)

Left: Giuditta Pasta as Anne in the Donizetti opera 'Anna Bolena'. (Karl Bryullov, Public domain, via Wikimedia Commons)

Below: Anne's body lies in the chapel of St Peter ad Vincula in the Tower of London; during Victorian times, it was exhumed and reburied. (From 'Memorials of the Tower of London' by Lieut. -Gen. Lord De Ros, 1866, Public domain, via Wikimedia Commons)

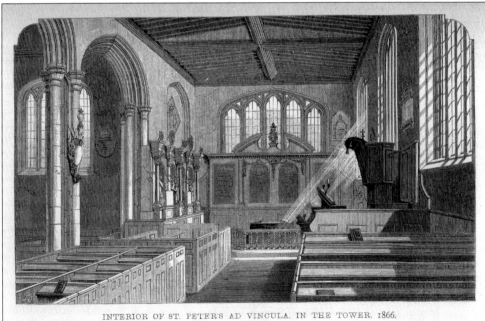

INTERIOR OF ST. PETER'S AD VINCULA, IN THE TOWER. 1866.

One of the first major feature films concerning Anne's life came in the form of 1920's 'Anna Boleyn'. (Public Domain, Wikimedia Commons)

Merle Oberon made a brief but striking appearance as Anne in 1933's 'The Private Life of Henry VIII'. (Everett Collection Inc / Alamy Stock Photo)

Geneviève Bujold became the onscreen Anne to beat in 1969's 'Anne of the Thousand Days'. (Movie studio, Public domain, via Wikimedia Commons)

Charlotte Rampling vied for screentime in 1972's 'The Six Wives of Henry VIII'. (Everett Collection Inc / Alamy Stock Photo)

Above: 'The Other Boleyn Girl' movie in 2008 gave the first substantial screentime to Mary Boleyn, even if the facts and the dates were all over the place. (United Archives GmbH / Alamy Stock Photo)

Below: Natalie Dormer defined Anne for a whole new generation and remains the version to beat in Showtime's 'The Tudors' (2007 – 2010). (Everett Collection Inc / Alamy Stock Photo)

Anne's legacy lives on in myriad forms, from pop culture references to pubs; this is the Anne Boleyn in Rochford. (Author's own)

The musical 'SIX' turned the story of Henry VIII's six wives into a talent show-style singing contest. (CC BY SA 4.0, via Wikimedia Commons)

attempting to address the nuns at Syon in December 1535. Initially, they refused Anne and her entourage entry, on the basis that she was a married woman and thus debarred by the rule of the order. But Anne persisted, and eventually the party were permitted entry, whereupon they found the accumulated nuns prostrate, their eyes staring down at the floor. That she apparently made them accept English primers instead of the Latin ones they were using (and which they did not seemingly understand) was a victory of sorts, but Anne departed having failed to secure their fealty to the King's newfound religious supremacy.

The 1535 progress also involved a stop at the Seymour family seat of Wolf Hall (or 'Wulfhall') in Wiltshire. It was here, so popular legend – and many, many novels – has it that Henry VIII first fell for Jane Seymour. If this is the case, then it came at a low point in Jane's own personal career, when she had been 'let go' from Catherine of Aragon's dwindling household and packed off home with scant chance of being relocated to the court in London. However, conflicting accounts – as ever, a terrible bane for the Tudor historian – have her already in Anne's household at this point and simply accompanying her mistress on a fortuitous visit to the family home. Either way, it seems likely that something sparked during the stop-off at Wolf Hall, because the court in London is most definitely where we find Jane in early 1536, several months later. But even if the King saw something in this semi-literate country girl with her excellent embroidering skills, he was still far from done with Anne. Despite the fact that they were quarrelling frequently, to the point where Henry apparently told her, 'I raised you up to your present exalted position and I can just as swiftly bring you down/undo you again,' they were also still sleeping together during the 1535 progress. In fact, by the end of 1535 Anne was pregnant again, although the pressure was beyond intense; if she lost this baby, or it proved to be another girl, then her days were doubtless numbered. Provided she kept calm, however, unburdened by trauma of one sort or another, then she stood a fair chance of carrying the child successfully.

On 7 January 1536, Catherine of Aragon died. Anne Boleyn was now undoubtedly *the* Queen of England. However, Catherine's death was a

poisoned chalice. With her passing, the King would, in the eyes of the Catholic Church, be free to remarry without any hint of illegality. In Catholic eyes, Henry was now a widower, leaving Anne's new position more perilous than triumphal. However, in the wake of his first wife's passing, 'Henry reacted with relief; "God be praised that we are now free from all suspicion of war". The hostility of the Emperor could now be expected to abate, which would reduce his dependence upon France, and make Francis more amenable to his wishes.' (Loades, 2013, p40.)

We can dismiss with some certainty the idea that Anne wore yellow as a sign of celebration at her predecessor's passing; Henry, yes, but not Anne, who apparently had the good taste to melt into the background whilst her husband made merry at losing such a weighty political millstone. The idea that yellow was the Spanish colour for mourning seems unsteady, but more likely the King wore it because the colour represented in Christian terms rebirth and renewal. Meanwhile, rumours soon circulated that Catherine had been poisoned; a post-mortem revealed that her heart was engulfed by a monstrous black mass, which some took as a sign of foul play. Given the narrow escape that her partisan Bishop Fisher suffered, one may at least acknowledge that such rumours were understandable. Far more likely, however, is that this was merely the outward manifestation of cancer of the heart. However, whilst this rather dispels the accusation of poison, one cannot help but consider the fact that poor Catherine did in some sense die of a broken heart. Given the danger her passing now posed to Anne as far as Catholicism was concerned, however, it seems unlikely that the Boleyns had anything to do with Catherine's death.

In a material sense, at least, Anne made some small profit from Catherine's passing. The deceased's belongings, stored at Baynard's Castle in London, were divvied up, with Anne bagging several choice items for her own household. It was around this time – or shortly beforehand – that Henry actually began courting Jane Seymour, but there appears to have been no indication that he was considering remarrying. In fact, his interest in Jane was on several occasions dismissed as nothing more than another one of the King's occasional dalliances.

Soon after Catherine's death, Henry was knocked unconscious in a jousting accident. Apparently, 'This latest jousting incident was far more serious even than it seemed at the time. His armoured horse reportedly fell on top of him as he was unseated by his opponent's blunted lance.'

(Hutchinson, 2006, p137.) He was unconscious for several hours and may have suffered some sort of brain damage. Several historians have posited that Henry's already unsteady personality further corroded in the wake of this incident, although speculating on possible brain injuries some 400 or so years after the fact is precarious at best. Anne was apparently informed of the incident by her uncle, the Duke of Norfolk, in his trademark tactless manner. What is less certain is whether Anne had previously discovered Jane Seymour sitting on Henry's lap in the days leading up to the accident. Either way, one or the other of these incidents, or perhaps even a combination, caused her to miscarry a male foetus on 29 January. 'She miscarried of her saviour' is perhaps the most poignant – and accurate – opinion of this sad event. From that moment, Anne's days were essentially numbered, although neither she nor even Henry really grasped it. For him, certainly, the whole stream of miscarriages must have seemed like a ghastly recreation of his life with Catherine. By the sort of macabre coincidence that historians delight in stressing, it was on the very day of Anne's miscarriage that Catherine was laid to rest in Peterborough Abbey. For Anne, the realisation that she had yet again gambled all on her fecundity but was in fact a busted flush must have been devastating.

Much controversy still surrounds this miscarriage, and whether or not the foetus was in some way deformed. The allegation that it was misshapen would lead to rumours that Anne was a witch. Witches, it was said, often delivered malformed or monstrous children; physical deformity apparently offered a window onto an equally monstrous soul. If there *was* a deformity, this may have been because the father was actually Anne's brother, George. Several historians have come to this conclusion and seen this as a confirmation of Anne's infidelity and incest. They are, however, generous enough to attribute it to the fact that she was so desperate to survive that she turned to her brother to help her conceive, given that Henry was losing interest in her, besides being – by then – partially impotent himself. However, such conclusions stem from an increasingly secular outlook. What these historians fail to realise is that Anne was an intensely spiritual woman, someone who baulked at the simple fact of a fling with the King, as her sister had so recklessly demonstrated, let alone bedding her own brother in the hope of producing a decoy baby. That Anne would consider damning her soul for the sake of prolonging her brief earthly life is therefore little short of ludicrous;

Hayley Nolan highlighted this discrepancy quite succinctly in her 2019 biography of Anne. However, it is worth stressing that we none of us know what we might succumb to when placed under the sort of pressure Anne was then facing. It's highly unlikely still that she transgressed thus, if not almost inconceivable to someone of such a religious bent, but not totally removed from the bounds of reality either.

Retha Warnicke argued strongly that Anne miscarried a deformed foetus, and that this was almost entirely responsible for her downfall; needless to say, such an opinion has left her far from being a fan favourite. She set the crisis which the miscarriage ignited against the general backdrop of superstition then prevalent throughout sixteenth-century Europe: 'Virtually all early modern Europeans believed in the existence of evil spirits; Satan was for them an actual demon who worked ceaselessly to lure mortals into becoming his followers. Among his worshippers, witches were considered such a menace that in 1542, less than six years after Anne's death, parliament enacted a statue that, among other prohibitions, specifically forbade the use of witchcraft to incite a person to illicit love.' (Warnicke, 1989, p192.) She then added that unrestrained carnality – often the province of the 'wanton' woman/witch – was in Tudor times apt to lead to adultery, sodomy, and even bestiality. The act of sodomy was made illegal by the Reformation Parliament in 1533, the year Anne married Henry. Warnicke then explains, 'A major reason for these restrictions was that illicit sexual acts were blamed for the birth of deformed children.' (Warnicke, 1989, p195.)

The legend of the deformed foetus has become as much an integral part of Anne's myth as the suggested sixth finger. Curiously, 'The Tudor mind was that most bizarre hybrid of the medieval and the Renaissance, in that it could juggle the concepts of taxes and loans and also witches and demons in the same thought process.' (Mayhew, 2022, p31.) Certainly, in Tudor times, women were seen as the more sexually voracious of the species. This was something for which Anne and her reputation would suffer when she went on trial for her 'crimes', even more so when issues of the King's own virility were called into question. In fact, besides being considered virtual simmering nymphomaniacs, women in the sixteenth century were also supposedly prone to suffering from 'wandering womb' syndrome, an apparently related side-effect of frequent female masturbation. This theory originated in ancient Greece, espousing the belief that the womb would go 'wandering' around the woman's body quite unchecked, pressing itself against other organs and causing no end of ailments, unless the woman was sexually sated. (Bullough, 2003, p22.) Even as late as the sixteenth century this was generally believed to be the case, until the invention of the microscope revealed that the womb was, in fact, quite stationary. Such theories, however ridiculous they might sound to the modern ear, nevertheless tally with Warnicke's own hypothesis about those issues of unnatural sexual acts which dogged Anne during the dark days of her trial.

In the days following her miscarriage, Anne and Henry's marriage apparently stabilised, this despite the fact that Henry apparently told her it had become clear he would have no male issue by her. Beyond that, no further 'threats' were made, and the royal couple resumed their relationship. In fact, for several months they seemed to 'coast along' at a fairly satisfactory pace, although Henry's courting of Jane Seymour certainly cranked up a gear between February and April 1536, a fact of which Anne was undoubtedly aware. Henry was also beginning to murmur that he been seduced into marrying Anne by means of witchcraft. This has led some to believe that she was actually charged thus, but this was not the case. Henry probably alleged it in a fit of pique, but it went no further than that, although such utterances dovetail nicely with Warnicke's deformed foetus theory.

Soon, however, real alarm bells would ring for the Boleyns when Jane Seymour was granted – by Cromwell – the use of his private apartments, which afforded her personal access to the King's own quarters. Then, George Boleyn lost out on being awarded the Order of the Garter, which was instead given to Sir Nicholas Carew (although oddly enough, several weeks previous, Thomas Boleyn had been granted the rights to the town of King's Lynn; truly, as a quasi-God, Henry VIII gave with one hand and then took away with the other). However, the royal marriage could still surprise with its rollercoaster lurches: 'As late as Easter, Henry also sought Imperial recognition of his marriage to Anne, and on Easter Sunday, Chapuys was finally, after three years, tricked into recognising Anne's position as queen, when he was manoeuvred behind a door through which she suddenly entered.' (Norton, 2009, pp63-64.) In reality, though, it seems that Chapuys was merely showing – according to the King, who was with Anne on this occasion – the proper reverence due a monarch. However, if the Boleyn faction were buoyed up by this apparent show of Imperial regard, it was to be a pyrrhic victory at best. You see, unfortunately, Anne had just picked the fight of her life...

Several weeks previously, Anne's almoner, John Skip, preached a fiery sermon which had her fingerprints all over it. It concerned the Old Testament story of Queen Esther, with Anne in the role of the aforementioned monarch, whilst Henry was cast in the role of her husband, King Ahasuerus, who was misled by his adviser, Hamon (Cromwell, of course), into sanctioning the slaughter of the Jews (or, in this case, the English clergy). Of course, the situation is saved by Queen Esther, who manages to change her husband's mind at the last moment, and as a result, Hamon is hanged. Skip's sermon was a direct answer from Anne to a recent argument with Cromwell concerning how monies from the dissolved monasteries should be used. She wanted the funds siphoned into educational endeavours, whereas his motives were slightly less altruistic and mainly involved pouring them into the King's coffers. And Anne had a point. Payments to the Pope had been slashed by an act passed by the Reformation Parliament, and those monies were now pouring into Henry's pocket as it was. He was getting richer by the day, even if the amounts weren't exactly eyewatering. Still, Skip's sermon was a direct challenge to Cromwell's plans, and he knew it. In fact, it couldn't have been clearer if Anne had come up and punched him in the face. Previously, 'As early as the previous July the Queen had threatened to have his head if he continued to obstruct her, and that time may now have come. She was far too formidable a politician to be shunted aside as Catherine had been, and it began to look as though it was her head or his.' (Loades, 2014, p118.)

Anne and Cromwell were both Reformers, but they had very different ideas about what to do with the spoils of restructuring. All that Cromwell's plans required were the stamp of royal assent. He had paved the way as far as Parliament was concerned, compiling a veritable catalogue of the abuses discovered whilst visiting the various monasteries. Those revelations were at the time met with almost universal condemnation, and Cromwell's plans thus seemed to have the aforementioned rubber stamp of approval. As far as Anne's threats were concerned, he was initially optimistic: 'I trust so much on my master, that I fancy she cannot do me any harm,' he told Chapuys.' (Borman, 2019, p264.) The question was, would the King love money more than he loved his wife? Cromwell prayed so, because there is some suggestion that Anne was also on the verge of taking her complaints to Henry, alongside assertions that Cromwell and his cronies were also lining their own pockets. As for Skip, he was seized after preaching his inflammatory sermon but soon released. In the meantime, Cranmer wrote a letter to Cromwell in which he echoed Anne's displeasure regarding the distribution of the monies from the monasteries.

At some point following Skip's sermon, Anne perhaps realised she had possibly gone too far. This moment, perhaps even more than the fateful miscarriage, was instrumental in sealing her fate: 'Poor Anne had divined how the wind blew and tried to trim her sails; but she was no match for the combined forces of Chapuys and her domestic enemies.' (Sergeant, 1924, p266.) How much Chapuys was also conspiring Anne's downfall is debatable. Historians are so familiar with his blatantly biased despatches that there seems to be a general consensus that what you saw was what you got, though, as previously stated, he was a man hardly likely to out himself in assisting any plot to usurp the Queen. He and Cromwell had a good working relationship and met often. Indeed, they were close neighbours, both living in the Austin Friars area of the City of London. Most of what we know of these meetings comes from Chapuys and the filter of his own self-interested discretion.

But it wasn't just Skip's sermon or even Chapuys that prompted Cromwell to act against Anne. In the wake of his close encounter with the Queen on Easter Sunday, Chapuys had an audience with the King, during which Henry rounded on Cromwell after being informed of the conversation Cromwell had conducted with Chapuys regarding the benefits of an imperial alliance, a path Cromwell had instigated without royal sanction. Henry disagreed with many of the points regarding said alliance and demanded of Chapuys that they be put down in writing. Cromwell, meanwhile, retired to a window embrasure in an attempt to recover his composure.

Quite possibly, Henry's mood on that day had been influenced by Anne, the last time that she managed to sway her husband in a direction favourable to herself. Anne may have sought to scupper the imperial alliance by insisting that Charles V recognise the new status quo in

England. This was optimistic at best, which Anne doubtless knew, which would then force Henry into a French alliance. Still, Cromwell championed the imperial alliance, reiterating the point when he reconvened with Chapuys later that day. Both men were still smarting from such a close call with the King's temper. Cromwell told Chapuys that he had since talked again with Henry and assured him that in future he would not proceed apace in brokering such suggestions without the assistance of a colleague, at the very least. Basically, Henry had rather indiscreetly reminded him just who really ran the country.

At this juncture, with Anne's star flickering uncertainly, both men *still* thought it prudent to favour an imperial alliance. Possibly they even mooted how much more smoothly said alliance might proceed if Anne were not around to scupper things. For Cromwell and Henry, however, from this point on, one detects a certain souring in their working relationship, although Cromwell continued to wield considerable power at court. In fact, despite the dressing-down, it would still be several years before Henry apparently took to plucking Cromwell's hat from his head and then swiping him about the face with it. Right now, Cromwell simply had to contend with the fact that Anne favoured a French alliance rather than an imperial one. It need not be reiterated that Anne was, because of her background, partial to such an association, never mind the fact that she was unlikely to find a friend in Charles V, nephew of the woman she had so successfully supplanted.

So, we have Cromwell leaning towards an imperial alliance and Anne favouring a French one, in addition to their pre-existing clash concerning the monasteries. But the imperial alliance wasn't without its dangers for Cromwell, either, and he began to waver when Charles V made it clear he wanted his cousin Mary – Catherine's daughter – to inherit the throne of England when her father was dead. In order for this to happen, it was in imperial interests for Henry to remain with Anne, whose great maternal gamble had backfired spectacularly. In that sense, Charles considered her no great threat in providing a boy to scupper Mary's chances, as opposed to having Anne replaced by some upstart who might usurp Mary's position by giving the King a son. Henry, however, was still vaguely optimistic about his chances of fathering a son by Anne, relaying to his ambassador in Rome on 25 April that '... he was opposing Charles' latest demands, due to the "likelihood and appearance that God will send us heirs male ... through our most dear and entirely beloved wife, the queen".'

However, the imperial stance, which favoured keeping Anne on the English throne, also left her, unwittingly, in a position to do Cromwell further harm. If Cromwell managed by some miracle to outlive his master, he would also then face Mary ascending to the throne, flushed with power and hardly likely to look favourably upon Thomas Cromwell, a man whose religious leanings jarred so much with her own rather rancorous form of Catholicism. When weighing all this up, Cromwell still considered removing Anne as the best option in terms of his immediate survival. If Henry did indeed remarry, Charles V would simply have to accept the fact that Mary would be shunted further down the line of succession if the King's new wife provided him with a son (as indeed she did). However, removing Anne by way of an annulment was out of the question; it would seem little short of ludicrous, given just how hard Cromwell and others had fought to have Henry's first marriage finished off. No, Anne had to be removed in such a way that there was no possibility of either recrimination or comeback. And Chapuys, for one, was in no doubt that Cromwell and not Henry was the author of that impending coup.

So, besides the basic tale of Henry VIII wanting to rid himself of yet another patriarchally unpleasing wife, it must be considered plausible that Cromwell engineered Anne's demise, and more for personal/financial reasons rather than because she had failed to provide England with a prince. Those reasons also included, as we shall see, 'minor details' like getting rid of some problematic courtiers. The orchestration of the entire thing was accompanied by the backdrop of Skip's sermon ringing ominously in his ears. Nothing would stop Cromwell from continuing to profit from the dissolution of the monasteries; even the ones that escaped restructuring were at risk, with Cromwell '...ordering them to obey impossibly restrictive regulations and then granting them exemptions in return for "cash" gifts.' (Randell & Turvey, 2008, p120.) Possibly, as Suzannah Lipscomb postulates, he was also in cahoots with the Seymours, as they began steering Jane in the King's direction: 'This view rests on an image of Henry as a king who could be manipulated and manoeuvred by the factions of his court, to "bounce" him into action and tip him "by a crisis" into rejecting Anne.' (Lipscomb, 2009, p75.) Several historians have considered these – the monies and the alliances – insufficient reasons to annihilate the Boleyn faction, but we cannot ascertain how much Anne may also have been 'heavying' Cromwell behind the scenes. As said, she had already threatened to 'have his head' before deploying Skip to reiterate just what a threat she was.

Several other scenarios elucidating Cromwell's reasons have been offered over the years, with varying degrees of success; they are mentioned here purely for the sake of completeness. To begin with, there is speculation that Anne was – several months previous to her arrest – apparently involved in the passing of new legislation which would seek to find employment for those trapped in a cycle of poverty and joblessness. It was, basically, 'Anne Boleyn's Poor Law'. However, the working of such a monumental apparatus would involve the creation of a governing council that would rival Cromwell's own department, with the inevitable possibility of further diminishing his powerbase. This theory has little real evidence to back it up, whilst again raising the question of why this would spur Cromwell into obliterating the Boleyns, unless one couples it with the Skip sermon, at which point he therefore feels that his entire position is suddenly under extreme duress. But the timeline doesn't quite fit for Anne to have been involved in the drafting of the aforementioned legislation; at that point, Anne had her fingers in enough Tudor pies without saddling herself with this sort of law-making. She certainly didn't have immediate access to the information, whilst Cromwell ended up taking credit for the thing anyway. What passed in Parliament in 1536 was legislation created in the Commons by those present, where Anne most certainly wasn't. In citing Anne's involvement with such legislation as an example of her beneficent charity, Ives (2004) is careful to use the words 'may also' and then 'perhaps' several times over; in other words, unproven. She certainly may have wanted to help, but she simply lacked the resources.

Regarding the next possible/unlikely theory for the coup, several historians have mooted the possibility of Anne's involvement in pushing for a defensive 'Protestant league' alliance with the Lutheran Princes of Germany, much to the chagrin of Charles V (his own negotiations had foundered), alongside her predilection for the French alliance. Other sources say Henry himself brokered this prospective alliance through his own agents, in return for providing the Lutheran princes with financial backing. When the negotiations went sour, so it is suggested, Henry turned on his wife (blame the woman, of course). This theory has more bite to it, even though most historians consider Cromwell the principal architect behind the negotiations. In that regard, he was hedging his bets on both sides, although perhaps leaning towards an imperial alliance, at least until he realised this would involve leaving Anne in power as an imperial path to pave a smooth succession for Mary. But even that, as said, was something he probably considered worth the risk when the chips were down. Either way, the feelers sent out in regard to the 'Protestant League' came to naught. By the time Henry's ambassadors returned to England, the Boleyns had been brutally deposed, and with them much of their hopes for the continuation of Anne's work for reform. When the Reformers reconvened around the King, after a brief surge for the conservative faction, they would be Cromwell's selection and not Anne's.

One major problem with the notion of Cromwell as sole engineer of the coup against Anne is that such an undertaking was a massive personal risk. If it backfired, he would be facing an irate Henry and also the Boleyn faction, and there would have been no way he would have escaped that combination with his life. Therefore, this author leans toward Henry evincing a rather insistent private dissatisfaction with Anne, with Cromwell concocting the evidence to do away with her on his own, free from the possibility of any ramifications from his master but quietly relieved at being able to eliminate his newfound enemy from the board. It has been suggested that had Anne given birth to a surviving boy, she would have been untouchable, but this completely underestimates the ruthlessness both of Cromwell and also of the Tudor times in general. With a boy securely in the cradle, there would have been no imperative to preserve the life of so troublesome a mother, and the fact remained that Anne had picked a fight with Cromwell, a man who had considerably more to lose than she did. A new wife could always provide a second son, after all, and Cromwell wasn't grooming Jane Seymour just because he was bored.

All of these theories are at risk from the historians who believe Anne may have been wholly or at least partially guilty of the crimes of which she was accused, and that instead of fabricating evidence against her, Cromwell merely took what rumour and innuendo actually already existed and moulded it into a convincing case for the prosecution. It is known that he faked illness in the weeks leading up to the coup that ousted the Boleyns, during which time he is said to have concocted or perhaps simply embellished the whole of what was to follow. But if Anne's failed fecundity/alleged amours had little to do with her downfall, then Cromwell's desire to rid himself of her becomes almost a compliment. Here was a woman shrewd enough to play him at his own game, and who had her own sources and spies when it came to the matter of monasterial monies and French versus imperial alliances. Therefore, it was either him or her.

It may be concluded then that Cromwell destroyed Anne because he saw her as a competent and credible threat and not simply because she couldn't carry a boy to full term. Who knows, perhaps the King's entire dalliance with Jane Seymour really was Cromwell's work, rather than some random chance. Certainly, Hilary Mantel made this the basis of the narrative of her first two books in the trilogy, wherein Cromwell himself pauses the 1535 progress at Wolf Hall. Probably, at the end of the day, it really was just personal; as said, Cromwell felt that Anne was making moves to get rid of him and so he got rid of her first. Henry was very suggestible, almost to the point of gullibility, and for the most part Cromwell – and Anne – could play him like the proverbial fiddle. By early 1536, however, Anne's musical fingers were rather spent in such matters. And by then, even the naïve Henry was weary of getting high drama from Anne instead of the sons she'd promised.

It was, therefore, most likely a lethal confluence of motives that served to remove her, first from power and then from this mortal coil.

The scant records provide little illumination, but clearly Anne soon realised that things were happening behind the scenes which didn't bode well. Perhaps the Seymour faction were openly boasting of the favour Jane was currying with the King, besides the fact of her using Cromwell's apartments, although demure Jane would of course be chaperoned on all such visits. Meanwhile, John Skip's sermon was still the talk of the court. Ironically, 'The text for Skip's sermon came from the New Testament parable of the woman taken in adultery and this may have inspired the Minister (Cromwell) with the idea to investigate or, more accurately, invent accusations of faithlessness against the embattled Queen. On 24 April, a special commission headed by Cromwell and Norfolk was set up to find damning faults in the Queen's character and behaviour.' (Hutchinson, 2008, p86.) Sadly, it seems it was shoddy form on Anne's part to pick a quarrel with a man who was said to have memorised the entirety of the New Testament by heart. She had, inadvertently, just given Cromwell the grist for the mill that would grind her to dust. In the immediate term, whatever Anne did or didn't know in regard to these machinations, *something* spurred her to seek out her chaplain and countryman, Matthew Parker, and to plead with him to mind her daughter's spiritual welfare in the event that anything happened in the days and weeks ahead. Parker was born in Norwich in 1504, making him not just a countryman of Anne's but also a contemporary. Many years after her death, Elizabeth would make him Archbishop of Canterbury.

Anne and Henry argued at Greenwich Palace on 30 April. An eyewitness, the Scottish Reformer Alexander Aless, relating the story to Anne's daughter decades later, recalled: 'Alas I shall never forget the sorrow I felt when I saw the sainted Queen your mother, carrying you, still a little baby, in her arms, and entreating the most serene King your father in Greenwich Palace, from the open window of which he was looking into the courtyard where she brought you to him. The faces and gestures of the speakers plainly showed the King was angry, though he concealed his anger wonderfully well.' (Jenkins, 1965, p12.) Whatever the conclusion of this quarrel, Anne spent the remainder of the day peaceably enough, watching a staged dogfight within the palace precincts before returning to her apartments, where her ladies would prepare her for a ball to be held later that evening. It was whilst attending this soiree that she was discreetly informed of the fact that one of the musicians in her household had been arrested. Whether she laughed this off as some trivial matter that didn't concern her – she set the best moral compass she could for her household, but she was not their mother, after all – or whether she sensed something decidedly ominous approaching is uncertain. The weather at the time was warm and sultry, in fact, almost overbearing; pleasures and pastimes were thus heightened, but so were tempers and nerves. When she retired for the night, it is doubtful, given the argument, the temperature and the arrest, that Anne actually slept at all.

Jane Seymour won Henry's affections in a matter of months by aping the vaguely coquettish techniques established by Anne, liberally sprinkled with some demure, 'maidenly' affectations that would probably have made Mademoiselle Boleyn retch. Whereas Anne's behaviour was *apparently* spontaneous and natural, Jane's 'technique' was calculatedly used to bring about the same effect, albeit in a far speedier timeframe. In so doing she drew far more on stereotypical Tudor norms of the submissive woman, in direct contrast to Anne's firebrand femininity, which was fast leaving Henry somewhat cold. When he had a purse of gold coins and an accompanying letter sent to her, Jane examined the contents of the purse before modestly replacing the clasp and then handing it back to the messenger; the seal of the letter she kissed, whilst leaving the missive unopened, protesting that, as an unmarried woman, she could not in all modesty accept such bounties and declarations. One can almost imagine Anne in the background, mimicking two fingers down her throat at the sight.

Jane's rapid success with Henry has recently resulted in some astonishingly personal attacks, even by prolific writers like Eric Ives. In his 2004 book *The Life and Death of Anne Boleyn*, he goes so far as to say that, in response to Jane's attire on her wedding day that '...anyone familiar with Holbein's portrait of Jane Seymour might be forgiven for feeling that she needed all the help she could get.' (Ives, 2004, p360.) Despite the fact that she achieved what Anne had in a fraction of the time (the seducing Henry part, certainly), modern historians tend now to paint Jane as another of the villains of Anne's downfall, whilst somewhat forgetting the worst excesses of what Catherine of Aragon and her daughter went through – even indirectly – at Anne's hands. Ives is one of Anne's few male biographers, and his impartiality, or rather startling lack of, he at least admits to earlier in the text: 'I have sometimes described Anne Boleyn as the third woman in my life, after my immediate family, and it is true that once she interests you, fascination grows, as it did for men at the time.' (Ives, 2004, pxiv.) Perhaps. However, back in 1536, that fascination was about to have catastrophic consequences for the Boleyn faction and their various hangers-on.

On 1 May the traditional May Day jousts took place at Greenwich Palace. Anne's brother led the challengers, whilst Sir Henry Norris, Henry's Groom of the Stool, spearheaded the defenders. The King was apparently in good spirits, on hand to offer the use of his horse to Norris when his own mare refused to move. Nothing seemed awry. Despite the argument of the previous day, Anne was also upbeat, if a little distracted. She certainly spent more time congratulating the participants of the joust than she did placating her husband, a preference that would play out rather badly given the events soon to unfold. At some point in the proceedings, a message was delivered to the King via a nephew of Cromwell. The contents of this explosive missive concerned the fact that a certain musician in the Queen's household had confessed to having sex with her. Henry set off at once for London, summoning Norris to his side as he did so. On the way, he would interrogate his 'friend' over alleged words which had passed between Norris and the Queen and which had then been reported to Cromwell. Anne was left behind in Greenwich, befuddled but not realising that she would never see her husband again.

Hayley Nolan's recent biography declares, at this juncture, that '...the following tales of adultery and scheming are the only element of Anne's married life that most writers care to focus on – not wanting to sully their story of sex and scandal with anything as dull as helping the poor and rescuing refugees.' (Nolan, 2019, p161.) For a book that touts the subheading '*500 years of lies*', this is a bit misleading. Countless books concerning Anne's life go into great detail regarding her relationship with Henry VIII, bearing in mind they were only actually married for three years.

After the joust, Anne returned to Greenwich Palace with her women, little realising that several – if not all – of them had been recruited by Cromwell to provide damning – but dubious – testimony about what went on in her household. Even the alleged words of a dead woman – Lady Wingfield, Anne's lady-in-waiting, who died in 1534 – were brought to bear, ominously cloaked in the near-mystical mantle of a 'deathbed confession'. However, some of the most condemning 'evidence' came courtesy of the Countess of Worcester, Elizabeth Browne, who had served Anne as far back as her coronation in 1533. When accused of being something of a flirt, the Countess had, apparently, asserted that her behaviour paled when compared to that of the Queen. Other sources have the Countess reprimanding a lady-in-waiting for flirting and receiving the same response that the original anecdote attributes to the Countess herself. Either way, in such a deeply patriarchal society it was bad form for a woman to behave thus, although the Tudors had a flimsy notion in regard to where court flirtations ended and the real heavy-duty dallying began.

Another woman who apparently gave evidence against the Queen was her antagonistic sister-in-law Lady Rochford, whose testimony, touching as it did on the supposedly incestuous relationship between Anne and her brother, stands head and shoulders above all the others for sheer venomous ingenuity. How much of it was twisted out of her by Cromwell is hard to say; it all depends on how much one believes that she and George Boleyn really loathed each other and whether or not Jane nursed a grudge against Anne for inadvertently getting her banished from court in the wake of the failed coup against Henry's mysterious 1534 mistress. Cromwell, after all, was a lawyer and might have reworked Jane's jealousy against such close siblings into something downright immoral. Even the slightest distaste for Anne was, in his capable hands, capable of being twisted into something treasonous.

Besides those mentioned here, many other women also gave testimony to the effect that Anne was a profligate adulteress. It gives the advice Margaret of Austria once bestowed upon Anne – 'Trust in those who offer you service, and in the end, my maidens, you will find yourselves in the ranks of those who have been deceived' – a bitter poignancy. But perhaps Anne's women were threatened into their statements. Perhaps some of them simply didn't like her and found this the ideal time to exercise their distaste. How any of them managed to look her in the face that night when they returned to Greenwich Palace, as they helped dress her for bed, beggars belief. Possibly their own demeanour sent yet another signal that something was seriously awry. We have no idea what Anne's bedtime ritual was, beyond the fact that she prayed each night, but one can only imagine the uncertainty she felt as she huddled beneath the sheets and gazed out the window. She had scant idea where her husband was or who he was talking to, and no way of contacting him. She didn't realise it, but it was actually her last night of freedom.

Anne was arrested on 2 May 1536. She was apparently – reports, as ever, tend to conflict – watching a game of real tennis when they came for her; or, rather, a messenger informed her that she was to present herself before the Privy Council forthwith. She repaired to the council chamber at Greenwich Palace and found herself faced with a formidable array which included her uncle, the Duke of Norfolk. She was then told in rather blunt terms that she had committed adultery with Sir Henry Norris and with a 'lowly' Flemish musician called Mark Smeaton; the aforementioned arrest thrust suddenly to the fore. Both men had already confessed their guilt, whilst a third man accused was currently being 'examined'. If Anne sensed that the end was approaching, that the incredible gamble she had played with her fecundity had backfired, she surely had no inkling that Henry would actually have her killed. Banished perhaps, like Catherine, but surely no worse than that? She argued her innocence, but was met with blank faces, shaking heads and the occasional 'tut-tut'. She was then told that she was under arrest.

That done, she was taken back to her apartments and given an hour or so in which to compose herself while the tide turned on the Thames. The barge would arrive to escort her to the Tower of London at two o'clock in the afternoon. In the meantime, a guard was placed on her room. When the time came, she was escorted down to the jetty and helped aboard the barge, the vehicle manoeuvred deftly about from whence it had come, before being propelled off towards the Tower. The journey took almost two hours, during which time no one seems to have spoken to her at all, save for a few more salvos of 'tut-tut'.

Anne Boleyn aficionados will be at great pains to point out that she most certainly did not enter the Tower through the famous Traitor's Gate, but through the royal Court Gate of the Byward Tower instead. She was, after all, still the Queen of England, albeit not for very much longer. She was received by the Constable of the Tower, Sir William Kingston, and his lieutenant, Sir Edmund Walsingham. Kingston was courteous but at great pains to pierce any illusions Anne might have harboured; she was now a prisoner, although she was at least to be housed in the rooms used for her coronation and not in some malodourous dungeon below the waterline of the Thames and within earshot of the Tower's many tortured inhabitants. It is said that she fell to her knees and declared that incarceration in such rooms was 'too good for me', alternately weeping and laughing as the enormity of her plight hit home; 'Jesu have mercy on me,' she reportedly added ('Jesu' being the Middle English way of referring to Jesus). Some have taken these statements as a blatant admission of her guilt (or of guilt concerning *something*, at the very least), but others disagree; people under sudden, immense stress often do say the most nonsensical things. As those who had escorted her to the Tower left, Anne beseeched them to petition the King to show her mercy. Meanwhile, the cannons boomed out to announce that a person of considerable rank was being incarcerated within those grim and forbidding walls.

Anne's apartments were located on the eastern side of the inner ward of the Tower, between the Lanthorn Tower and the Wardrobe Tower. Sadly for the fervent fanbase – not to mention the hardened historian – they were dismantled in the eighteenth century. The rooms included a presence chamber, a dining chamber and a bedchamber. Anne was concerned when she reached the apartments that the sacrament would be available in the adjoining closet, so that she might pray for mercy; for, as she assured Kingston, she was most surely free from any guilt in regard to the accusations levelled against her. She also asked after her father and her brother, becoming particularly fretful over the latter's location. Although she would soon experience the upset of George's arrest, she would take cold comfort in the fact that he was then lodged nearby. Her mother, she lamented, would surely die of shame when she heard what had become of her daughter. Later that day, Anne asked Kingston if she would die without justice. He replied with confidence that even the meekest of the King's subjects had justice. At this, a clearly ludicrous statement when applied to an autocrat of Henry VIII's increasingly irascible nature, well, Anne simply laughed in his face. This see-sawing between hysteria, despair, and, on occasion a little of her former savvy, became the hallmark of her tenure as a prisoner: 'She has much mirth at being incarcerated thus'.

Once settled into her new lodgings, the sheer unreality of the situation also caused her normally sardonic wit to misfire spectacularly: 'In her incoherent babblings in the Tower, all carefully noted by Kingston and the unsympathetic ladies set to serve her, Anne unwittingly presented the King's chief minister with more and more circumstantial froth that he was only too happy to use against her, and against any man whose name tripped from her tongue.' (Fox, 2008, pp186-187.) At other times, Anne was heard to declare that it would not rain until she was released; that, or some other catastrophe of Biblical proportions would befall the country in divine retribution for these unjust accusations. Such statements seem to cement the idea that she considered herself the receptacle of a divine mission against Catholic corruption. Sadly, it may at this point have begun to dawn on her that perhaps her part of the mission was now concluded. Then, oscillating from one extreme to the other, she tried to convince herself that the whole thing was a test conspired by the King – although for what bizarre purpose the mind boggles – and that she would actually be spared and sent to live out the rest of her days in a nunnery. However, these 'incoherent babblings', alongside the confessions of Sir Henry Norris and Mark Smeaton, had already sealed her fate.

As to those 'unsympathetic ladies set to serve her', they included Anne's old nurse, Mrs Orchard (recent research has provided some cause to doubt her presence; nay, her entire existence, even), as well as Mrs Stonor or 'Stoner'; these women would act as domestic servants for the duration of Anne's stay. Four other women were positioned in the role of ladies-in-waiting/spies, including Anne's aunt, Lady Shelton, mother of the Margaret/'Madge' with whom Henry had dallied several years previously. Lady Shelton had also acted as a governess to Catherine's daughter Mary, during which time Anne had encouraged her to be as strict with the girl as was required – i.e., rough her up a bit if necessary. There is speculation that Lady Shelton may have resented the position she was put in by her niece and thus used her newfound role as Anne's keeper to exact a vague sort of revenge upon her. Also in attendance on Anne was another aunt, namely Elizabeth Wood – Lady Boleyn – wife of Thomas Boleyn's younger brother, Sir James Boleyn. Another of these women – 'wardresses', Anne called them – was Mrs Margaret Coffin or 'Cosyn', wife of the Queen's Master of the Horse. Also, Mary Scrope, Lady Kingston, wife of Sir William, a woman then suffering from some undisclosed malady. She was also a former lady-in-waiting to Catherine, so not much of a sympathetic ear there either. So, we have a 'Mrs Stoner' and also a 'Mrs Coffin' attending – and in Mrs Coffin's case also sharing Anne's bedchamber – and guarding a woman accused of adultery and soon to be executed. You couldn't make it up.

Despite the somewhat sly and underhand nature of their mission, these women actually treated Anne with the courtesy and respect due a monarch, even one in the process of being prised free from her exalted station. As a 'guest' of Sir William Kingston, Anne took her meals with him, during which time she frequently enquired as to the whereabouts of the other players in her rapidly unfolding drama. She apparently remarked on the first night of her captivity, 'I hear say that I should be accused with three men, and I can say no more but nay, without I should open my body.' She then opened her gown and spread her skirts in a dramatic, almost a theatrical gesture, before adding, 'Oh, Norris, hast thou accused me? Thou art in the Tower with me, and thou and I shall die together.' Such words, smacking as they did of some sort of bond or closeness with Sir Henry, merely served to harden the suspicions of her custodians. Anne then turned her somewhat indiscreet tongue towards the fate that had befallen that 'lowly' Flemish musician Mark Smeaton, when she said, 'And Mark, thou art here too.' She then began to weep, lamenting the condition of her friend the Countess of Worcester – 'Her child did not stir in her body' – unaware that the woman was, in fact, among her principal accusers. Anne seemed to be labouring under the misapprehension that her friend's baby had died because of the grief the mother had taken when Anne herself lost her own child back in January. It was then that Anne apparently finished off her laments by enquiring of Kingston as to whether or not she would receive justice, bursting into peals of laughter upon receiving her jailer's rather po-faced response.

Meanwhile, word soon spread across London that the Queen of England had been arrested, although it seems that initially no one knew quite what for. As Cromwell's agents got to work, that would soon change. The French diplomat and scholar Lancelot de Carle wrote that the citizens of London were quite overjoyed to hear of Anne's arrest and hoped shortly to hear some favourable word regarding the return of Catherine's daughter to the succession. Upon hearing word of Anne's arrest for himself, Chapuys wrote to his master what he knew of the matter thus far, although this hasty despatch shows that he was not quite as well informed as he imagined, declaring that Norris had been taken merely for failing to disclose details of Anne's affair with Mark Smeaton:

> Your Majesty will be pleased to recollect what I wrote to you early in the last month touching the conversation between Cromwell and myself about the divorce of this King from the Concubine. I accordingly used several means to promote the matter, both with Cromwell and with others, of which I have not hitherto written, awaiting some certain issue of the affair, which in my opinion has come to pass much better than anybody could have believed, to the great disgrace of the Concubine, who, by the judgement of God, has been brought in full daylight from Greenwich to the Tower of London, conducted by the Duke of Norfolk, the two chamberlains, of the realm and of the Chamber, and

only four women have been left to her. The report is that it is for adultery, in which she has long continued with a player on the spinet of her chamber, who has been this morning lodged in the Tower, [along with] Master Norris, the most private and familiar body servant of the King, for not having revealed these matters.

Although he would eventually peer above the parapets of his latest marital drama in the most peculiar style, Henry initially kept his head down in the wake of Anne's arrest. The only tears he seemingly shed over the entire sorry affair came when he comforted his teenaged son – the illegitimate Henry Fitzroy – over the fact that Anne had apparently been plotting to poison both him and his half-sister, Mary. After all, the King maintained, she had form on this score, with the Boleyn faction now under renewed suspicion for the attempt on Bishop Fisher's life, alongside resuscitated whisperings regarding Catherine of Aragon's death. When Henry Fitzroy himself died of natural causes some several months after Anne's downfall, even that particular passing was quickly blamed on rogue elements of the Boleyn faction.

Anne's downfall occurred with such swiftness and severity that it sent shockwaves throughout the court. Besides the arrest of her brother, George, several other prominent courtiers were also hauled in for questioning, including the poet Thomas Wyatt. But perhaps the most prominent among those arrested was the 'lowly' Flemish musician Mark Smeaton, singled out with vitriol for his role in Anne's alleged 'harem' precisely because he was of low or common birth. Smeaton originally held a place in Cardinal Wolsey's household but was transferred to Henry VIII's troupe upon the presuming prelate's downfall, whereupon he seems to have garnered a middling interest from Anne herself. Smeaton was in his early twenties and quite handsome, besides being a genuinely talented musician; one didn't enter Cardinal Wolsey's household without at least a generous helping of flair. The one real anecdote we have of Mark in relation to Anne is that she once apparently scolded him for presuming that she might speak to him as she would to someone of noble birth. Anne was very self-conscious – one might almost say 'touchy' – where her queenly status was concerned.

Mark has been portrayed in various onscreen media either as a snivelling little creep – *Wolf Hall/Bring Up the Bodies* – or as rather a likeable, soft-hearted individual – *The Tudors* – and one who may have enjoyed a brief dalliance with Anne's brother. Certainly, in financial terms, he was considerably better off after entering Anne's household than when he arrived. Much was made of this financial fact, but it stands to reason that someone who provided music for the Queen of England wouldn't be standing around in rags and toddling off a tune on a second-hand lute. He was arrested on 30 April 1536 – as mentioned previously, Anne was informed of his arrest that evening – and taken to Cromwell's house at Stepney, where he may have been tortured into confessing an adulterous relationship; 'popular' lore depicts a length of knotted cord wound around his head and then pulled fast over his eyes. Later, disputed, reports claim that he was then racked at the Tower of London. It was possibly as a result of these interrogations that the other men in Anne's circle – including her brother – were then seized.

Sir Francis Weston was only in his early twenties when he was informed of the fact that his life was effectively over, and he was taken to the Tower. He was a Gentleman of the Privy Chamber, besides having been made a Knight of the Bath at Anne's coronation in 1533. His sole crime, at least according to the testimony Anne is supposed to have indiscreetly divulged whilst herself imprisoned in the Tower, was that he accused the betrothed Sir Henry Norris of paying more attention to the Queen than to his own sweetheart, Anne's cousin Margaret/'Madge' Shelton. In return, Anne apparently accused Weston of lusting after 'Madge' himself and thus of neglecting his wife. Weston retorted by declaring that there was one whom he loved better than both those women, and that was Anne herself. During his imprisonment, Weston's family made various efforts to free him, but to no avail.

Sir Henry Norris was considerably older than Smeaton or Weston. Besides having served as the King's Groom of the Stool (which basically involved waiting on Henry VIII while he busied himself upon the toilet, before then checking said 'stool' for anything detrimental to the King's health), he was also a good friend to the King; at least, inasmuch as Henry VIII ever knew what friendship really was. Despite the scatological nature of the job, the position of Groom of the Stool actually afforded almost unprecedented access to the monarch, even if you had to watch him straining and groaning whilst trying to pass on your own particular petitions. To his credit, Norris also attended on Henry in various other capacities. But it was the intimacy which blossomed over the pan of a Tudor latrine that served, as said, to form a genuine bond of friendship between them, and which thus makes his arrest all the more shocking. Or not, if you subscribe to the idea that Henry VIII was the sort of sociopath who would quite literally turn on anyone who happened to hamper his plans.

Like the others accused of adultery with Anne, Norris was charged with having sex with her multiple times in multiple places even when the records stated quite clearly that on most occasions neither he nor Anne – nor indeed the others accused – were actually anywhere near the royal residence in question. The most damning piece of evidence against Norris emerged from an exchange he had with Anne on 29 April, shortly before her very public spat with the King at Greenwich Palace. Given that she must have had at least an inkling of which way the wind was beginning to blow, the fact that Anne let rip as she did shows both the pressure she was under and also that she had quite a temper when tested. Basically, she accused Norris of being in love with her, declaring, 'You look for dead men's shoes, for if aught came to the King but good, you would look to have me.' Norris was aghast. For one thing, he was betrothed to 'Madge' Shelton, although his delay of making an honest woman of her was what had apparently piqued Anne's temper in the first place. Of course, Sir Francis Weston was alleged to have commented on Norris' preference for the Queen. In the exchange on 29 April, Norris retorted to Anne that if indeed he harboured any such insalubrious thoughts about her then he wished that his head might be struck off. Anne rapidly realised that she had given voice to the possibility of the King's death, a treasonous offence, never mind suggesting aloud that her little clique was full of people at sexual cross-purposes. Only a few hours were to pass before she summoned Norris and admonished him to report himself forthwith to John Skip, and to swear for her that she was a good woman.

Sir William Brereton was a Groom of the Privy Chamber to the King, besides being deputy to Henry Fitzroy, the King's illegitimate son. He was younger than Norris but older than Smeaton or Weston. He had married the daughter of the Earl of Worcester and had two sons by her – Henry and Thomas. The beneficiary of various royal grants in Cheshire and the Welsh Marches, Brereton could be ruthless when crossed. When one of his retainers was murdered, Brereton had the man he believed guilty of the crime slain in return. Several sources – not to mention novels – have suggested that Cromwell added Brereton's name to the list of those accused of adultery with Anne simply to remove him from the trouble he had caused amidst those lucrative landowning grants. However, other sources maintain that Anne's chief accuser, the Countess of Worcester, definitely cited Brereton as one of those who had committed adultery with the Queen.

When these men were put on trial, the outcome was almost a foregone conclusion. Several specimens of the male sex had to take the fall with Anne in order to make it look convincing, and these poor souls just happened to be the right men in the wrong place at the wrong time (or the right place at the right time, given how ludicrously inaccurate were those dates regarding their alleged indiscretions). Tried in Westminster Hall on Friday 12 May, they were initially sentenced to be hung, drawn and quartered, before their sentences were commuted – as ever – to the more merciful beheading. Brereton has perhaps one of the best fictionalised portrayals amongst Anne's accused lovers, appearing in *The Tudors* as a radicalised Jesuit who confirms his accusation of adultery simply because he knows it will bring Anne down, even at the cost of his own life. The fact that the men were found guilty before Anne herself had even stood trial sealed her fate, whilst also explaining why her executioner – the Swordsman (occasionally, 'The Hangman') of Calais – was summoned before she was even declared guilty. If they were adulterers, then logically it followed that she, the source of all their seductions, was doubly so. Her trial was to be a mere formality, the worst kind of kangaroo court.

Besides Thomas Wyatt, those who were arrested but actually managed to survive the brutal coup against the Boleyns also included Sir Richard Page, a gentleman of the privy chamber said to have been on friendly terms with Anne. Amidst the arrests, almost every man who had ever crossed paths with the Queen must have been occupied with preparing himself for a possible accusation. Poor Page was actually one of Cromwell's men, but such details mattered little at this time of heightened drama, when lives were cheap and expendable. Wyatt and Page were both released without charge, a month or so after Anne's execution. Wyatt would eventually recover something of his career, but it was initially curtains for Page, who was soon 'forever banished' from the King's presence. However, the mercurial Henry soon changed his mind and Page was, over the next decade or so, to do quite well out of his unpredictable monarch.

On 3 May Cranmer wrote to the King, declaring that he could scarcely believe that the accusations against the Queen were true. However, he rather deviously covered his own back by adding that 'I think your highness would not have gone so far if she had not been culpable.' Perhaps he was simply reasoning that it was bad enough for the Reformation to lose Anne, without Cranmer joining her in her captivity. On 6 May Anne apparently wrote her own letter to the King, all but begging for mercy:

> Sir, your Grace's displeasure, and my Imprisonment are Things so strange unto me, as what to Write, or what to Excuse, I am altogether ignorant; whereas you sent unto me (willing me to confess a Truth, and so obtain your Favour) by such a one, whom you know to be my ancient and professed Enemy; I no sooner received the Message by him, than I rightly conceived your Meaning; and if, as you say, confessing Truth indeed may procure my safety, I shall with all Willingness and Duty perform your Command.
>
> But let not your Grace ever imagine that your poor Wife will ever be brought to acknowledge a Fault, where not so much as Thought thereof proceeded. And to speak a truth, never Prince had Wife more Loyal in all Duty, and in all true Affection, than you have found in Anne Boleyn, with which Name and Place could willingly have contented myself, as if God, and your Grace's Pleasure had been so pleased. Neither did I at any time so far forge myself in my Exaltation, or received Queenship, but that I always looked for such an Alteration as now I find; for the ground of my preferment being on no surer Foundation than your Grace's Fancy, the least Alteration, I knew, was fit and sufficient to draw that Fancy to some other subject.
>
> You have chosen me, from a low Estate, to be your Queen and Companion, far beyond my Desert or Desire. If then you found me worthy of such Honour, Good your Grace,

let not any light Fancy, or bad Counsel of mine Enemies, withdraw your Princely Favour from me; neither let that Stain, that unworthy Stain of a Disloyal Heart towards your good Grace, ever cast so foul a Blot on your most Dutiful Wife, and the Infant Princess your Daughter.

Try me, good King, but let me have a Lawful Trial, and let not my sworn Enemies sit as my Accusers and Judges; yes, let me receive an open Trial, for my Truth shall fear no open shame; then shall you see, either mine Innocency cleared, your Suspicion and Conscience satisfied, the Ignominy and Slander of the World stopped, or my Guilt openly declared. So that whatsoever God or you may determine of me, your Grace may be freed from an open Censure; and mine Offence being so lawfully proved, your Grace is at liberty, both before God and Man, not only to execute worthy Punishment on me as an unlawful Wife, but to follow your Affection already settled on that party, for whose sake I am now as I am, whose Name I could some good while since have pointed unto: Your Grace being not ignorant of my Suspicion therein.

But if you have already determined of me, and that not only my Death, but an Infamous Slander must bring you the enjoying of your desired Happiness; then I desire of God, that he will pardon your great Sin therein, and likewise mine Enemies, the Instruments thereof; that he will not call you to a strict Account for your unprincely and cruel usage of me, at his General Judgement-Seat, where both you and my self must shortly appear, and in whose Judgement, I doubt not, (whatsover the World may think of me) mine Innocence shall be openly known, and sufficiently cleared.

My last and only Request shall be, That my self may only bear the Burthen of your Grace's Displeasure, and that it may not touch the Innocent Souls of those poor Gentlemen, who (as I understand) are likewise in strait Imprisonment for my sake. If ever I have found favour in your Sight; if ever the Name of Anne Boleyn hath been pleasing to your Ears, then let me obtain this Request; and I will so leave to trouble your Grace any further, with mine earnest Prayers to the Trinity to have your Grace in his good keeping, and to direct you in all your Actions.

Your most Loyal and ever Faithful Wife, Anne Bullen
From my doleful Prison the Tower, this 6th of May.

It would be no surprise to the layperson to hear that this letter is of somewhat dubious authenticity. And to be perfectly honest, when you're reaching several hundred years into the past, there isn't all that much that isn't somewhat precarious. The letter was found in Cromwell's papers after his own execution in 1540. Those who argue against the authenticity of the letter point to the familiarity used in the language, which is, however, perfectly understandable for a woman writing to her husband, whatever their 'straitened' circumstances. Perhaps Cromwell concocted the letter, the contents of which were designed to make sure that Anne's forthright manner ensured there would be no mercy on the King's part; or perhaps it was genuine and merely intercepted before it reached Henry. Of course, there is also the handwriting to consider, a script which apparently doesn't match the extant documents written by Anne, although this aspect is easily explained by the fact that Anne may have dictated the letter and that it was written by one of the women who were guarding her. As ever, it seems safest simply to trot out that well-worn cliché that comes with so many things concerning the Tudors; in other words, *we shall likely never know.*

So, the majority of historical opinion – G. W. Bernard and Retha Warnicke aside – agrees that Anne and her 'harem' were framed for varying reasons. Elizabeth Norton, for instance, pointed out that '...whilst many people in England did believe in Anne's guilt, the charges against her were laughable. An English queen, as both Henry and Jane (Seymour) were well aware, was never alone and it would have been impossible for Anne to have committed adultery on so many occasions.' (Norton, 2009, p69.) However, Henry's fifth wife, Catherine Howard, managed it, though she had connivance from several of her ladies-in-waiting.

As stated, the locations where Anne's various adulteries were alleged to have taken place were so arbitrary as to be almost beyond ludicrous, unless knowledge of her misdemeanours was actually true but precise dates escaped verification; better to put forth a spurious date as evidence than no date at all, after all. But this too is an absurdity. To have so many extramarital liaisons, and for word of them to have remained hidden for so long – some of the charges stretched back several years – stretches an already strained credulity almost to breaking point. When Catherine Howard was discovered to have had a somewhat 'chequered' sexual past, besides her relationship with a current courtier, word reached Henry within a year or so of their marriage. Apparently, we are led to believe by Anne's prosecutors, that she was enjoying several illicit liaisons *for years* before anyone thought to furnish Cromwell with the facts; the testimony of the conveniently deceased Lady Wingfield, for one thing.

There is, however, the disturbing fact that the publication of Anne's adulteries had the knock-on effect of turning the macho Henry VIII into a public cuckold, not an enviable position for any man in Tudor times. Just ask Mary Boleyn's first husband, William Carey, how it felt to be such a monumental cuckold. And yet, Henry apparently gave Cromwell carte blanche to do just that, even going so far as to compile a diary of his lamentations, ready to read aloud to whomever might listen. On one occasion, conferring with the Bishop of Carlisle during the course of a banquet, Henry allegedly confided that he thought it possible that Anne had enjoyed upwards of a hundred lovers. The bishop later told Chapuys that 'You never saw prince nor man who made greater show of his horns, or bore them more pleasantly.' The reference to 'horns' comes from the sign of the horns, which derives from 'the cuckold's horns', a gesture in which two fingers are placed over or behind the head of a man whose wife has been unfaithful. This is an allusion to the mating habits of stags, who surrender their mates when they are defeated by another, often more virile male. That someone would risk public humiliation in such a fashion – and when that someone is the near-mystically masculine Henry VIII – seems almost incredible, unless he genuinely believed that his piteous efforts might elicit some sympathy. After all, Henry reasoned, if Anne really was the monster of sexual depravity that the charges painted, then even the best of men might find themselves cuckolded by her at some point.

Still, this aspect of the case sits somewhat uncomfortably, not merely with regard to what we know about Henry VIII, but also of what is known about the sexual psychology of men in general. And that doubt, so at odds with the popular narrative, remains one of the reasons why Anne's downfall continues to fascinate. Because, as sure as we are of her innocence, there are some aspects of the case that continue to defy cold, rigorous definition.

She *was* innocent. Probably.

10

The short journey to the scaffold

'It is at least possible that Anne Boleyn was not as innocent as she claimed. It may be that she pursued other men in desperate search for a male child who could be hailed as the heir to the throne, thereby saving herself and her family for the foreseeable future.'

(Ackroyd, 2012, p97)

Anne and her brother George were tried at the Tower of London on 15 May in the King's Hall and found guilty. Anne was condemned on all counts of adultery – including incest with George – as well as treason, by plotting to poison the King and then to marry one of the members of her fictional harem. The trial was presided over by their uncle, the Duke of Norfolk, in his role as Lord High Steward. For the occasion, he was sat upon a special throne underneath the canopy of estate. In his hand he held the white staff of office, whilst at his feet, in rather a bizarre position of subservience, sat his son, the Earl of Surrey, holding – on his father's behalf – the golden staff of the Earl Marshal of England. Sir Thomas Audley, the Lord Chancellor, and Charles Brandon, the Duke of Suffolk, were placed on either side of Norfolk.

None of these men were in any way sympathetic to Anne's plight, and that theme seeped on into each and every one of the jurors summoned to condemn her. The Earl of Worcester was there, the man whose wife had provided such damning evidence. Also present was Baron Morley, Lady Rochford's father, and Lord Cobham, possibly the husband of the elusive 'Nan Cobham', another of Anne's ladies-in-waiting who poured scandal upon her mistress (in *The Tudors*, she was almost a supporting character, played by actress Serena Brabazon). A relative or two of the incoming queen of England were also present on the jury, including Lord Wentworth, a cousin of Jane Seymour's. Contrary to some of the less salubrious legends that have blossomed around Thomas Boleyn over the last several hundred years, he was not present and did not speak in any way against his two children during the course of the trial. We do not know whether or not he petitioned Henry or Cromwell for mercy behind the scenes, and whether or not he was warned off as a result. After all, there was room enough on the scaffold at Tower Hill to accommodate a great deal more Boleyns, if need be.

Certainly, Thomas Boleyn had taught his daughter how to conduct herself in the midst of a fiery debate. By all accounts, Anne managed herself so well at this kangaroo court that she succeeded in making the charges look even more ridiculous than they already were. However, the fact that the other men – except George – had already been found guilty meant that there was scant chance she would come out of the trial a free woman. Some 2,000 spectators had assembled in the King's Hall in order to watch this particular slice of history unfurling. During the course of the proceedings, although maintaining her innocence with some considerable verve, Anne admitted to giving money to Sir Francis Weston, but elaborated that she had often made monetary gifts to young gentlemen of the court. With hindsight, it is painfully apparent how such an admission might be further construed as a sign of her habit of procuring buoyant young bucks for their sexual favours. However, this was as nothing when the specific charge of incest was read out to her, namely that she had enticed her brother to have sex with her, specifically on 2 November 1535, but also on several previous occasions. The emphasis on the siblings exchanging a tongue-twisting French kiss has become a staple of Anne Boleyn lore. Added to that, Anne is alleged to have conspired with various other members of her harem to do away with the King and then marry one of them by way of a reward. Even the deceased Lady Wingfield's slanderous diatribe was trundled out and added to the evidence. Then, as if such a tally of treasonous charges were not enough to condemn her, it was added that she had scoffed at the King's sense of dress and possibly also his poetic efforts; where Henry VIII's preposterous codpiece is concerned, she may have had a point.

George, meanwhile, pleaded not guilty and then proceeded to acquit himself as capably as his sister – in fact, it was said that he acquitted himself better than Thomas More – but he sealed his fate when he read aloud a missive that called into question Henry VIII's much-vaunted virility, despite strict instruction not to repeat the contents of this highly compromising missive. There is a certain absurdity in this, given that the

King was apparently quite proud of parading his freshly minted status as a cuckold to anyone willing to lend him an ear. Now, word soon spread that not only was Henry a cuckold, but also that he was a pretty poor lover to boot, besides possibly not being the father of Anne's daughter. The letter was apparently hearsay regarding a conversation Anne had conducted with George's wife, aka Lady Rochford, during which the Queen was said to have scoffed at Henry's potency. That joke was then – so George's accusers maintained – shared liberally between sister and brother, with George adding fuel to the fire by apparently having gossiped that the King, given his potency problems, couldn't possibly be the father of Elizabeth.

Questioning the paternity of the King's issue was tantamount to treason. However, despite George's flagrant disregard for the admonitions of the court in regard to this explosive missive, there were many – including even Chapuys – who considered his defence so spirited that they were convinced he would be found not guilty, clearly without having much idea of the stuff going on behind the scenes regarding the coup against the Boleyns. George, for the most part, shrugged off the allegation of incest, despite the fact that he had at one point been privately in his sister's company for some considerable time. This was perfectly natural, he maintained, for siblings as close as he and Anne were. However, when the guilty verdict was read back to him, George became resigned and admitted that he deserved death. One may deduce from this the slight but not insubstantial possibility that he was confessing to some indiscretion with Anne after all, but more likely he was simply admitting that he had led a dissolute life up until that point. He would repeat such sentiments upon the scaffold, mere moments from death. Henry Percy, Anne's former amour, was among the jurors who delivered their unanimous verdict to the siblings; when the sentence was read aloud, he collapsed and had to be carried from the room. He died eight months later.

The aplomb of both Anne and George in the courtroom, however, failed to help their plight. Anne was condemned to death, either by burning or beheading. The King would later commute the sentence to beheading, and by the more merciful stroke of a swordsman imported from Calais as opposed to the dull axe reserved for the others. Anne's uncle read out the sentence of the court to her, apparently with tears in his eyes (one finds this somewhat hard to credit to such a cantankerous individual, a man who had previously referred to her as 'The big fuck'):

'Because thou hast offended against our sovereign the King's Grace in committing treason against his person, and here attainted of the same, the law of the realm is this, that thou hast deserved death, and thy judgment is this: that thou shalt be burned here within the Tower of London on the Green, else to have thy head smitten off, as the King's pleasure shall be further known of the same.'

Anne kept her cool as this grisly fate was laid before her, although she was heard to comment that she had been condemned for some reason other than the one alleged. Basically, this was Anne saying that she – and indeed they – all knew the real reason she was being disposed of, and this was because of her clash with Cromwell, because of Jane Seymour, and so on and so forth. Besides that, she delivered a speech of some power and eloquence to those assembled, of which various versions have since surfaced:

> O Father, O Creator! Thou who art the way, the truth, and the life, knowest that I have not deserved this death!
>
> My lords, I will not say your sentence is unjust, nor presume that my reasons can prevail against your convictions. I am willing to believe that you have sufficient reasons for what you have done; but then they must be other than those which have been produced in court, for I am clear of all the offences which you then laid to my charge.
>
> I have ever been a faithful wife to the King, though I do not say I have always shown him that humility which his goodness to me, and the honours to which he raised me, merited. I confess I have had jealous fancies and suspicions of him, which I had not discretion enough, and wisdom, to conceal at all times. But God knows, and is my witness, that I have not sinned against him in any other way. Think not I say this in the hope to prolong my life, for He who saveth from death hath taught me how to die, and He will strengthen my faith.
>
> Think not, however, that I am so bewildered in my mind as not to lay the honour of my chastity to heart now in mine extremity, when I have maintained it all my life long, much as ever queen did. I know these, my last words, will avail me nothing but for the justification of my chastity and

honour. As for my brother and those others who are unjustly condemned, I would willingly suffer many deaths to deliver them, but since I see it so pleases the King, I shall willingly accompany them in death, with this assurance, that I shall lead an endless life with them in peace and joy, where I will pray to God for the King and for you, my lords.

Even at this, undoubtedly her darkest hour, Anne cleaved to Jesus and his message of forgiveness. There is some evidence that this parting speech stirred emotion in some of the jurors, but it was too late to change the verdict, and too dangerous where their own lives were concerned. In fact, short of summoning Jesus himself to act as a character witness, there was nothing that could save Anne now. Even Chapuys commented that she had been convicted '...without valid proof or confession'. He himself had been unable to attend the trial, having been taken ill at the time, possibly with gout, or possibly with a snivelling case of tact.

With the proceedings concluded, Sir William Kingston then escorted Anne from the room, an axe now turned against her to signify that she had been sentenced to death. George, meanwhile, was sentenced to the traitor's death of hanging, drawing and quartering, the punishment read out to him by his uncle, presumably with another smattering of crocodile tears. Shortly thereafter, the sentence would be commuted to the more merciful beheading. In the meantime, Anne was returned to her rooms in the Tower, and to the eager ears of her jailers. At this point, it might have appeared that there was little left for those women – those 'wardresses' – to do in regard to listening to Anne's every utterance, but still they were kept in position. Anne also continued to receive visits from John Skip, doing his best to offer her what spiritual sustenance he could under such straitened conditions.

Cromwell, meanwhile, made sure there was scant chance of the case against her crumbling when he '...pretended to flinch from disclosing any further details of the case because they were so shocking. "I write no particularities, the things be so abhominable, that I think the like was never heard."' Even after Anne's trial, when all the lurid details had been revealed, he claimed that there was still more that had remained hidden. 'In good faith I wrote as much and as plainly of the matters that chanced here as I could desire unless I should have sent you the very confessions, which were so abhominable that a great part of them were never given in evidence but clearly kept secret.' (Borman, 2014, p247.) We can doubtless dismiss this as simply Cromwellian spin, making absolutely sure that Anne didn't miraculously bounce back and then set him in her sights. For the morbidly curious, it does make one wonder quite what Cromwell was alluding to, what further depravities that could have been considered much worse than sleeping with one's own brother, for instance. A lesbian love affair with one of her ladies, perhaps? Or perhaps something more scandalous still? We shall likely never know quite how far Cromwell was really willing to go in order to close the book on Anne Boleyn.

The documents relating to the trial of Anne and her brother can be viewed at the National Archives, where they are held in a file of the proceedings of the court of King's Bench, KB 8/9. These are records of the special commissions of oyer and terminer, or the court of the Lord High Steward and peers, which tried peers of the realm who were accused of treason. The records were originally kept separately from other indictments, in a bag known as the '*Baga de secretis*', or 'Bag of Secrets'. This was due to the fact that it was a state trial, in this case the trial of a crowned queen, and was therefore considered exceptionally important. Needless to say, the mere mention of the word 'secrets' in relation to such a monumental slice of Tudor history, especially when one mixes in Cromwell's cryptic remarks about the uncharted depths of Anne's depravity, has served to cause even the most cynical historian to salivate with anticipation. When one adds that the records for the trial, as well as the transcripts, records of evidence and the statements of those testifying are all missing, well, this merely fuels the Boleyn mythos, mainly for the worse. In such a kangaroo court, anything as yet uncovered by some enterprising historian would probably only serve to tally with Cromwell's cryptic statement regarding possible further depravities on the part of the Queen. Perhaps the loss is for the best.

Archbishop Cranmer, meanwhile, was instructed to declare Henry and Anne's marriage null and void, thereby making their daughter Elizabeth a bastard, alongside Catherine's daughter Mary. Anne was thus required to confess to an impediment to her marriage. In the end, it was the King's relationship with Mary Boleyn which seems to have put an end to the royal matrimony. Mary 'had been Henry's mistress; and as illegitimate relations, there was a forbidden degree. Scandalous as the proceeding might be, the marriage was to be annulled on this ground.' (Friedmann, 2013, p272.)

Possibly, Cranmer had been instructed to broker a deal, whereby Anne would be released and sent to live in a nunnery if she consented to the annulment of the marriage. Whether Cranmer was conned into making this offer or whether he knew it and lied to her face remains a mystery. At dinner that night, Anne was certainly nursing the possibility of a nunnery, although her illusions were soon to be brutally shattered. Meanwhile, Henry was busy signing the death warrants of her various 'lovers', whilst Sir William Kingston was fretting about whether the scaffold upon Tower Hill was quite prepared for such a conveyor belt of star turns.

On 17 May 1536 Anne's brother and the others accused were beheaded. Whether or not Anne was able to see her beloved brother lose his life upon Tower Hill, from her vantage point in the Tower itself, has been open to some speculation; *The Tudors* depicts that she did, in some harrowing detail. Certainly, Thomas Wyatt apparently saw the whole thing from his confinement in the Bell Tower, as his verse makes clear:

Innocentia Veritas Viat Fides Circumdederunt me
inimici mei

Who list his wealth and ease retain,
Himself let him unknown contain.
Press not too fast in at that gate
Where the return stands by disdain,
For sure, circa Regna tonat.
The high mountains are blasted oft
When the low valley is mild and soft.
Fortune with Health stands at debate.
The fall is grievous from aloft.
And sure, circa Regna tonat.
These bloody days have broken my heart.
My lust, my youth did them depart,
And blind desire of estate.
Who hastes to climb seeks to revert.
Of truth, circa Regna tonat.
The Bell Tower showed me such sight
That in my head sticks day and night.
There did I learn out of a grate,

For all favour, glory, or might,
That yet circa Regna tonat.
By proof, I say, there did I learn:
Wit helpeth not defence too yerne,
Of innocency to plead or prate.
Bear low, therefore, give God the stern,
For sure, circa Regna tonat.

A further poems laments each of the convicted in turn:

In Mourning wise since daily I increase

In Mourning wise since daily I increase,
Thus should I cloak the cause of all my grief;
So pensive mind with tongue to hold his peace,
My reason sayeth there can be no relief:
Wherefore give ear, I humbly you require,
The affect to know that thus doth make me moan.
The cause is great of all my doleful cheer
For those that were, and now be dead and gone.
What thought to death desert be now their call.
As by their faults it doth appear right plain?
Of force I must lament that such a fall should light on
those so wealthily did reign,
Though some perchance will say, of cruel heart,
A traitor's death why should we thus bemoan?
But I alas, set this offence apart,
Must needs bewail the death of some be gone.
As for them all I do not thus lament,
But as of right my reason doth me bind;
But as the most doth all their deaths repent,
Even so do I by force of mourning mind.
Some say, "Rochford, haddest thou been not so proud,
For thy great wit each man would thee bemoan,
Since as it is so, many cry aloud
It is great loss that thou art dead and gone."
Ah! Norris, Norris, my tears begin to run
To think what hap did thee so lead or guide

Whereby thou hast both thee and thine undone
That is bewailed in court of every side;
In place also where thou hast never been
Both man and child doth piteously thee moan.
They say, "Alas, thou art far overseen
By thine offences to be thus dead and gone."
Ah! Weston, Weston, that pleasant was and young,
In active things who might with thee compare?
All words accept that thou diddest speak with tongue,
So well esteemed with each where thou diddest fare.
And we that now in court doth lead our life
Most part in mind doth thee lament and moan;
But that thy faults we daily hear so rife,
All we should weep that thou are dead and gone.
Brereton farewell, as one that least I knew.
Great was thy love with divers as I hear,
But common voice doth not so sore thee rue
As other twain that doth before appear;
But yet no doubt but they friends thee lament
And other hear their piteous cry and moan.
So doth eah heart for thee likewise relent
That thou givest cause thus to be dead and gone.
Ah! Mark, what moan should I for thee make more,
Since that thy death thou hast deserved best,
Save only that mine eye is forced sore
With piteous plaint to moan thee with the rest?
A time thou haddest above thy poor degree,
The fall whereof thy friends may well bemoan:
A rotten twig upon so high a tree
Hath slipped thy hold, and thou art dead and gone.
And thus farewell each one in hearty wise!
The axe is home, your heads be in the street;
The trickling tears doth fall so from my eyes
I scarce may write, my paper is so wet.
But what can hope when death hath played his part,
Though nature's course will thus lament and moan?
Leave sobs therefore, and every Christian heart
Pray for the souls of those be dead and gone.

George Boleyn's last days were apparently spent less worrying about having his head lopped off than with settling his debts before he died. In fact, that all his debts might be settled via means of his confiscated assets troubled him so much that petition was made to Cromwell to ease his conscience in this regard, after he'd raised his concerns in the immediate aftermath of his trial. He and Anne were permitted no contact whilst they were held prisoner; or, if they were, then it was done with such discretion that history has left no record of it, although given what they were charged with, such an indulgence seems unlikely. When actually upon the scaffold, George made an impressive final speech:

> Christian men, I am born under the law, and judged under the law, and die under the law, and the law hath condemned me. Masters all, I am not come hither for to preach, but for to die, for I have deserved to die if had 20 lives, more shamefully than can be devised, for I am a wretched sinner, and I have sinned shamefully.
>
> I have known no man so evil, and to rehearse my sins openly it were no pleasure to you to hear them, nor yet for me to rehearse them, for God knoweth all. Therefore, masters all, I pray you take heed by me, and especially my lords and gentlemen of the court, the which I have been among, take heed by me and beware of such a fall. And I pray to God the Father, the Son and the Holy Ghost, three persons and one God, that my death may be an example to you all. And beware, trust not in the vanity of the world, and especially in the flattering of the court.
>
> And I cry God mercy, and ask all the world forgiveness, as willingly as I would have forgiveness of God; and if I have offended any man that is not here how, either in thought, word or deed, and if you hear any such, I pray you heartily on my behalf, pray them to forgive me for God's sake. And yet, my masters all, I have one thing for to say to you, men do come and say that I have been a setter forth of the word of God, and one that have favoured the Gospel of Christ; and because I would not that God's word should be slandered by me, I say unto you all, that if I had followed God's word in deed as I did read it and set it forth to my power, I had not come to this.

I did read the Gospel of Christ, but I did not follow it; if I had, I had been a living man among you: therefore I pray you, masters all, for God's sake stick to the truth and follow it, for one good follower is worth three readers, as God knoweth.

In this speech, George followed the usual execution convention, acknowledging that he had been condemned by the law – however unjustly – and that he deserved death because he was a sinner. He also used the moment to preach a sermon to the rather bloodthirsty crowd before him, urging them to learn from his mistakes. Most likely it fell on deaf ears; those gathered to watch a good beheading wanted gore, not a Sunday school speech. The 'deserving death because I'm a sinner' angle has been seen by some as a veiled allusion to the fact that George was homosexual, or, as said, that he was guilty of some sort of overfamiliarity with his sister. Most Tudor historians baulk at the idea of George as a gay man – run a snap poll and you'd come away thinking homosexuality didn't even exist then – and insist there was no evidence for the fact. However, there isn't an awful lot of evidence for an awful lot that Anne's partisans insist she did and didn't do, and yet they're happy to run with that when the occasion suits. One detects a certain subtle but lingering hint of homophobia in this regard. If George Boleyn was gay then he was gay – so what? Retha Warnicke, for one, was very much an adherent of the idea that George was at the summit of a virtual gaggle of Tudor queens, and not one of them were his sister. Even the insinuation against George could be damaging, if indeed someone suggested it or had secret knowledge of such a clique. Homosexuality was seen mainly as a vice of monks in their monasteries, although the reality barely kept place with the slurs. As for George being perhaps simply bisexual, well, it adds a bit of diversity to an otherwise drearily conformist Tudor court.

As to the other executions, Sir Francis Weston, whilst prostrate upon the scaffold, apparently said, 'I had thought to have lived in abomination yet this twenty or thirty years and to have made amends.' Given that he apologised profusely to his wife in a letter sent whilst under arrest, it can be fairly interpreted that Weston was a bit of a rake. In fact, the words 'in abomination' seem to constitute something a lot worse than simply even an excess of extramarital affairs. Had he engaged in homosexual relations, perhaps with George Boleyn? – 'You shall not lie with a male as with a woman; it is an *abomination*.' Whether Weston was being so specific we shall never know. He was about to have his head lopped off, so he may have been less than lucid at that point. Also, there is the natural tendency the Tudors had to speak in what to modern ears sounds like overblown or flowery language. Either way, Anne showed a distinct lack of judgement in associating with such a well-known womaniser, even at a 'courtly' distance. Likewise when it came to her ill-advised exchange with Sir Henry Norris. Norris himself reportedly went to his death with scant comment, other than the standard – but to the modern mind bizarre – lip service mention regarding the mercy of the King and the general benevolence of the brutal Tudor regime as a whole. Sir William Brereton apparently came to the closest to challenging the accusations laid against him, when he said, 'I have deserved to die if it were a thousand deaths. But the cause whereof I die, judge not. But if ye judge, judge the best.' In fact, he repeated the last sentence some several times over, the very same words Anne herself would emphasise when she too stood upon the scaffold. Poor Mark Smeaton, whatever taste of Tudor torture he had perhaps endured, had the good sense to maintain his guilt until the very end. Perhaps, even atop the scaffold, he feared that Cromwell or one of his adherents might turn up and start plucking his fingernails out by the root. To his bloodthirsty audience, the last one for whom he would ever perform, he said simply, 'Masters I pray you all pray for me for I have deserved the death.' Needless to say, such a statement only added to the ardour of those rejoicing in the fall of the King's concubine. When his words were relayed back to Anne herself, she apparently said, 'Alas! I fear that his soul will suffer punishment for his false confession.'

As was the case with Bishop Fisher, the corpses were left on the scaffold for some several hours, although this time they were mercifully half-dressed. What indignities the gathered hordes might otherwise have heaped upon them before they were removed one dares not imagine. Eventually, they were stripped and then prepared for burial. All but George Boleyn were laid to rest in the churchyard of the church of St Peter ad Vincula. George was buried inside the building itself, his decapitated remains being interred just before the altar.

With her brother despatched, Anne knew that she herself had only days left to live. John Skip visited her rooms, at the ungodly hour of 2am, to pray with her, and they were still praying when Cranmer arrived to perform mass and to hear Anne's final confession. Anne then took the sacrament and swore twice, with Sir William Kingston as a witness, that she was innocent of all the charges laid against her. She was adamant that the fact should be reported to Cromwell, and from there it was short work before Chapuys was talking about it: 'The Concubine, before and after receiving the sacrament, affirmed to her (one of the women guarding Anne), on the damnation of her soul, that she had never been unfaithful to the King.' Whether she was leaving this declaration as a simple matter for posterity or whether she actually thought it might prick Cromwell's conscience is a matter of opinion. Perhaps she hoped to do both.

Anne was brought to the scaffold within the grounds of the Tower of London and decapitated by the Swordsman of Calais on 19 May 1536. This pivotal moment in history took place directly between the White Tower and the Waterloo Block, the latter being the location wherein the Crown Jewels are currently housed. Despite what some of the Beefeaters and several less well-informed books about Anne Boleyn might try to tell you, she was most certainly *not* executed on the site of the lovely glass memorial erected to those beheaded within the walls of the Tower: 'Gentle visitor pause a while, where you stand death cut away the light of many days. Here jewelled names were broken from the vivid thread of life. May they rest in peace while we walk the generations around their strife and courage under these restless skies.'

The actual, authentic spot of her execution isn't marked. Before the beheading, Anne delivered a short but eloquent speech to the assembled onlookers, telling them, among other things, that Henry VIII was in fact the most kind and loving prince that a wife and a kingdom could ever hope to have. As obscene as this may sound, it was, as said, the polite protocol for someone facing a traitor's death in Tudor times. Anne had a daughter and a wider family to think of, so badmouthing her beastly husband in the last few minutes of her life simply wasn't in her best interests. There are several versions of that short but eloquent speech, the most widely reported of which is as follows:

> Good Christian people, I have not come here to preach a sermon; I have come here to die, for according to the law and by the law I am judged to die, and thereof I will speak nothing against it. I am come hither to accuse no man, nor to speak of that whereof I am accused and condemned to die, but I pray God save the King and send him long to reign over you, for a gentler nor a more merciful prince was there never, and to me he was ever a good, a gentle, and sovereign lord.

> And if any person will meddle of my cause, I require
> them to judge the best. And thus I take my leave of the world
> and of you all, and I heartily desire you all to pray for me.

She was apparently calm and composed throughout, but once her words were done and she knelt and awaited the blindfold, she was seen to glance repeatedly over her shoulder at the swordsman, her prayers half muttered against a rising wave of anxiety. The man whose name she uttered as she stooped there upon the scaffold was not that of her brother, her father, and most certainly not her husband: 'O Lord have mercy on me, to God I commend my soul. To Jesus Christ I commend my soul; Lord Jesu receive my soul,' she mumbled, over and over again.

As said, rather than being subjected to the blunt humiliation and often botched brutality of the axe, Anne was shown a special 'mercy' by being allowed to lose her head in the quicker 'French style'. In this instance, the prisoner would kneel at the front of the scaffold rather than being required to sprawl themselves out in an ungainly manner over a bloodstained block of wood. The actual beheading itself was thus usually achieved in one swift stroke, rather than the usual awkward hacking of the axe.

The Swordsman of Calais was late in arriving in both England and then in London, as will shortly be explained, meaning there were several unintentionally sadistic false-starts to Anne's final days. She had mentally prepared herself for death on several occasions only to be told that her execution had been delayed because the swordsman was, in terms of timekeeping, seemingly something of a slacker. Besides the blindfold, his special, 'civilised' method of execution also involved wearing soft-soled shoes as he scurried about the scaffold, so as not to alarm his victim unduly; as if they weren't most likely in enough of a state already. He would then distract them by calling out for his sword to an assistant, who would be standing nearby. In fact, the sword was secreted elsewhere and the swordsman would retrieve it as his victim turned their head to track his request. At that precise moment, the fatal blow would be struck, the sinews on the neck of the victim being exposed to the maximum effect when the head was turned.

Anne was finished off in exactly this manner, her head removed so swiftly and so efficiently that many of the witnesses – quite a crowd, by all accounts – briefly doubted what they had actually seen. The pain would have been intense when the sword struck, but mercifully brief. However, scientific studies show that Anne may have survived her decapitation by several seconds or even by a minute or more; equally, the shock of the blow may have killed her outright. Perhaps the blindfold was administered in order to prevent a post-decapitation view on the part of the victim, to save their remaining dignity from the curious faces of the crowd. Some reports of the seconds following Anne's beheading have alluded to her lips murmuring for several minutes whilst her ladies were busily bundling her body – followed by the head – into a nearby arrow chest. No provision had been made for Anne's body following her death, unbelievably, although whether this was an intentional slight or simply a gruesome oversight has never been adequately explained. However, some sources say that an extremely basic coffin was in fact provided.

The graphic reality of decapitation, regardless of the mercy of a sharp sword versus a blunt axe, was amply illustrated by Alison Weir, in the closing pages of her book *The Lady in the Tower*. Therein, she cites the work of several French doctors whose experiments regarding decapitation concluded that almost every element of the brain survives beheading, however briefly, and that consciousness was quite possible for the victim for some several minutes afterwards. For instance, 'In 1989, the face of a man decapitated in a car accident registered shock, then terror, then grief, as the living eyes looked directly at the witness before dimming.' (Weir, 2009, p272.) This sort of evidence thus leads to the dreadful thought that the victims of beheadings, including Anne, may indeed have been conscious, albeit briefly, after their head was separated from their body. Indeed, when the head of the victim was held up by the executioner as proof of his success – as it so often was – the victim may have still been 'alive' and thus staring out at the astonished crowd, hence the testimony that Anne's lips were said to have murmured for some several minutes after the actual beheading. In *The Mirror and the Light*, Hilary Mantel deftly walks the reader through the well-trodden aftermath of this, perhaps the most famous beheading in English history: 'The women have done well. Anne would have been proud of them. They will not let any man touch her; palms out, they force back those who try to help them. They slide in the gore and stoop over the narrow carcass. He hears their indrawn breath as they lift what is left of her, holding her by her clothes; they are afraid the cloth will rip and their fingers touch her cooling flesh.' (Mantel, 2020, pp3-4.)

The Swordsman of Calais was paid £23 6s 8d for his services, a handsome sum for the times. His real name remains generally unknown and nor is it certain he even originated from Calais; most movies and TV shows covering the event give him a rather formulaic French accent, thus forgetting that the place was then almost entirely English. However, there may be logical reasons for his anonymity. In Tudor times, the identities of executioners were often kept secret, for fear of retribution by the families of their victims. However, this author's research both in Calais and St Omer (another purported hometown for the Swordsman) has uncovered the fact that the Swordsman of Calais was of English descent, although born in Calais to a long-standing trading family. As an adult, he was simply a well-trained English (speaking) executioner versed in the art of beheading in the French style for offenders in Calais and the surrounding area; a great many historians seem to forget that Calais was, in 1536, '... in most respects an English colony.' (Turpyn, 1846, pXXIII.) He was not Jean Rombaud of St Omer; Charles V's sister, Mary of Hungary, was merely exhibiting some vengefully minded wishful thinking on that score. Also, the fact that this was reported in the notoriously 'flexible' Spanish Chronicle should come as no surprise to those seeking the truth regarding the Swordsman's identity. Never mind the fact that the identities of executioners were simply not bandied about in polite society, or what passed for it in Tudor times; they were, quite succinctly, '...one of the most reviled and feared members of society.' (Larson, 2014, p95.) Our Swordsman still lived in Calais when the summons for his services was sent (by Cromwell, as a final gesture to his former Reformist comrade; not by Henry, as has been reported ad nauseum, although the warrant was issued in his name). The Swordsman was escorted to his ship by the Calais man-at-arms, Mr Hyfeldh. The previous night, the Swordsman was discreetly hosted by the Lord Deputy of Calais, wherein certain scruples of conscience regarding Anne's execution were smoothed over by the Lord Deputy; basically, it was simply not good form for a Frenchman to be cutting off the head of the Queen of England; no, an Englishman must do it. On that score, Anne certainly knew who she was getting – and realised the somewhat awkward sentiment – hence her laughter, when commenting to William Kingston that she had heard that the executioner was good and that she only had 'a little neck'.

The tale that the Swordsman's horse slipped a shoe as he galloped through Kent – hence the delay in the execution – is nonsense. He was given a considerable escort, both to ensure his safety and also to guarantee that any of the aforementioned scruples of conscience did not return to waylay him. As it was, the delay was still caused by the simple fact of the Swordsman casting doubt about whether he was cut out – pun unintended – for so momentous a task. But regardless of who he really was – or perhaps because of it – the Swordsman of Calais went to his grave without ever apparently disclosing how he felt in regard to performing one of the most famous beheadings in history. Even at the time, the execution of Anne Boleyn was quite astonishing – she was the first queen of England ever to suffer such an ignominious fate – and thus the Swordsman of Calais can have been in little doubt that he had secured his own particular place in history for having performed such an act.

Once secured in that 'discarded' arrow chest, Anne was buried inside the church of St Peter ad Vincula, but not before a further slight to her dignity occurred, when it was discovered that the space reserved for her in the chancel – the area around the altar – required a man to be summoned to lift the paving stones in order to place the arrow chest inside. This involved a wait of some several hours, during which time her jewellery was removed and handed over to officials. It would then be redeemed by Henry for whatever he could get for the various pieces. Whilst all of this was going on, the crowd began to disperse, with diplomats hurrying to pen their despatches, whilst others made for court, for the King and for Cromwell, to tell them exactly how Anne had died.

Once interred, Anne would remain undisturbed for some several hundred years, until, in 1876, Queen Victoria gave permission for renovations to be carried out on the premises. What was presumed to be the arrow chest containing Anne's remains was exhumed, along with the containers carrying various of the other unfortunate traitors. Once this was done, an examination of their remains was carried out. None of the skeletons removed and examined showed the 'deformity' of a sixth finger. However, several of the bodies had long since dissolved, and it may be that Anne's was among them, and that she may indeed have had some sort of telling mark on her hand after all. Although most historians would recoil at the merest suggestion of such a thing, the fact remains that, even now, such a specific physical slight may indicate at least a kernel of truth upon which to base it.

Today, a plaque marks what is generally assumed to be the 'correct' spot where Anne's body is thought to lie. When the Victorian renovators had finished unearthing the various bodies, the remains were placed inside lead coffins which were then encased in protective oaken coffins and reburied, although perhaps not in the spots in which they were originally found. To this end, there remains a certain doubt as to whether Anne's body now lies in repose in the chancel area. For all we know, her many fans may instead be paying yearly homage to Lady Rochford – aka Jane Boleyn – instead. After all, the Victorians were amateur archaeologists at best, and they were working with badly decomposed bodies, all of which were missing their heads. Regardless, flowers are laid for Anne in that spot on the anniversary of her death, including, so it has been suggested, blooms sent by a certain person or persons in rather high and exalted places.

As for Anne's husband, well, Henry VIII was betrothed to Jane Seymour the day after Anne lost her head. The 'happy couple' tied the knot a mere ten days later.

For the knowing modern audience, helped by a hefty dose of historical hindsight, there is a twist to the tragic tale of Anne Boleyn, a sense that somehow, in the end, history 'evened things out' by making Anne's daughter Elizabeth perhaps the most successful and famous female monarch in history. However, for Anne's detractors (and Catherine's supporters), there is also the sense that history evened things out in the manner of her downfall. Although Anne became known – both in her lifetime and subsequently – as the archetypal 'other woman', she eventually fell victim to Jane Seymour; thus was Anne ousted in the self-same manner by which she had come to power. Jane played the same 'game' with the King's affections, but at a ruthlessly accelerated rate, and then went on to achieve the greatest goal of all by giving him the son he so desired. However, this is to subscribe to a narrative that pits woman against woman, the tired old 'Team Aragon'/'Team Boleyn'/'Team Seymour' narrative. The fact remains that Anne's greatest legacy – besides Elizabeth – was bending Henry's ear to her message of Reformation, even though, ironically, it would be under the reign of Jane Seymour's son that England would, for the first time, become what we now think of as a Protestant state. But it was Anne's daughter who rescued that narrative when Catherine's daughter Mary pulled the country back toward Catholicism. Before that, no doubt England would have reached the Reformation sooner or later, but it happened when it happened because Anne Boleyn jostled it in that direction. And that was why she married the King of England.

'The Sword of Calais'

The so-called 'Sword of Calais' was four feet long; the blade was one-and-a-half inches in width and double-edged. It was not blunt-tipped, as was the standard for a good heading sword, but the tip has worn slightly over time and has also been – rather inexpertly – honed away, the damage in this regard being clearly visible to the naked eye; to the layman it would thus appear to be of the standard blunt-tipped variety. The handle was leatherbound, but all of the leather has now frayed away, save for the odd strip; where the metal beneath has been exposed, the handle has been inexpertly repaired with a small length of string and in some sections, what appears to be almost an entire roll of bog-standard Sellotape. There is a fuller – or groove – on the flat side of the sword, but, contrary to the assertions of Alison Weir, the purpose of this was not to draw blood away from the blade. The purpose of the fuller was in fact to reduce the weight of the weapon but not the strength; however, the weight was still sufficient – in tandem with the momentum of the swing – to decapitate a person quickly and cleanly. Without the fuller, the sword would have proven too unwieldy. The fuller on the 'Sword of Calais' is damaged, by way of several intermittent indentations. The middle of the 'Sword of Calais' is missing and what remains is the aforementioned handle, to which is still attached around a foot of blade. Another foot of blade – including the aforesaid blunt tip – is also extant. The two sections are unmistakeably part of the same weapon. They are held in separate locations; what became of the middle section of blade remains a mystery, but the most likely explanation is that it was lost when the sword was initially damaged. The extent of the mutilation is so severe in this regard that it leaves one with the impression that someone deliberately tried to destroy the thing.

Following the execution of Anne Boleyn, the 'Swordsman of Calais' spent several days in England before returning home; contrary to conventional etiquette (he was an executioner, after all), he was hosted at several locations during his progress back towards the English coast, including one stop that may have placed him uncomfortably close to the Boleyn family seat at Hever. According to his own family lore, he no longer used the sword after the execution of Anne Boleyn; another heading sword of a similar design was employed for later executions, but, being English, the Swordsman still alternated between that and the axe for offenders at Calais, dependant on their nationality. Needless to say, most of these offenders were English and were thus executed with an axe; as always, many historians forget that Calais was then an English outpost, certainly when it comes to this particular point. Most of the people in Calais were then English.

Several of the Swordsman's children lost their lives when Charles V besieged Therouanne in 1553 (these offspring – two sons – were living there at the time). In 1558, Calais was recovered by the French. As brief as the reclamation was (a mere several days), it was still protracted enough for the-then English Queen, Mary I, to send a 'discreet verbal request' for the sword. The request was ignored; by then, quite possibly, the Swordsman's family had already fled. He himself had passed away a year or so previously, at which point several more 'discreet verbal requests' had already been fielded. The replacement heading sword was, however, sold in the wake of the Swordsman's death, to pay off outstanding debts; there was some talk of selling *the* sword, but it came to nothing and the thing was apparently left behind when the family fled Calais. Once settled, they later requested the return of the sword but were now themselves the subject of a refusal. To that end, the general consensus seems to be that whoever found the sword was of a mind to make a Catholic relic of it, but that the family would in no way aid and abet that action. The religious identity of the Swordsman's family at this time remains opaque but, given his own misgivings in regard to Anne's execution, one imagines that they were – even as early as 1536 – of a distinctly Reformist bent.

Quite who it was who recovered the sword and how – and who also recognised the provenance of the thing – remains uncertain. Certainly, it was not thrust into the public sphere in any meaningful way. The notion that several Popes haughtily dismissed the idea of considering it a Catholic relic I have yet to ascertain; more 'discreet verbal requests', or, in that case, verbal refusals. Thereafter, the trajectory of the sword runs along a similar pattern to the so-called 'Holy Lance' that pierced the side of Jesus Christ during the Crucifixion. For several hundred years, the sword seemed to vanish. Even as the literature regarding Anne Boleyn proliferated, still no historian seemed to evince the slightest curiosity regarding its whereabouts (not much has changed on that score). Those given to flights of fancy conjectured that it was nevertheless secreted in a submerged Vatican vault, perhaps near Henry VIII's love letters to Anne; certainly, a relic purporting to be the 'Holy Lance' can be found there. Then, quite suddenly (in June 1919), the sword resurfaced, now – as detailed – broken, with the greater part of the blade (the aforementioned middle section) missing.

I am visiting a small private apartment in Turin, nestled somewhere between the Porta Susa and the Porta Nuova stations. It has been a long trip (five or so hours from Paris for the nervous non-flyer), although the scenery as the train skirted the Alps was never less than spectacular. Now, adrenaline dismisses the immediate desire to return to my hotel and rest; here, I am assured, is part of the blade that beheaded Anne Boleyn. To be clear, my host is not related to the Swordsman of Calais; however, she assures me that the family did not simply vanish in a puff of smoke after 1558. Indeed, the Swordsman of Calais had ten children; their descendants pepper parts of Italy to this day, although, peculiarly, you will not find a single one of them in France. They have no interest in the sword; several deny the provenance of the thing altogether. In such spartan surroundings, I am briefly unsure of it myself. For those descendants, the tale is something blithely passed around amidst family gatherings along with the sliced fruits and the plates of cubed Taleggio cheese, to be considered and then airily dismissed. On that score, they have no interest in talking to historians either. I doubt even a researcher of bestselling proportions and infinite resources might winkle them out. I could've made up a family name for them, for the sake of this book, but I didn't. Quite honestly, they positively bask in the utter indifference shown by most Anne Boleyn aficionados in regard to this particular part of her story. But, rather delightfully, the surname name of their illustrious forebear to this day still brands several branches of the family. His first name, meanwhile, was *Bartholomew*. One of his descendants – the only one who deigned to talk to me, in fact – is a Franciscan monk who positively recoils at the thought that his great-great-great-great (and several more 'greats' besides) grandfather once removed the head of the Queen of England.

Now, in that small private apartment in Turin, I find myself gazing down at roughly a foot of badly discoloured metal, including the honed down tip; that final foot of blade. It nestles on a bed of cheesecloth, crammed inside a nondescript cardboard box; so tight is the fit that when I am permitted to lift the box up, the blade does not slither either way or indeed move at all. For a fragment, it's remarkably heavy; I wonder briefly what the whole thing would have weighed, the thought accompanied by brief images of Bartholomew's heavily sinewed forearms curving in mid-air, whilst nearby a kneeling Anne Boleyn blinks and shudders behind her blindfold.

Several days later I am in Florence, in an apartment approximating the modest, slightly claustrophobic airs of the Turin residence. The man retaining the handle of the sword sits, watching me gaze at the thing; me, anxious and taut, he slumped in an armchair, fanning himself with a rolled-up copy of yesterday's paper. A thorough forensic examination it most certainly isn't. The handle – replete with the shoddy string and Sellotape repair job – is also snuggled on a bed of cheesecloth, the whole ensconced in some cloudy Tupperware. It looks like an exhibit in a cheap museum. I am not allowed to touch it, nor to photograph it; to that end, I was required to hand in my phone before entering the apartment, although my earlier hostess made no such demands, but clucked and waved an admonishing finger at me when I attempted to take a picture. There followed – from her – a brief little instruction about the horror of insuring such an item, most of which went over my head. Both, however, did at least smile when I turned to them and mouthed my wonder at the pieces; they certainly look old enough, at least. I'm no expert on Tudor weaponry – on heading swords – but I've researched enough to the point where I know what I'm looking for; that research helped furnish the opening paragraph of this little piece.

'No bloodstains?' I ask him.

He waves a hand dismissively; 'Don't be ridiculous.'

'Might I buy it?'

Now he shrugs, breaking suddenly into a Central Italian patois. 'Is priceless.'

Glancing around, one gathers rather rapidly that he isn't the type to be tempted by the promise of swift monetary gain. Some collectors, I conjecture, simply like to bask in the fact of possessing something of great historical import. To that end, I spend the remainder of my visit confiding almost every detail I can to memory. My earlier hostess was at least gracious enough to offer me tea, but now I am offered nothing. The courtesy of the former aside, both received me – so I felt – under a sort of vague sufferance, wary perhaps of a wave of Anne Boleyn fans following on in my wake. Only later, via email, will they begin to unfurl the great tapestry of happenstance that allowed the item to fall into their laps in the first place; their affinity with the descendants of the Swordsman, and so on and so forth. It is enough, I assure you, to fill a volume all on its own.

11

Erasing Anne

After her death, all things Anne Boleyn became forbidden. In fact, 'All traces of her were then obliterated with a Stalinist ruthlessness: all of the pictures, but perhaps for one, all of the images of her crest of arms. Henry had his "H" and her "A" carved entwined on panels and embossments throughout Hampton Court Palace. They were all removed – though one was missed: it can be seen in the Great Hall, high up to the right on the wooden screen.' (Brenton, 2011, p5.) For her daughter, the sudden demotion in rank positively rankled: 'She was a precocious child, and soon noticed the change in her life, asking her governor why she had been addressed as my Lady Princess one day and merely as my Lady Elizabeth the next.' (Weir, 2008, p12.) Before she eventually became queen, things would get a great deal more uncertain than that. Elizabeth would endure demotion, promotion, imprisonment and countless other slights, surprises and ordeals besides. In the meantime, however, by appearance alone – never mind the temperament – all those of sensible mind could tell that she was definitely Henry's daughter: 'A royal father was parentage enough: it could glorify the bar sinister, remove the taint of an adulterous mother.' (Neale, 1960, p14.) Meanwhile, Cromwell was urged by another of Anne's appointees, Nicholas Shaxton, to continue with the Reformist project, regardless of the fact that the main benefactress was now dead.

Meanwhile, Thomas Boleyn died at Hever Castle in 1539. His mother, Lady Margaret Butler, passed away a year or so before. He is buried in the nearby St Peter's Church, with a fine monumental brass marking his final resting place, to the left of the altar. He is clad in his robes and wearing his insignia as a Knight of the Garter, an honour bestowed upon him back in 1523. It is not the brass of someone suffering any sort of disgrace at his daughter having the ignominy of being the first queen of England ever to be executed. As recently as 2022, historian Lauren Mackay gave a talk in St Peter's Church on the life and rather sullied legacy of Thomas Boleyn. Anne's mother died several years before her husband, in 1538, and was laid to rest in the Howard family chapel in St Mary's Church, Lambeth, which is now the site of the current Garden Museum. Mary Boleyn met her maker several years later, but her children carried on the Boleyn bloodline, a blessing when it later transpired that Anne's daughter intended having no children of her own whatsoever. In fact, the descendants of Mary Boleyn are so prodigious that you can hardly venture onto your average Tudor-related social media platform without meeting with someone who claims to be her great-great-great-great-great granddaughter/fourth cousin twice-removed. The Queen Mother and Queen Elizabeth II are, however, direct and verified descendants of Mary Boleyn. For the stories of those who came inbetween, well, their tales would fill another book all on its own.

To return to the Tudor court, Henry VIII's new wife, Jane Seymour, continued to act in a manner contrary to that of her predecessor, despite the fact that her prize was now essentially won (perhaps she wasn't quite so contrived after all). Where Anne was opinionated, Jane was pliant to the point of indifference; all of the frivolity and the playfulness of Anne's court was dismissed in favour of a more austere royal household. There were no lusty lute players hanging around Jane Seymour, that's for sure. Jane also did away with Anne's French fashions, including her signature French hood, and reintroduced the rather medieval gable hood favoured by Catherine of Aragon (Anne did on occasion sport one). Jane wasn't around long enough to have any real contact with or impact upon the life of Anne's daughter, but she scored a far greater success where Catherine's girl was concerned, reconciling Mary to her father in a slow and often painful process which included having the poor demoted Mary sign a document which declared her mother's marriage to have been all but invalid.

The one time Jane dared raise her head above the patriarchal parapets, in order to garner pardons for some of those involved in the rebellious Pilgrimage of Grace, saw Henry VIII scolding her for not knowing her place and reminding her of the fate of his previous wife. Jane was more successful in that latter department at least, providing the King with his much-desired legitimate male heir a year or so after their rather ill-timed nuptials. Unfortunately for Jane, the excruciating birth left her body so damaged that she died a few days later. Her loss was a cruel blow to

Henry, but it removed another player from the chessboard upon which Anne herself had once occupied so pivotal a position. When Henry married Anne of Cleves in 1540, she brought with her nothing regarding Anne Boleyn whatsoever (apart from sharing the same name, of course). The fallout from the Cleves marriage saw Thomas Cromwell removed from the board, severing yet another link with the past, and adding a further blow to the cause of the Reformation. As for the son whom Jane had provided for the King, this poor boy – briefly Edward VI – died whilst still in his teens; another of history's great ironies, wherein the sickly son is survived by the neglected daughters, the latter of whom – Elizabeth – goes on to preside over a veritable 'Golden Age' of English history.

Henry VIII's fifth wife, Catherine Howard, was a first cousin of Anne Boleyn. Her marriage to the tempestuous Tudor monarch proceeded similarly to Anne's, with accusations of adultery culminating in an eventual beheading at the Tower of London. At times, given the kinship the two women shared, the parallels were decidedly pointed. The main difference was that poor Catherine was almost certainly guilty of some sort of extramarital relationship, besides her previously mentioned 'chequered' (or abusive) sexual past, and the combination of these factors meant that her head had to roll in order for Henry to maintain what precious little dignity he had left. As his now-infamous marital life unfolded, it perhaps became clear that allowing the world to see him as an almighty cuckold in the wake of his marriage to Anne wasn't quite as preposterous as one imagines. Indeed, when married to his fourth wife, Anne of Cleves, Henry had thought nothing of confiding that he found her so unattractive that he was unable to consummate the marriage. Now, with Catherine Howard, he was left a laughing stock by a wife some thirty years or so his junior, ridden with gout and an ulcerated leg – not to mention becoming morbidly obese – while Catherine dallied with her handsome young beau, Thomas Culpepper. Matters weren't helped by the fact that Catherine's accomplice in arranging her trysts was none other than George Boleyn's widow, Jane; her role in the car-crash that was Henry VIII's fifth marriage earned her the unenviable tag of 'The infamous Lady Rochford'. When Catherine was executed in 1542, Lady Rochford joined her in losing her head within the precincts of the Tower of London.

After Catherine Howard, the ghost of the Boleyns was forever laid to rest for Henry VIII. Even after his death in 1547, there was no real movement to champion Anne's life and achievements, or even to pay lip-service to her memory. She continued to be a 'non-person'. In fact, 'A revealing remark made in 1549 by Jane Seymour's brother, Thomas, shows that, even then, the mere mention of Anne's name could provoke sniggers.' (Somerset, 1997, p9.) One would imagine that when her daughter finally ascended to the throne in 1558 that things would change, but they didn't. For the most part, on the surface at least, it was still as though Anne Boleyn had never existed.

12

A daughter's silent pride – Anne Boleyn through the lens of Elizabeth I

Elizabeth I was without a doubt Anne's greatest triumph, her gift from beyond the grave. Elizabeth became queen when her half-sister, Mary, Catherine of Aragon's daughter, died in 1558. Over the five years of her brief but brutal reign, Mary – or 'Bloody Mary', as history recalls her – did her level best to steer England back towards Catholicism, burning several hundred Protestants at the stake in the process. In recent years there have been several attempts to rehabilitate Mary's image, which on the one hand is fair enough; why should she be nicknamed 'Bloody Mary' but her father not 'Horrible Henry'? But then again, Henry VIII still gets plenty of stick, even if he hasn't got such a catchy alias. However, one need only avail oneself of the case of Perotine Massey of the Guernsey Martyrs to understand why Mary earned herself such an unenviable reputation. Perotine was heavily pregnant when she was burnt alive in 1556. She gave birth in the flames and eventually her baby, after initially being plucked free, was cast back into the fire and roasted alive along with its mother. Mary Tudor doesn't get a free pass to sanction the burning of pregnant women simply because she was a woman herself. Her adherents would do well to allow her legacy to own that fact, unpalatable as it may be.

After she became queen, Elizabeth slowly but deftly dismantled all of the harm her half-sister had wrought in that brief but now infamous reign. Indeed, Elizabeth's tenure on the throne was, as said, a veritable 'Golden Age'. However, she rarely made any mention of her mother – although Tracy Borman has challenged this assertion – nor ever sought to have her tarnished memory reevaluated. In fact, whenever the moment required it, she always cleaved more to her father, evoking his image perhaps most famously during her famous Armada speech in 1588, when she maintained that she had '...the heart and stomach of a king, and of a king of England too!' However, historians disagree as to the actual extent of Elizabeth's familial fealty/indifference. 'Philippa Berry argues that Elizabeth's early appointments to her court and her choice of coronation iconography show that she saw herself as Anne Boleyn's daughter no less than as Henry VIII's, and knowingly allowed her father's dynasty to die out; David Starkey suggests that Elizabeth hero-worshipped her father uncritically and would have remembered her mother's death primarily as a temporary impediment to her acquisition of new clothes.' (Dobson & Watson, 2004, p6.) This doesn't mean that she wasn't to stumble upon various reminders of her mother's life and legacy, however. As early as her coronation procession in 1559, Elizabeth was confronted with a life-sized effigy of Anne, suspended as part of a three-stories-high arch. The Houses of Lancaster and York were represented by the union of Henry VII and his wife, Elizabeth of York, whilst above them were featured Henry VIII and Anne Boleyn. And above them sat a figure on a throne descended from these lofty forebears, namely Elizabeth herself.

Still, regardless of who was invoking Anne's memory, Elizabeth was a masterful politician, a veritable maestro of the soundbite speech, someone who knew perfectly well that to publicly raise the spectre of her disgraced dead mother would open up the whole Catholic can of worms about Anne and Henry's child being, basically, an illegitimate bastard. After all, 'Catholics could not accept the legitimacy of Henry's marriage to Anne Boleyn, nor of the child that had resulted from it. Bizarrely, opponents of Elizabeth's claim to the throne could cite the King himself in their support. Henry had annulled his union with Anne when presented with evidence of her adultery, making Elizabeth illegitimate by royal proclamation as well as the strictures of the Catholic Church.' (Cooper, 2012, p50.) And so, at least in the public sphere, Elizabeth left well enough alone.

However, whilst she was perhaps rather prudent in this regard, others were less concerned with letting deceased queens lie, and still harboured resentment for what Anne Boleyn stood for in terms of the Reformation. It was during Elizabeth's reign that Nicholas Sanders' 'seminal' work entitled *Rise and Growth of the Anglican Schism* (c.1573) was published, creating an image of Anne – the witch and the scheming woman with that niggling sixth finger – which still persists today; as recently as 2009, Anne was commemorated in a 'Witch's Garden' at Hampton Court Palace. Sanders, a Catholic priest born around 1530, was perhaps Anne's most ardent detractor during the reign of her daughter. He reinforced the notion maintained by Catholics that Elizabeth Tudor was a bastard, but also that she born of an incestuous union, maintaining that Anne Boleyn was in fact Henry VIII's daughter, conceived during an affair with her mother (this one often does the rounds, but not as frequently as the sixth finger tale).

Many other paternal slanders exist in regard to Elizabeth I, including that she was the result of Anne's incest with her brother, or that she was the daughter of Mark Smeaton, the only man condemned to die for his affair with Anne who actually confessed his guilt. Some people have said that poor Sir Henry Norris was Elizabeth's father; for some reason, no one ever really ventures forth the names of Sir William Brereton or Sir Francis Weston in this regard. It was said of Sanders that '...as a result of the scandalously immoral nature of the union between Henry and Anne, Elizabeth herself was not only a bastard but a monster of sinfulness. He (Sanders) directly set himself against recent Protestant texts which acclaimed Elizabeth as a messianic figure presiding over England as the new Israel'. (Hackett, 1995, p131.) By modern standards, Sanders' work can in no way be interpreted as a serious attempt to document the life of Anne Boleyn, but by the touchstones of the time it was seen as the definitive history of the English Reformation, at least from a Catholic – and therefore badly biased – point of view. And the mud it slung at Anne was to stick for centuries.

As said, during the course of her long reign (1558-1603), Elizabeth mentioned her mother merely once or twice, but after she died a ring she was found to be wearing was opened, revealing a small miniature portrait of both herself and her mother. This ring is currently kept in the official country house residence of the British prime minister, Chequers. Of course, several Tudor historians have suggested that the woman supposed to be Anne might in fact be her stepmother, Catherine Parr – Henry's sixth wife – to whom Elizabeth was especially close.

13

Anne Boleyn Bibles

The overall situation of Anne as persona non grata during her daughter's reign meant that a purely academic work, or even a first appearance in fiction, escaped her until several years after the Tudor reign ended. Indeed, this first notable foray for Anne Boleyn into the world of fiction came in the form of Shakespeare's Henry VIII (c.1613). However, her daughter is the real heroine of the piece, promising the reform of religion in England, despite only appearing at the very end as a baby at her christening. Purely for the sake of completion, it is worth mentioning here that the ballad 'Greensleeves', traditionally attributed to Henry VIII mourning a rejection by Anne, actually first surfaced several decades after his death and some several decades before Shakespeare's play. Still, like the sixth finger and the incest allegation, the ballad continues to be associated with Anne, even to the point of Patricia Routledge performing it as the crazed psychic medium 'Madame Fontana' in an episode of the BBC's Steptoe and Son.

It would be some considerable time before Anne's real life was correctly documented, with Agnes Strickland's *Lives of the Queens of England* published in twelve bulky volumes between 1840 and 1848. This became one of the first full-bodied and most popular pieces of research concerning the monarchy, covering the Tudor era in some considerable detail. It was also one of the first such works widely available to the general public and came at a time when both more rigorous and also more popular historical research was emerging, with historians increasingly accessing ambassadorial despatches and the like. Agnes was assisted in her great endeavour by her sister Elizabeth, who wished, for the most part, to remain anonymous.

The series was unusual for the time because it was serious historical work researched and written by a woman/women. It was around this time that the popular image of Henry VIII as a tyrant and a lech who slew various wives on a whim came into sharper focus (earlier indications include Sarah Fielding's in her brother Henry Fielding's 1743 *Journey from This World to the Next),* and for the first time, female writers, in particular, began to question the evidence against Anne Boleyn regarding her purported adultery. Jane Seymour, initially lauded on becoming Queen of England, was said by Strickland to have been 'loaded with panegyric' (Ives, 2004, p. 305). Alison Weir says of the Stricklands that they were all but spellbound by La Boleyn: 'There is no name in the annals of female royalty over which the enchantments of romance have cast such bewildering spells as that of Anne Boleyn' (Carrick, 2013, p. III). As a result of the labours of the Stricklands, it was Anne who began to be somewhat re-evaluated by Victorian society, whilst Jane, who died in childbirth and perhaps ought to have solicited on that score a more sympathetic hearing, became more generally derided. Of course, the Stricklands weren't the only Victorian writers availing themselves of a heightened level of access to the source material: Selina Bunbury's 1844 *The Star of the Court or the Maid of Honour* and *Queen of England, Anne Boleyn* is a worthy addition to the canon.

But how was Anne presented, both then and now? Alison Weir initially refers to Anne in her 2001 work *Henry VIII King and Court* as being '...driven by ambition rather than virtue' (Weir, 2001, p. 262). Suzannah Lipscomb introduces her as the 'witty and captivating Anne Boleyn. Although not particularly beautiful' (Lipscomb, 2009, p. 37). In her biography of Katherine Parr, Linda Porter describes Anne as '...a mercurial, difficult woman who made enemies easily' (Porter, 2010, p. 76). This gives some insight into how Anne was written from the Stricklands onwards as a woman, not of exceptional beauty, but of great character and wit, but rather a difficult personality at that. Still, better for a woman to be renowned for her wit than for her wiles, although Anne's religiosity has taken longer to come simmering to the surface. That isn't to say it isn't there at all, however; Philip W. Sergeant's 1924 *The Life of Anne Boleyn* took the facts uncovered by the Stricklands and ran with them, adding a little religiosity in the process. Several decades previously, P. Friedmann's *Anne Boleyn* (1884), meanwhile, offers some good political details. In 1908, Edred and Elfrida Arden witnessed a May Day celebration involving Anne in Edith Nesbit's novel *The House of Arden*, via a time travelling technique that also saw them visiting the circumstances surrounding the Gunpowder Plot. Already, Anne's rehabilitation by the Stricklands was paying dividends in terms of reimagining her as a Reformist heroine of lofty proportions. But as we shall see, the sixth finger and the tales of incest and intrigue would prove alarmingly hard to ignore.

By 1939, Anne's stature was such that she could hold the narrative of a historical novel all on her own; Francis Hackett's *Queen Anne Boleyn*, for starters. Jean Plaidy's *Murder Most Royal* (1949) contrasts Anne's rise and fall along with that of her cousin, Henry VIII's fifth wife, Catherine Howard. From there, the novels flowed thick and fast; *Anne Boleyn* by Evelyn Anthony (1957) and *Anne, Rose of Hever* by Maureen Peters (1969), among others. Anne has also adorned the covers of countless historical magazines over the years, but one of her most prominent appearances was on the cover of the 29 October 1956 issue of *Life* magazine. Inside, her tale was put forth by no less a personage than Sir Winston Churchill himself.

Second-wave feminism in the 1960s and '70s coincided with a proliferation of Tudor TV and film projects, among them *The Six Wives of Henry VIII* (1970) and *Elizabeth R* (1971), both acclaimed BBC miniseries, as well as the film *Anne of the Thousand Days* (1969). Together, these contributed to a general shift in how Anne was portrayed – and therefore, a shift in the tone of her biographies – especially with the works of Antonia Fraser and Norah Lofts. Fraser focused more on the personal lives of Henry VIII's six wives, but because of her pivotal role in the Reformation, Anne received the lion's share of the attention. Likewise, in David Starkey's book on the six wives, published several decades later, almost the entirety of the book is given over to Catherine of Aragon and to Anne, with the following four wives relegated almost to the status of footnotes. Norah Lofts' entertaining biography of Anne (1979) makes much of the mythic status of its subject, giving a good indication of the fact that even by the 1970s, Anne was already viewed as something of an iconic figure. The book also links Anne firmly to her Norfolk roots - Lofts was a native - so, Anne reincarnated as a hare, as mentioned in Chapter 1, is pure Lofts. Lofts also wrote the novel *The Concubine*, as well as a novel concerning Catherine of Aragon, *The King's Pleasure*, in which Anne herself plays a major role while sporting all of her stereotypical 'adornments': 'Many of the other ladies – not one of whom liked the newcomer – were envious, constantly asking themselves, and one another, what he (Percy) could possibly see in her. "She's not even amiable," Maria de Moreto said. "And that great mole on her neck and that extra finger"' (Lofts, 2006, p. 130). Still, Lofts was merely working with what was then pretty much the established narrative – the novel was originally published in 1969 – 'warts and all'. The same has to be said for *The Concubine* (originally published in 1963): 'Anne Boleyn had no looks to speak of, no bosom even. One of the Court gallants had dismissed her with the words, "All eyes and hair," and that was a truer saying than were most such slighting remarks' (Lofts, 2006, p. 9). However, Lofts does use Anne's French experience to highlight a vague sense of unease at the prospect of a virtual 'foreigner' turning up at the English court and making such a splash (such themes would be expanded some sixty years later when Jodie Turner-Smith was cast as the first ever black actress to play Anne). In the course of *The Concubine*, Lofts relates Anne's meteoric rise to power and her fall from grace with some aplomb, narrating how, in regard to the latter, Anne disguises herself during a series of masques following the birth of Elizabeth and in the face of Henry's increasing impotence, to get herself pregnant by sleeping with a succession of courtiers, none of whom realise it is her. Thereby, Anne uses sex as a means by which to save herself, with Lofts attempting to turn the charges of adultery on their head, although they end up being the means by which Anne is, of course, still brought to the block.

Nearly twenty years later, she is still steeped in such tricks and traits, courtesy of Margaret George's *The Autobiography of Henry VIII*: 'Her voice was low – unlike the fashionable high voices of our court ladies. Her gown was also different; it had long, full sleeves which almost completely obscured her hands. She had designed it herself. Then I though it charming. Now I know why she needed to do so – to hide her witch's mark! But as I took her hand to dance, I did not discern the small sixth finger, so skilfully did she conceal it beneath the others' (George, 1988, p. 269). Over a decade later, in *The Other Boleyn Girl*: 'And Anne, who had come in with her head very high, and her arrogant dark look darting everywhere' (Gregory, 2001, p. 5). Several years later, Gregory does make sure that Anne's dedication to the Reformation gets a cursory mention in *The Boleyn Inheritance*: 'Those dark Boleyn flirtatious looks, their high living: such gamblers, such lovers of risk; both so fervent for their reform of the church, so quick and clever in argument, so daring in their reading and thoughts' (Gregory, 2007, p. 2). Of course, in the midst of all these books, one must never forget that Anne is also often the guest star in works with almost no connection to the Tudors whatsoever. A favourite of this author's casts her as the progenitor of the spirit 'Lasher' in Anne Rice's *Lives of the Mayfair Witches* series. In this sumptuous trilogy, Anne Boleyn – who is naturally, a six-fingered witch – gives birth to one of the monstrous 'Taltos', a race of giant humans, of whom Lasher is one: 'My mother rose up and stared at me through her tears. She held up her left hand. I saw there the mark of the witch, the sixth finger. I knew that I had returned through her because she was a powerful witch, yet she was innocent as all mothers' (Rice, 1993, p. 527). He is murdered by the followers of the Scottish Protestant firebrand John Knox during the reign of Anne's daughter but is reincarnated as a spirit when he is called back into being by the village healer, Suzanne Mayfair, around 1664. Although Suzanne is burnt as a witch, Lasher goes on to serve her daughter, Deborah, before passing to each successive female in the family line, until he finally brings himself to the attention of the current 'designee', Rowan Mayfair, a talented neurosurgeon living in San Francisco. Lasher yearns to be reborn through Rowan but is eventually despatched by Rowan's husband. Regardless of the pedigree of Anne's involvement, when they come as classy as this, it almost doesn't matter that the legends about six fingers and sorcery are regurgitated, used as they are to frame such an opulent narrative.

Two of the foremost modern factual works studying Anne's life are Retha Warnicke's *The Fall of Anne Boleyn* (1989) and Eric Ives' *The Life and Death of Anne Boleyn* (2004). As well as doing her best to pinpoint the exact date of Anne's birth, Warnicke's book offers the previously mentioned idea that Anne's supposedly deformed foetus was responsible for her downfall. It also puts forward the idea that her fall was also sped up by the presence of a homosexual clique in court, headed by her brother George, a clique said to be comprised of several men accused of adultery with her and who were eventually executed. As said, the evidence for homosexuality among the men accused with Anne is scant – not the sort of thing one would flaunt when the law banning sodomy had just been passed – although, given the passage of time, unfortunately, it is not entirely possible to refute either. With the deformed foetus, Warnicke holds to Nicholas Sander's view of Anne's monstrous miscarriage whilst dismissing his other allegations elsewhere in the text.

The Life and Death of Anne Boleyn, meanwhile, is still considered the authoritative work on the subject. Ives was an expert on Tudor history, and on the Boleyns in particular, and his study of the religious nature of Anne's character and her charitable works is almost without compare. The book lingers less on the reasons for Anne's downfall than Warnicke's, offering a more satisfactory overview of her life. However, in the main, Ives steadfastly sticks to the noncontroversial idea that Anne was framed. The original edition of his work was considered to have 'provoked' the 'response' work of Retha Warnicke, and later of G.W. Bernard and his excellent book *Fatal Attractions* (2011), which also offered the hypothesis that Anne was guilty of adultery, but only because of her ardent desire to survive.

Karen Lindsey's book *Divorced, Beheaded, Survived ~ A Feminist Reinterpretation of the Wives of Henry VIII* (1995) was probably the first work situating Anne Boleyn in that particular socio-political movement, although again at the expense of Jane Seymour. Regarding Anne's charity to the poor and her help to Reformist refugees, Lindsey says, 'It's nice to have these images of a caring, thoughtful Ann Boleyn to juxtapose with the more common picture of her that emerged during the three years of her marriage, that of the vicious shrew. It's true that she was often nasty to Henry, but her irritability doesn't deserve censure. Whatever Henry suffered in his new marriage he had brought on himself, and the power in the relationship was all his' (Lindsey, 1995, pp. 101-102).

Also published during the last thirty years were Joanna Denny's *Anne Boleyn* (2004) and also the aforementioned G.W. Bernard's *Fatal Attractions* (2011). With Bernard – and perhaps Warnicke – the intention seems to be not to 'blacken' Anne Boleyn's character but perhaps to understand the circumstances of her downfall from a different stance. Bernard suggests that Anne was only of peripheral importance to the Reformation – which is rather unlikely – as well as hypothesising that it was Henry VIII who refused to sleep with her until they were married rather than the other way around. Also suggesting that Anne may have been guilty of adultery, Bernard postulates that the pregnancy which resulted in the deformed foetus – the Warnicke theory – came about from relations with her brother, hence why the body aborted the 'unnatural' result of their liaison. For most of his evidence, Bernard refers to the records of Anne's trial at the Tower of London, always a tricky area because some of them are missing. Meanwhile, 2008 saw the publication of Elizabeth Norton's *Anne Boleyn – Henry VIII's Obsession*, a competent and thorough piece that perhaps does its subject the greatest service in the closing lines, wherein Norton says that Anne was '...no helpless victim, she was a politician and she was the most exceptional woman of her time' (Norton, 2008, p. 197).

Following on from Warnicke, Ives and Bernard, a major shift in the perception of Anne Boleyn occurred in the twenty-first century with the advent of *The Tudors* TV series (2007–2010) and also *The Other Boleyn Girl* movie (2008), adapted from the novel of the same name. Before that, Anne popped up as the heroine in the rather grimly titled

Doomed Queen Anne (2002) by Carolyn Meyer, a young-adult novel in which Anne is rather oddly ostracised by her parents and spends far too much time obsessing over her 'deformities'. Of course, any of the novels concerning Henry VIII – and there are plenty – usually also feature Anne. There are too many to list here, but among the top-tier efforts is H.M. Castor's *VIII*, another entry in the young-adult range of Tudor tomes. Just for a change, we are treated therein to an Anne who is as much, if not more, a religious Reformist rather than a fiery vamp: 'She has shown me book and pamphlets setting out arguments about the role of the Church. Saying that ancient histories and chronicles declare this realm of England to be an empire. That, as such, it is free from the authority of any foreign ruler. And that I, as king of England, have no superior except God' (Castor, 2005, p. 298). Also appearing during this period of high-profile film and TV series were the first serious works exploring the idea of Anne as an icon, usually as a feminist icon. Susan Bordo's *The Creation of Anne Boleyn* (2013) was Foremost among these.

For the fictional works of Phillipa Gregory and even Hilary Mantel, Bordo is critical, although the depictions of these authors have helped create the greater part of Anne Boleyn's mythic status. Bordo also acknowledges the cyclical nature of much of the material concerning Anne and how it also reflects the social mores of the times in which it was produced. In the wake of *The Tudors*, books not only concerning Anne (and indeed Mary Boleyn) but the entire Boleyn clan began to emerge. Of particular note is *The Boleyns – The Rise and Fall of a Tudor Family,* by David Loades (2011). This work begins with Blickling and then takes the reader all the way up to Elizabeth I, although it stumbles somewhat in conclusion by stating that '...the Boleyns were unique in that they owed their influence to the sexual prowess of their women rather than to the military or political talents of their men' (Loades, 2011, p. 225). The entire point of Anne – not just for Henry VIII but for countless others – wasn't so much her appearance but rather her wit, her conversation and her accomplishments. Besides that, Loades suggests that Thomas Boleyn owed his entire career at court to his wife, without taking into account his mother, Lady Margaret Butler's status as co-heiress to the Ormond Earldom. Another book showcasing the entire Boleyn clan came in 2013, courtesy of Elizabeth Norton; *The Boleyn Women – The Tudor Femme Fatales who Changed English History* is a wonderful work, even if the aforementioned tagline dredges up Anne as a scheming sexpot and also lumps in the entirety of her female relations with her. Still, the work bookends the Boleyn women from start to finish satisfactorily and provides the reader with a good grasp of what they achieved when they weren't hitching up their gowns and giving the nearest randy monarch a sly wink.

In fiction, following Philippa Gregory's *The Other Boleyn Girl*, Anne became the 'calculating concubine' in Hilary Mantel's *Wolf Hall* (2009), and its sequel *Bring Up the Bodies* (2012). *Wolf Hall* and *Bring Up the Bodies* form part of a trilogy (*The Mirror and the Light* concluded the series in 2020), and, as previously stated, Mantel won the Booker Prize for the first two books. This was an unprecedented achievement, one which also allowed Mantel to fling forth a series of articles in various newspapers regarding the present state of the monarchy, besides offering her own insights in a comparison between the role of the future queen consort Kate Middleton and that of Anne Boleyn. However, Mantel's work has come in for criticism from historians like John Guy (who penned his own contribution to the cannon in 2023) and Alison Weir, who believe that these fictional takes on the Tudors, i.e., *The Tudors* TV series and also Mantel's novels, are somehow diluting real, rigorous research and blurring the lines between fiction and reality (Brown, 2017, paragraph 5 of 25). Despite this, the main focus of Mantel's books is Thomas Cromwell, and it was with this in mind that Mantel was quoted on the whole issue of Anne Boleyn eclipsing the star of her novels: 'Mantel knows that with Anne Boleyn, she's on both well-trodden and controversial ground. She acknowledges that people are "obsessed" with Anne, and "they're going to hate that I haven't presented her as a victim" – indeed, Mantel leaves the whole question of Anne's supposed adultery "hanging in the air"' (Penn, 2012, paragraph 13 of 22). In regard to how she actually writes Anne, Mantel's richly drawn depiction isn't a world away from the fare offered by Nora Lofts: 'He closes his lips on the topic of Anne and has no more to say. Mary Boleyn says she has noticed him, but till recently Anne gave no sign of it. Her eyes passed over him on their way to someone who interested her more. They are black eyes, slightly protuberant, shiny like the beads of an abacus; they are shiny and always in motion, as she makes calculations of her own advantage' (Mantel, 2009, p. 166). By the time we get to *Bring Up the Bodies*, Anne is at it again: 'Once sinuous, she has become angular. She retains her dark glitter, now rubbed a little, flaking in places. Her prominent dark eyes she uses to good effect, and in this fashion: she glances at a man's face, then her regard flits away, as if unconcerned, indifferent. There is a pause: as it might be, a breath. Then slowly, as if compelled, she turns her gaze back to him. Her eyes rest on his face. She examines this man. She examines him as if he is the only man in the world' (Mantel, 2012, p. 36). The first two books in the trilogy were adapted for the stage by the Royal Shakespeare Company and enjoyed sell-out runs in London's West End (British actress Lydia Leonard played Anne). More recently, they were turned into a lavish six-part drama for the BBC with Claire Foy as Anne Boleyn (2015).

Meanwhile, Anne has positively blossomed into a heroine of monolithic proportions in a veritable plethora of 'Young Adult' fictional ventures, including Dawn Ius's *Anne & Henry* (2015), which offers a modern take on the Tudor romance. *Anne Boleyn and Me: The Diary of Elinor Valjean, London 1525-1536* by Alison Prince (2014) offers the perspective of a daughter of one of Catherine of Aragon's ladies-in-waiting. *Tarnish* by Katherine Longshore (2014) takes the reader through Anne's journey in a first-person perspective. And finally, the upliftingly titled *Doomed Queen Anne* by Carolyn Meyer (2004), which follows pretty much the same track as the previous offering, with the opening pages documenting Anne's final night in the Tower of London (books about beheaded heroines inevitably open with the despicable denouement first). These are just the tip of the iceberg; one could fill a small catalogue with the ever-increasing numbers of fictional takes on Anne's life, particularly for the 'Young Adult' market.

Moving back to the factual offerings, Alison Weir concentrates on Anne's tenure as a prisoner awaiting execution in the Tower of London in the factual *The Lady in the Tower – the Fall of Anne Boleyn* (2009). Weir provides a brief overview of Anne's life and the possible reasons for her downfall without committing herself to a definite answer on whether or not she was guilty. She then turns her efforts into documenting the last several weeks of Anne's life in as much detail as the records show. Several years later, commencing with Catherine of Aragon, Weir would then set herself the task of writing a novel about each of Henry VIII's wives in a series called *Six Tudor Queens*; for the purposes of this narrative, we need only concern ourselves with the first three offerings. Stretching to over 600 pages, the first book is – at least in length – a worthy rival to Hilary Mantel's mammoth offerings. When Anne first appears, the narrative plots the impending rivalry between the two women by focusing on Catherine's opinion of Anne's looks: 'Anne Boleyn was not as beautiful as she liked her ladies to be' (Weir, 2016, p. 321). By the time we reach Jane Seymour, Anne is cracking: '"He never comes near me!" Anne wailed. "His unkindness grows. And it's all your fault!" She flung a quill pen at Jane. The nib scratched Jane's cheek as it hit her. She put her fingers to the place and found them streaked with blood and ink. She stood there frozen, horrified at the vehemence of Anne's attack and the wound. All the women were looking at her. "Has the witch's cat got your tongue?" Anne spat. "He's fucking you, isn't he?"' (Weir, 2018, p. 229). As for Weir's actual novel concerning Anne, well, it clocks in at an impressive 529 pages, beginning in 1512 as Anne is due to depart Hever Castle for the court of Margaret of Austria. The brilliant black eyes are there, as is the extra finger, pared down now and described as little more than an extra fingernail ('accessory nail') on the little finger of her right hand. Perhaps the most interesting section of the novel is the Author's Note at the end, wherein Weir says, 'I am aware that in some circles, particularly on the Internet, she (Anne) has acquired celebrity status, and that she has become many things to many people and, in the process, controversial. During the writing of this book, an admirer of Anne Boleyn expressed the hope that I would portray her accurately, to which I answered that historians might well differ when considering what 'accurately' might mean. There is so much room for conjecture' (Weir, 2017, p. 508). When it comes to Anne's execution, Weir harkens back with grim detail to her diagnosis of the immediate aftereffect of decapitation, as detailed in The Lady in the Tower – the Fall of Anne Boleyn. The book is a stonking good read, if hampered somewhat – by Weir's own public admission – by the fact that much of what we know of Anne comes courtesy of Chapuys, one of her biggest detractors.

A more recent factual effort is Sylvia Barbara Soberton's *Ladies-in-Waiting: Women who served Anne Boleyn*, which is a spirited exploration of the lives of a set of women who had at least the chance to make something of their relationship with their mistress. Soberton understands her task only too well when she says, 'The aspects of Anne Boleyn's life and death are fiercely debated by historians, yet her ladies-in-waiting remain an understudied topic... By concentrating on a previously neglected area of Anne Boleyn's female household, this book seeks to identify the women who served Anne and investigate what roles ladies-in-waiting played in this Queen's household' (Soberton 2022, p. 1).

This selection is just the tip of the iceberg; there are jewels out there aplenty, just waiting to be discovered.

14

Anne Boleyn at the movies, on TV, in song and on the stage

Anne Boleyn has enjoyed a long and illustrious career on both the big and the small screens, and also on stage. Her fate has been alluded to in the plays of Shakespeare, besides being adapted for the stage several times in the centuries immediately following her death, in other works of varying quality. In the early 1680s, a new genre called the 'she-tragedy' saw a veritable slew of plays about the likes of Mary Queen of Scots, Lady Jane Grey, and of course Anne. *Vertue Betray'd* premiered in 1681 or 1682. 'Through the suffering female victims at their centers, she-tragedies explored predicaments of feeling in ways that had not been possible in the ranting heroic tragedies popular earlier in the Restoration, and they marked also a new interest in the heroic possibilities of helplessness.' (Lewis, 1998, p88.) Anne's life has also been the subject of an opera: *Anna Bolena* was first performed in Milan in 1830 as part of a quartet of Tudor-related pieces, another of which focused on Mary Queen of Scots. The Italian soprano Giuditta Pasta played Anne initially. *Anne Bolena* then premiered in London a year later; the first American performance was in 1839. As recently as 2015, it was being staged at the Lyric Opera of Chicago. Jane Seymour features heavily in the piece, but of Anne's alleged 'harem', only Mark Smeaton – besides George Boleyn, of course – has any real presence.

One of the first feature films with Anne as a main character was 1911's *Henry VIII*, with the Scottish silent screen actress Laura Cowrie as Anne. In 1912 there was a short film about Cardinal Wolsey, in which Anne was played by the American actress Clara Kimball Young. There is some evidence that Laura Cowrie then returned to the role in 1913 or 1914 for *Anne de Boleyn*, but specifics prove difficult to trace. In 1920 *Anna Boleyn* debuted, seemingly the first full-length feature based entirely on Anne's story. The German actress Henny Porten took the title role, with Emil Jannings playing Henry VIII. The silent film was a German production.

Stylistically, it might appear to modern audiences as something of a black comedy, with the lack of dialogue offering an almost macabrely madcap slant on the ravenous monarch as he pursues a rather unenthusiastic Anne around a variety of scenic locations (imagine Benny Hill's 'Yakety Sax' playing as these scenes unfold). The silent nature of the film has proven something of a turn-off to the majority of the modern fanbase, and with an almost two-hour running time, it might tax even the most ardent of Anne's enthusiasts. Therefore, for the purposes of this narrative, it serves more as a curiosity of a bygone age of movie-making, as opposed to being a pivotal piece of Boleyn movie memoire.

The next film to feature Anne was the 1933 *The Private Life of Henry VIII*, with Merle Oberon as Anne. Disappointingly for Boleyn enthusiasts, Oberon only appears in the beginning of the film, which opens with Anne's execution (unusually, the majority of the narrative is concerned with Henry VIII's marriages to Anne of Cleves and Catherine Howard). The film was both a critical and a commercial success and was therefore likely the first time that a cinematic version of Anne received such worldwide exposure. Charles Laughton won an Academy Award for his portrayal of Henry VIII, which then became the default onscreen template for the character for the next several decades; lecherous, boozy and tossing half-eaten chicken drumsticks over his shoulder, basically. Whilst 1920's *Anna Boleyn* might now appear as an unintentional farce, *The Private Life of Henry VIII* is very definitely played as a black comedy. The opening scene of Anne's execution cements this notion quite neatly, with an unnamed but pointedly henpecked husband observing the event, envious at the panache with which the King of England disposes of his unwanted wives, a remark that was ultimately trimmed from the final cut. Merle Oberon was a classic beauty of her time, with promotional shots relaying something of their subject's notorious sexuality; she was actually of Anglo-Indian descent, but, given the less inclusive times in which the picture was made, decided to pass herself off as Australian. From this film onwards there would be a steady increase in the sexualisation of the onscreen Anne, before it reached what appears to be a peak with *The Tudors* in 2007. A cinematic vamp was much more appealing, clearly, than the more realistic ardent religious Reformer, which probably explains why almost all of the onscreen depictions of Anne spend little or no time troubling themselves with her possible past dealings with the likes of Marguerite d'Angoulême and Louise of Savoy.

Besides a cameo in *Young Bess* (1953, played by American actress Elaine Stewart), an appearance as a headless doll in American black comedy sitcom *The Addams Family*, and a small role in *A Man for All Seasons* (1966, played by English actress Vanessa Redgrave), the next major screen outing for Anne was not until 1969, with the seminal *Anne of the Thousand Days*. The title refers to the numerically perfect length of her tenure on the throne of England. Based on a 1948 Broadway play in which the part of Anne was played by Joyce Redman, the film has gone on to become one of the most popular and enduring depictions of Anne Boleyn, besides being a frequently cited favourite among fans. The film stars the-then relatively unknown Canadian actress Genevieve Bujold as a feisty but desperately feminine Anne, this being Bujold's first role in an English language film. There are several large but not intractable liberties taken with the truth of the tale, but you'll find that even in the most faithful of film and TV adaptations. Anne's mother, Elizabeth, makes a rare but relatively low-key appearance, played by Katharine Blake. In this adaptation, Elizabeth is an equal partner in her husband's pimping of his two daughters. Particularly painful for the modern viewer is the scene in which Richard Burton's Henry literally prises a kiss out of a clearly unenthusiastic Anne, a move that elicits an approving round of applause from her family. Valerie Gearon plays Mary Boleyn, whilst Michael Johnson is almost invisible as brother George. Also featured – albeit in *very* minor roles – are the entirety of Anne's alleged 'harem'; of Anne's religiosity there is almost nothing. The film was successful enough to be nominated for ten Academy Awards/Oscars although in the end it won just the one, for best costumes. The segments set at Hever Castle were shot at the actual location, lending it a lasting sense of authenticity. Thematically, the film portrays Henry VIII as an insatiable sexual predator, as in the 1920 *Anna Boleyn,* but unlike the 1920 portrayal of Anne Boleyn, Bujold is far feistier, holding the King and his advances at arm's length and succumbing more it seems to the lure of power than at the prospect of his personal charms. When Anne finally falls from grace, Bujold makes the most of a fiery speech in the Tower of London to castigate Henry for his shortcomings and to remind us, the viewers, of things that undoubtedly seemed almost impossible at the time: 'Elizabeth shall reign after you! Yes, Elizabeth – child of Anne the whore and Henry the blood-stained lecher – shall be Queen! And remember this:

Elizabeth shall be a greater queen than any king of yours! She shall rule a greater England than you could ever have built! Yes – my Elizabeth shall be queen! And my blood will have been well spent!'

Given that forty-nine years separate this and the 1920 offering, it is not remarkable that the portrayals of the respective Annes are wildly different; as we shall see, onscreen she is reinvented cyclically for each new generation, generally more empowered with each performance but also equally sexed-up. Susan Bordo devotes an entire chapter to the mythos of the movie in her book *The Creation of Anne Boleyn*, where she says of Bujold's performance that 'I loved fiery, rebellious Anne. I loved the way she bossed Richard Burton's Henry around like a surly twentieth-century teenager. I loved the fact that Genevieve Bujold's hair was messy as she delivered that speech to Henry, loved her intensity, loved her less than perfectly symmetrical beauty, loved the fact that someone that small could pack such a wallop.' (Bordo, 2013, p190.) Genevieve Bujold remains the only actress nominated for an Academy Award/Oscar for playing Anne Boleyn.

Following on from *Anne of the Thousand Days*, there was something of a lull in appearances by Anne on the big and small screens in the 1970s. The one noteworthy addition to the onscreen lore was that of English actress Dorothy Tutin in the acclaimed BBC drama *The Six Wives of Henry VIII*. However, the actress, so Bordo felt, was a little 'too old' to be accurately portraying the character; one occasion perhaps where the seductress aspect of Anne's character wasn't considered the most important element to feature onscreen, perhaps. Nevertheless, Tutin was nominated for a Bafta for her restrained but powerful portrayal. The episode in which Anne features is definitely worth a watch, but it suffers from symptoms typical of your early 1970s BBC costume drama; slow, stagey, over-lit and on occasion ploddingly po-faced. Shortly after, Anne appeared in what was essentially a cinematic abridgment of the aforementioned *The Six Wives of Henry* VIII series; *Henry VIII and His Six Wives* saw Keith Michell again giving his generation-defining performance as the infamous English King, with English actress Charlotte Rampling as a competent but undistinguished Anne. In the course of the narrative, Anne's story is unsurprisingly pared down to fit with the condensed cinematic retake on the successful six-part BBC drama. In other media, in 1973, Rick Wakeman's second studio album, *The Six Wives of Henry VIII*, was released; Anne is featured on the fifth track.

Together, these various endeavours marked the end of what had been a brief but glorious cinematic revival, not only for Anne but really for the historical epic genre as a whole. In fact, it would be almost thirty years before Anne would be portrayed on either the big or small screen to any significant degree. She did however pop up – portrayed by comedian Candice Bergman – in a sketch on *Saturday Night Live*. Then, the way would be paved by the cinematic success of *Elizabeth* in 1998, starring Cate Blanchett as Anne's daughter. Anne herself is referenced only obliquely, whilst Henry VIII pops up as a portrait shoved away in a darkened room, taunting his daughter with her pressingly patriarchal inheritance. Nevertheless, this film revived interest in the cinematic historical epic, both as an experience and as an acceptable form of entertainment for what was by then a far more sophisticated audience. Meanwhile, Anne herself was still popping up in places where you'd least expect to find her, certainly where popular culture was concerned; in 1997, she was one among several 'decapitated women' appearing on the artwork for the cover of the American alternative rock band Hole's album *My Body, the Hand Grenade*. The artwork itself was collated by lead vocalist/frontwoman Courtney Love.

Philippa Gregory's pivotal novel *The Other Boleyn Girl* was released in 2001. Two years later the BBC adapted it for the small screen with Jodhi May playing Anne; this version tends to be overshadowed by the later Natalie Portman offering. Between adaptations, Anne's portrait made a cameo in the film *Harry Potter and the Philosopher's Stone* (2001), where it was seen hanging on the wall of the fictional 'Hogwarts School of Witchcraft and Wizardry'. Before that, actress Natasha Little played Anne in a dream sequence for the opening of the comedy *Kevin & Perry Go Large* (2000), starring Harry Enfield and Kathy Burke in the title roles. In a 2001 episode of *The Office*, during a tour of the nightclubs of Slough, viewers are told of a themed nightclub called 'Henry the Eighth's', which included an Anne Boleyn bowling alley, whilst a sign outside the toilets read 'Mind Your Head'; underneath someone had written, 'Don't get your Hampton Court'.

2003 offered the two-part TV drama *Henry VIII*, starring Ray Winstone. Helena Bonham Carter played Anne, with her story commanding almost the entirety of the first 100-minute episode, which meant that the subsequent four wives were squeezed into part two with alarming rapidity; a little like a televisual version of David Starkey's 2004 book, really. When American company CBS were approached for funding for the project, they stipulated that Bonham Carter should be replaced by American actress Sarah Michelle Gellar (of *Buffy the Vampire Slayer* fame), and that all of the accents be dubbed from British into American; funding, thankfully, was soon sought elsewhere. In 2004 Anne appeared in an episode of *The Simpsons* ('Margical History Tour'), where she was voiced by actress Tress MacNeille. In the episode, Anne wins Henry's favour when she observes him lamenting his ever-increasing waistline, informing him that this means there is simply more of him to love. In *The Simpsons* universe, Anne has been dubbed 'Anne of the Child-Bearing Hips' by *Wench Magazine*. After divorcing 'Margarine of Aragon', Henry marries Anne but has her beheaded when she gives birth to a girl and not the son promised on her 'A son'll come out – tomorrow!' calling card. In 2007, the English pop band McFly released their single 'Baby's Coming Back/Transylvania', with the latter song namechecking Anne in the lyrics as well as featuring an accompanying video in which bandmember Dougie Poynter drags up as Anne.

In 2008 *The Other Boleyn Girl* became a feature film with Natalie Portman playing Anne and Scarlett Johansson as Mary Boleyn; Eric Bana played Henry VIII. Certainly, the movie is better remembered than the TV adaptation, although more as a romp than as a genuine attempt to portray the story of these remarkable sisters in any significant fashion. To be honest, the chronology of the film is so awry that it makes *The Tudors* look like a discerning historical document. Needless to say, both the film and also the book are notorious among Anne Boleyn fans for the sheer number of historical inaccuracies they purport to pass off as fact. In her book *The Creation of Anne Boleyn*, Bordo even goes so far as to provide a handy checklist for readers to strike off the various inaccuracies against the 'truths'; tellingly, she does not provide a similar checklist for *The Tudors*. Apparently, Bordo found Natalie Dormer's portrayal in the aforementioned series to be of sufficient repute to avoid too much mudslinging. Natalie Portman, meanwhile, does an adequate job in the movie but plays second fiddle – for once – to her sister. The plot pivots around a rivalry between them for which there is not a shred of historical evidence, although many touching moments prevent it from descending into sheer vindictiveness. Anne is clever and headstrong, whilst Mary is compassionate but rather wet. In fact, Mary remains true to the novel, and it is interesting to note once more that, via Gregory's fiction, there has been a definite move in recent years to rehabilitate her image. Alison Weir has led the way in this regard with her biography of Mary Boleyn, which attempts to sort the fact from the fiction where her life as the supposed concubine of the King of France is concerned.

The Other Boleyn Girl film is also unusual in being one of the few onscreen productions to feature a prominent role for Anne and Mary's mother, Elizabeth. Therein, she is portrayed by Kristin Scott Thomas, souped-up as a moral antidote to her weak husband – *Wolf Hall's* Thomas Cromwell, aka Mark Rylance – who virtually pimps out his two beautiful daughters without a second thought and comes across as nothing less than a colossal wet weekend. David Morrissey smoulders as the Duke of Norfolk, portrayed more in this outing as the senior pimp, alongside Rylance's simpering Thomas. George Boleyn is played by Jim Sturgess, performed far more sympathetically than either of his siblings; the scene where he confronts Anne's incestuous advances – her life hangs in the balance, after all – is particularly heart-wrenching. Watching that scene, one might almost entertain the notion that the desperate thought must have crossed Anne's mind, even if only for a moment, although at the time Henry VIII had yet to behead any of his wives and hadn't therefore gone down in history as the murdering tyrant that we know and love/ loathe today. Still, as Anne saw her goal of religious reform going up in smoke, it is not impossible to imagine the lengths she might have gone to preserve her part in it. However, those yearning to see – just for a change – the spiritual side of Anne coming to the fore will be sorely disappointed with *The Other Boleyn Girl*. Anne displays absolutely zero Reformist tendencies, whilst the whole matter of the King's marriage and the break with Rome is reduced to a few trite sentences, courtesy of Kristin Scott Thomas. Meanwhile, Spanish actress Ana Torrent offers a rather restrained performance as Catherine of Aragon, but one cannot help cheering her on as she confronts 'the Boleyn whores' on her way to court, to battle for the fate of her marriage. Meanwhile, Juno Temple puts in a particularly snide performance as George's wife, the 'scheming' Lady Rochford. Benedict Cumberbatch plays perhaps the biggest Tudor cuckold of all time, aka William Carey, whilst Eddie Redmayne – in one of his earliest screen roles – plays Mary's second husband, William Stafford.

In 2010 Howard Brenton's play *Anne Boleyn* premiered at the Globe Theatre in London. Concerned less with the salacious side of her character – almost ground-breaking, therefore, and some several years before Hayley Nolan claimed to be blazing a trail in that regard – the piece concerns itself almost entirely with Anne's Reformist leanings and her enthusiasm for William Tyndale's translation of the Bible. British actress Miranda Raison played Anne. Susan Bordo commented, 'Judging from the reviews, for many in the audience – even the critics – Brenton's Anne was their first acquaintance with Anne the religious reformer.' (Bordo, 2013, p258.) Still, such pieces remain sadly in the minority. And when Anne wasn't gracing the stage in England, her accessories were busy appearing in a certain hit American sitcom called *Ugly Betty*; the title character wore the famous 'B' necklace sported by Anne on several occasions. In the 'Big Finish' range of *Doctor Who* audio adventures, Anne pops up in the story 'Recorded Time', voiced by actress Laura Molyneux. In the story, the 6th Doctor's companion, Peri, almost replaces Anne as the next Queen of England when Henry VIII takes a shine to her.

The adaptation of Hilary Mantel's *Wolf Hall/Bring Up the Bodies* was screened in 2015, with actress Claire Foy playing Anne in the six-part production. The series was, overall, a fairly faithful interpretation of the novels. Initial reviews praised Foy's restrained but 'pained' performance as a woman clinging desperately on to what one commentator called the 'oily rope' of power (Raeside, 2015, paragraph 3 of 7.) Initially smug and self-satisfied, Foy's Anne quickly succumbs to tantrums and then outright insecurities as Jane Seymour inveigles her way into Henry's life. Mary Boleyn was played by Charity Wakefield, in a role that might have slipped into Weir's 'slutty stereotype', were it not for the fact that the actress manages to make her version of Mary far more likeable, and a lot less simpering than Scarlett Johansson's. Bernard Hill chews scenery as their uncle, the Duke of Norfolk, whilst Thomas Boleyn – David Robb – is almost invisible, which is better, still, than Elizabeth Boleyn, once more relegated to invisible/non-existent status. But the story, of course, belongs to Thomas Cromwell, succeeding – as do the books – not merely in making him sympathetic, but actually downright likeable; an easy feat when you have an actor of the calibre of Mark Rylance in the role. Whatever Reformist sympathies united Anne and Cromwell in real life, here they are almost non-existent; Anne treats Cromwell like a cretin, and she pays for it dearly. In return, he spends an entire dream scene peering down at her heaving cleavage. The reform of the monasteries is left entirely in his hands, whilst Foy's Anne spends most of her time embroidering and making snide remarks about her various ladies-in-waiting. Matters aren't helped by the fact that her court 'harem' – including brother George – send up Cromwell's master, the disgraced Cardinal Wolsey, in the costumed masque performed in the wake of the prelate's sudden death. This, much more than Anne clashing with Cromwell over the monasteries, forms the basis of her fall from grace; that and the occasion when he has the temerity to tell her 'No' to one of her requests/orders. And whilst Cromwell's family are seen as tightly knit, the Boleyns are portrayed – as ever – as a bunch of self-interested, quarrelsome backstabbers. The fact that Cromwell loses his wife and two daughters due to the Sweating Sickness adds to the sorrow and thus the sympathy for the star of the show, whereas the most Anne gets upset about is losing her mark in an archery contest. When she suffers the first of her miscarriages, the audience cannot help but feel that they might need to mine a little sympathy in order to get on side with her. By the time the second miscarriage occurs, the audience is treated to the unedifying sight of Anne's fool, Jane, trying to beat life into an aborted fabric doll foetus. It all comes crashing down in the final episode, but even then, any sympathy the viewer might have sequestered for Anne is roundly squashed when she proceeds to reduce Mark Smeaton to tears with her imperiously snidey asides. When it comes to her execution, kudos must go to the production for being one of the few to remember that Anne was blindfolded when kneeling on the scaffold at the Tower of London. Meanwhile, throughout the earlier episodes, Charity Wakefield's Mary Boleyn makes a series of passes at Cromwell, in a desperate bid to escape from the machinations of her ambitious kin; one can hardly blame her, really.

Throughout, the viewer is never left in any doubt as to where Hilary Mantel's sympathies lie, and it certainly isn't with the woman working her all to become the second wife of Henry VIII. In fact, through the lens of Cromwell's relationship with the Queen, we see Anne and her family almost as the villains of the piece. Still, as period dramas go, it is an absolute masterpiece, and one of the few which also remembers that most of the Tudors read by candlelight and not thanks to the benefit of some strategically placed studio floodlights. Reviewers were quick to recognise what separated the series from Showtime's admittedly raunchier offering: 'They also don't go in for much exposition or explicitly libidinal kicks, à la Showtime's "The Tudors," rarely showing us the sex that's on every character's mind. Instead, we are privy to something realistically ugly: a hellscape of gossip, dominated by old men making mean remarks about the miscarriages of potential queens.' (Nussbaum, 2015, paragraph 3 of 11.) Also in 2015, Anne appeared as a ghost, played by Fleur Keith, in the short *I am Henry*.

Besides her serious onscreen outings, Anne has also – on rare occasions – starred in something a little lighter, in this instance as part of the famous rhyme about the six wives of Henry VIII (made into full verse by the *Horrible Histories* TV series, with lyrics by Terry Deary):

> Young Anne Boleyn, she was two
> Had a daughter, the best she could do
> I said she flirted with some other man
> And off for the chop went dear Anne

The actress Gemma Whelan played Anne in a 2017 episode of the series.

It might also be worth mentioning the other televisual medium in which Anne has often been depicted, namely the documentary. Documentaries featuring Anne proliferated in a range roughly in tandem with the explosion of interest which occurred around the publication of *The Other Boleyn Girl* and the advent of *The Tudors* TV series. For instance, *Henry VIII: the Mind of a Tyrant* aired in 2009, midway during *The Tudors* run, with Sophie Hunter playing the role of Anne. As the title suggests, the programme was more concerned with conveying the entirety of the King's life, but an entire episode – episode 3, 'Lover' – was given over to retelling the story of his relationship with Anne. The programme was presented by David Starkey, who also fronted a documentary on Anne's daughter, entitled simply *Elizabeth*. These and the various other documentaries all follow a similar format, interspersing a simple retelling of historical facts by a suitably qualified presenter – David Starkey, Suzannah Lipscomb, Lucy Worsley – with scenes re-enacted by a guest cast, enabling the end product to boast the title 'docudrama'.

In 2013's *The Last Days of Anne Boleyn*, Tara Breathnach starred as Anne, whilst 2016's offering from the BBC, *Six Wives with Lucy Worsley*, featured Claire Cooper as Anne. *The Guardian*'s Joel Golby gave the latter a considerable panning, suggesting a general 'dumbing-down' of historical documentaries in order to give them a more populist slant:

> It is my sad duty to announce that the series contains acting. This is in order to liven up proceedings. To make it feel like olden days, actors swish around in period dress delivering intense dialogue only vaguely directed at each other, as Worsley, clad in a simple maiden's cloth cap, watches rapt in the background. It's weird: the historian peeks around corners, eavesdrops on romantic encounters, tends to fires as people storm across rooms. As Henry's pursuit of a son becomes an ever more intense narrative, you keep expecting Worsley to pop her head up into a stiffly acted sex scene and shout-whisper "HE REALLY WANTS A BOY ONE" to the camera. (Golby, 2016, paragraph 4 of 7.)

In 2021, *The Boleyns: A Scandalous Family* again featured talking head historians peppered with dramatical re-enactments charting the rise and fall of the Boleyns; Rafaëlle Cohen played Anne. Reviews were generally favourable, but several viewers cited the dramatic scenes as either unnecessary or even downright distracting; more 'dumbing-down', really.

Right up to the present day, Anne continues to pop up in the most unexpected places. The 2021 biopic *Spencer*, based around the unhappy married life of Princess Diana, features Anne in what is considerably more than a cameo role; Amy Manson plays Anne, who is first introduced to Princess Diana via a book left at her bedside. As the film progresses, reading the book provokes firstly dreams and then hallucinations in Princess Diana, whilst in real life she is confronted with the reality of her royal rival, Camilla Parker Bowles. Here the film strikes something of a bum note; really, it ought to have been Catherine of Aragon who spent the majority of the movie heckling Princess Diana, unless part of the purpose is to lead the audience to believe that the royal family had some hand in having the latter 'executed'. Meanwhile, at one point, Anne's ghost actually prevents Princess Diana from committing suicide. Mixed messages, to say the least.

15

The Tudors

Showtime's *The Tudors* occupies a special place in the heart of many Anne Boleyn fans. This much I know from having studied these enthusiasts as the thrust of my PhD, examining in particular the online spaces in which Boleyn fans congregate and share their facts and their fictions. Perhaps this fondness for the Showtime series stems mostly from the fact that Natalie Dormer gave such a bolshy performance as Anne – rather like a homage to Genevieve Bujold – or perhaps because she had more time than almost all the other actresses in which to flesh out the role; almost twenty hours, overall. In fact, Dormer's performance seems to have been given as much, if not more, credence for creating a cult around Anne Boleyn than Genevieve Bujold's, at least according to the efforts made by Susan Bordo in that regard. Bordo interviewed Natalie Dormer extensively during the research for her book *The Creation of Anne Boleyn* and wrote of her performance as Anne, among other things, that she was '...sexy, but brainy, politically engaged and astute, a loving mother, and a committed Reformist.' (Bordo, 2013, p216.) Admittedly, there was considerably less time spent on scripture than on sex in the show's content, but that may have been why it was such a runaway success. Bordo also commented on the sheer number of websites created by fans, particularly to praise Dormer's performance, as well as penning a comment from the actress herself on the amount of fan mail she received as a result of her onscreen impact.

However, even though Bordo herself skirted around the issue, the fact remains that the chronology of *The Tudors* is all over the place. Anne and Mary are first glimpsed in France (fair enough), before Mary ends up in bed with Henry VIII, having been recommended by the King of France. Given that the show relied heavily on sex appeal to stir the ratings, it comes as no surprise that Mary's main scene therefore involved giving Henry VIII a blowjob. When he later loses interest, Thomas Boleyn – played with gleefully sadistic relish by Nick Dunning – promptly propels his remaining daughter toward the royal bed: '*The Tudors* adores a searching pause. There's a good cheesy-creepy one when Thomas Boleyn strokes the head of his daughter Anne and gives her a pep talk about snagging her man: "Perhaps you could imagine a way to keep his interest more ...*prolonged*." In the quiet of those caesuras, you can hear the spirit of the show at work. It's underwritten and ... *overripe*.' (Patterson, 2007, paragraph 6 of 6.)

Anne and Henry thus meet during the Shrove Tuesday pageant 'The Chateau Vert', with plenty of sideways glances, heaving bosoms and suggestive leers. There follows several episodes of breathless pursuit – including a borderline wet dream – before the couple declare their respective stances; Henry wants her body and offers her the role as his premiere mistress, known in France as *Maitresse-en-titre*, but Anne is guarding her virginity for her future husband, *whomever he might be*. And so it goes. *The New York Times* commented, 'Yet somehow one young woman, a commoner, managed to keep Henry ensorcelled for more than seven years, perhaps the most effective use of the "just say no" strategy in history. Natalie Dormer, whose sly, feline beauty is well suited to the role, is given many lingering close-ups, but Anne Boleyn's withholding ways and cleverest wiles are unexplored.' (Stanley, 2007, paragraph 5 of 19.) However, not enough is made of the patriarchal demands placed upon our heroine. Yes, the King wants a son and when Anne presents him with Elizabeth, he is understandably crushed, but the real high-stakes scenarios behind Henry's reason, as archaic as they may be, are never satisfactorily fleshed out. Likewise, Anne's Reformist agenda is either underplayed or irregular: 'Her evangelical leanings are inconsistent. Earlier episodes depict her as merely a hypersexualised political schemer, but by the second season she becomes a major proponent of the Reformation.' (Robison, 2016, pp214-215.)

Meanwhile, Irish singer and actress Maria Doyle Kennedy makes for such a strong, sympathetic Catherine of Aragon that one almost finds oneself rooting for her as much as one is for Anne; their exchanges are tantalisingly brief, but full of ire and defiantly uptilted chins. Various events marking the arduous marital annulment are played out onscreen, and although the chronology of several of these are again questionable, the scope of the show nevertheless allows for their inclusion, whilst in many cinematic versions they are omitted altogether. Given the show's raunchy remit, Henry and Anne come perilously close to consummating their relationship ahead of their actual wedding. Come season two and all the doomed players are in place – apart from Sir Francis Weston – including Sir William Brereton, now, as said, portrayed as a radicalised Jesuit intent on assassinating Anne whilst wearing a Darth Vader-esque cloak and hood ensemble. However, for some, despite the addition of Peter O'Toole as a rather prematurely placed Pope Paul III, the emphasis seemed still to be rather more on style than substance:

> "The Tudors" makes it seem as if the entire creation of the Anglican Church boiled down to Henry's wish to remarry and sire a male heir. (When Anne gives birth to a daughter this season, the future Elizabeth I, Henry looks as if he were a little boy who got the wrong kind of tricycle at Christmas.) "The Sopranos," "The Wire" and "Big Love" all have derived their potency from dramatizing the preservation of failing institutions. The paradox of "The Tudors" is that it takes on one of the most powerful and protested institutions in human history – the Catholic Church during the Renaissance – and provides little sense of what the English people have to gain or lose by breaking with it. (Bellafante, 2008, paragraph 7 of 8.)

This very much tallies with the earlier comments regarding the lack of patriarchal stakes at play in the show.

When Anne fails to provide a male heir, Henry's attention wanders to the fictionalised 'Lady Eleanor Luke', standing in for the mysterious mistress of the real-life timeframe. Anne then enlists her brother to frame the interloper, whilst in real life she involved her sister-in-law in the intrigue. When Jane Seymour does finally appear (played by Icelandic actress Anita Briem), the scenes between her and Dormer positively drip with vaguely distilled venom; Anne completely loses her rag at one point and draws blood on her rival when she yanks off the pendant Henry has given her. Meanwhile, Anne miscarries 'her saviour', in one of the most heart-wrenching scenes of the series, literally clasping her hands between her legs to try and stop the pregnancy from aborting itself.

Following that, the show runs deftly with the deformed foetus theory, whilst Anne's fall from grace is as rapid and as brutal as it was in real life. Mark Smeaton has his sinews ripped apart upon a rack in the Tower of London, whilst Lady Rochford delights in telling an interrogating Thomas Cromwell – by way of a derisive smile – that her husband and the Queen were indeed far too close for comfort. However, even at this crucial point certain liberties are taken with the truth; that Anne's father spent time in the Tower of London is utter rot, likewise that Brereton confesses to adultery with the Queen, even at the cost of his own life, simply so that he can become a Catholic martyr. After that, an entire episode is devoted to Anne's actual execution, including the demoralising postponements before the Swordsman of Calais finally puts in an appearance. Her scaffold speech is pretty near the mark, but rinsed clean of those tell-tale Tudor aphorisms, and the audience is spared seeing her decapitated corpse being hurriedly bundled into the waiting arrow chest. Natalie Dormer returned for the finale of the series in season four, along with several other deceased wives, playing a ghost chiding Henry VIII for all of his mistakes, including the fact that she was '...innocent of all the accusations against me; I thought you knew?'

In other interviews that Dormer gave in regard to her time on *The Tudors*, she was said to have, '...developed a sympathy for the woman so often dismissed as a scheming minx, seeing several parallels with Princess Diana. "Anne was a pawn in a man's world, and it's so easy for us in this postfeminist era to take female rights for granted." Anne was the first consort of a British monarch to be aware of image, as Diana was, and they both had this enormous polarising effect on people, who were either staunch supporters or who demonised and criticised them. As fallible human beings, women fall foul of that polarisation. And what happens to people, particularly women, in the spotlight has not changed in 500 years.' (Paton, 2008, paragraph 17 of 53.) So, perhaps there is some link in the popular imagination between Anne Boleyn and Princess Diana after all. That bond would, as said, be explored in *Spencer*, several years after *The Tudors* ended its dynamic and ground-breaking run.

16

Looking to the future: '*SIX*' & Jodie Turner-Smith

The current popular intertextual (i.e., the relationship between texts – usually literary texts, but now moreso between varying mediums) portrayal of Anne Boleyn, fusing the work of Eric Ives, the portrayal by Natalie Dormer, and perhaps the fiction of Philippa Gregory, have formed a consensus composite of what this historical woman 'ought' to have been like, at least when viewed through the looking-glass of twenty-first-century feminism. Now, besides being historically significant, Anne is to the current generation not only a general feminist icon but also a symbol of women maltreated treated due to their intelligence, religious ambition, and their refusal to conform to male expectations. Meanwhile, the historical figure of Anne Boleyn has now been 'transformed' – for the twenty-first century – into a veritable consumer commodity, her image utilised for a variety of different purposes and functions. In fact, Anne's persona has become so commercialised through various films and novels that she is now as recognisable, in this multitude of media formats, as one of our contemporary reality TV stars.

In his book *Celebrity Society*, Robert van Krieken suggests that the Tudors were actually the first genuine 'historical celebrities', and that this serves to explain much of their appeal to a modern-day audience, with the emphasis on pomp and pageantry, alongside the ruthless exercise of power, of course:

> Elizabeth I embodied many of the features of modern celebrity in her relationship with her subjects, both powerful as a monarch and acutely conscious of how dependent her power was on how she was represented and how she was perceived by the English public. Henry VIII

before her was also excellent at stage-managing his public persona, and this was not a merely superficial aspect of his power and authority. I explain what Norbert Elias meant by "court society", and how we should understand the ways in which the structure of celebrity society emerged from, and remains continuous with, the social and interpersonal world of the aristocracy in early modernity. (van Krieken, 2012, p11.)

However, even Henry VIII's carefully stage-managed court could never have envisaged the turn that Anne's tale would take in 2021, when her story was brought to a whole new audience – not to mention a whole new level of media attention – when a black actress, Jodie Turner-Smith, was picked to play her in a new three-part drama from Channel 5 (Fable Pictures was the production company). The casting caused a veritable online sensation, with some claiming it to be the most progressive piece of television possible, whilst others decried it as either purely sensationalist or else wildly historically inaccurate. To be fair to the latter argument, they had been saying the same thing about *The Tudors* for years; it wasn't simply that the actress in question was black. In the drama itself, Turner-Smith's race actually serves to underscore Anne's status as an outsider, although for the real Anne this resulted in her coming from the French court to the English and thus exchanging a world of sophistication for one still half-muddied with medieval mores. Jodie Turner-Smith said of playing the role:

> The filmmakers really were interested in doing something called identity-conscious casting, which allows the artists to bring their identity to the role and add something that has not yet been seen to it. I think as creatives, as artists, we have the opportunity to tell human stories. When we transcend this concept of race, we understand that we are telling a story about humanity. As human beings, we all experience love, loss, longing, familial ties, loyalty, betrayal, fear, grief. This was just an opportunity to do that, to not be confined to colour, and to invite actors of colour to tell a story that they have not been invited to tell before. (Legardye, 2021, paragraph 10 of 14.)

However, as ambitious as the show was, it wasn't without faults. Once the caption 'Based on truth ... and lies' vacated the screen, the sour temperament of Turner-Smith's Anne soon left some viewers cold, whilst others questioned various liberties taken with what the production termed 'historical truth', especially with regard to some simmering lesbian tensions between Anne and Jane Seymour. To that end, several websites declared, if you're going to tout the thing based on 'truth' then don't invent things, because the simmering lesbian tensions don't even come under the 'lies' heading; there is about as much evidence for them as there is for George Boleyn's homosexuality. The first episode begins almost at the end of Anne's journey, finding her at the pinnacle of her success and pregnant – rather too heavily, one wonders – with the boy she will soon miscarry; in fact, she almost carries the baby to full-term before losing him.

Despite being touted by some as a feminist interpretation of Anne's life, the first episode still ends with her dashing out of the palace in pursuit of a departing Henry, plaintively calling his name as she does so, the scene rather an unedifying one given the edict. Some critics commented that the drama didn't really have anything ground-breaking to give to the story, regardless of Turner-Smith's casting: 'Yet it's debatable whether the series as a whole truly adds anything new to its heroine's legacy. By the end of the show's first episode, we have discovered that Henry's wives were powerless baby receptacles who were also deeply sad and endlessly cheated on. To call it revelatory would be a mistake. It's almost as if a woman famously beheaded by order of her husband lived quite a miserable existence. Who'd have thought?' (White, 2021, paragraph 6 of 7.) Episode two takes the viewer all the way up to Anne's arrest, inventing a fictionalised affair for her brother in the process, as though to push home yet again the notion George Boleyn *absolutely definitely* wasn't even vaguely homosexual. Also, Anne and Henry almost come to blows, as Anne's life post-miscarriage really begins to unravel. Needless to say, this doesn't make for particularly edifying viewing either.

The final episode involves an extended stay in a rather squalid version of the Tower of London, although it does give a fairly gutsy account of Anne's trial. At the end of the episode, further captions explain how Anne's daughter would come to the throne amidst a 'succession crisis' – she didn't; her half-sister, Mary died, and Elizabeth was the next-in-line and so she ascended the throne. It seems a strange misstep for a show that prided itself on truth (and lies!), but it raises a smile if nothing else for sheer novelty value. But as White's review makes clear, there is nothing here that really adds anything to Anne's legacy or has anything truly feminist to offer. In fact, it seems almost as though the producers expected the casting of a black actress to compensate for the fact that there was nothing new on offer; it seems even more a publicity stunt than a real attempt to try and twist something fresh from Anne's tragic tale.

The musical *SIX* premiered at the Edinburgh Festival Fringe in 2017, with Ashleigh Weir as Anne. The lives of Henry VIII's six wives are presented therein as a pop concert, with each wife singing her story to the audience in succession, in an attempt to convince them that she has suffered the most and thus deserves to be the lead singer of their little six-piece pop band; 'The whole thing is staged as a deeply unsisterly competition, each wife getting a song in which to prove they're the biggest victim, the one who suffered the most at Henry's hands. This is treated weirdly as comedy though, OTT shrieks and snarks escalating until they're actually in a catfight, pulling each other's hair.' (Williams, 2022, paragraph 4 of 10.) Some might wince at the idea of 'competitive suffering' served up as entertainment, whilst others might see it as a wry commentary on the fact that Henry VIII's six wives have long been pitted against one another in various formats, from novels to TV shows and so on. Only at the end of the production do the women realise they have become mere appendages to the King's tale, deciding thus to form together as a group without a specific lead singer, before going on to mull what their lives might have been like had they never met or married the famous Tudor tyrant.

Despite being a modern production, *SIX* plays on many of the familiar tropes where Anne is concerned: she mocks Catherine of Aragon for stealing her husband, before admitting to flirting with other men in order to make the King jealous, which then causes Henry to have her head cut off. Anne's main musical number in the proceedings is the rather crassly titled 'Don't lose ur head'. Unfortunately, the problems run deeper than this, as countless critics have observed, especially when trying to push across such an important feminist message in so trite a package:

> So at the end, when Catherine Parr says that approaching
> the story in this way is all wrong, *Six* manages to come off

only as smug, hypocritical, and scolding. It wants to reap the rewards of making a feminist deconstruction of history without having put in the work to get either its feminism or its history correct. You just know that at some point in the development process, someone said, "I really think this show can be *Hamilton* for women!" and the finale operates as though we have all agreed that this is in fact what *Six* has pulled off, even though it hasn't. (Grady 2021, paragraph 25 of 27).

Other reviews sound a similar note: 'Indeed, the musical proclaims its feminism so loudly that it's less fourth wave than sonic wave. But it feels more for show than out of conviction. Unlike "Hamilton," [a musical based on the life of the American Founding Father Alexander Hamilton] where hip hop culture is placed into service on behalf of history; in "Six," history is placed into service on behalf of pop culture. An example: Andrea Macasaet, who is making an impressive Broadway debut in the role of Anne Boleyn, Henry's second wife and the first that he decapitated, makes a lot of beheading jokes. (It's hard to imagine any duelling jokes in "Hamilton".)' (Mandell, 2021, paragraph 9 of 10.)

However, despite the misgivings of some critics, *SIX* has gone on to some considerable success, currently enjoying an extended West End run as well as on Broadway. Several actresses have portrayed Anne over the course of these stints, including Courtney Bowman and Millie O'Connell.

Quite where Anne's tale will be taken next – onscreen or onstage – is anyone's guess. In the months and years to come, it may well be that we see her in a 'roles reversed' depiction for the first time, which tells the tale of a tyrannical queen who works her way through six unfortunate husbands in the hopes of siring a suitable heir. And maybe we'll even see 'Man Boleyn'. With Thomas Boleyn's darling daughter, literally anything is possible.

171

17

Merchandising, marketing and schooling – Anne Boleyn and the essence of English nostalgia

Someone as obviously marketable as Anne Boleyn has, unsurprisingly, been merchandised to within an inch of her (after)life in recent years. Replica costumes of various accuracy are sold online and in specialist high-street boutiques – some examples are exquisite, whilst others are just trash – whilst among other weird and wonderful Boleyn paraphernalia, as mentioned in the introduction, eBay offers rings that '...allegedly have been infused with the spiritual essence of Anne Boleyn.' (Weir, 2009, p 335.) Doubtless it gets a great deal weirder than that, depending on how hard you're prepared to delve. One imagines with a shudder the prospect of Anne Boleyn sex dolls or genuine replica Tudor dildoes (one may not wish to envision such a thing, but the first dildoes were actually being wielded in England some several decades before Anne was even born).

In venues like the Tower of London and Hever Castle, you can buy Anne Boleyn mugs (indeed, a mug for each of the six wives!), as well as replica 'B' necklaces (the *Ugly Betty* version is available online, yours for an eyewatering $200!), brooches, notebooks, headed notepaper, Christmas baubles, greetings cards, cushions (some on the remarkably expensive side, but quite beautiful to behold), and toy ducks moulded into a grotesque mimicry of Anne's head. You can find hoodies, tank tops and t-shirts with every image of Anne conceivable emblazoned upon them, as well as an Anne Boleyn swimsuit; paperweights, resin figures (of varying and sometimes dubious quality), candles, soaps, umbrellas, bookmarks (one for each wife, naturally), compacts, fridge magnets (including a reproduction of 'The Moost Happi' coin, also available as a pendant), beanies (in various stylish colours), nail files, lip balms, pin trays, wrapping paper, vintage dolls (some, like the cushions, touted at eyewatering prices – the Peggy Nisbet pieces are particularly collectible); fragrances, essential oils, purses, earrings, makeup bags, tote bags, chocolates (a bite for each wife!), stationery, stamps, mobile phone covers, watercolour prints (framed, if it takes your fancy), costume prints from the designers of the various TV shows, and plenty more besides. There is even an Airfix Anne Boleyn model kit. Besides that, you have also those countless books – the factual ventures as well as the novels – and the DVDs and the Blu-Rays of the movies and the TV shows, and so on and so forth. Then you have all the memorabilia from those onscreen ventures, like cinema programmes and costume tour booklets. There was even an exhibition in Portsmouth in 2011 featuring various costumes from *The Tudors* TV series, several of which were worn by Natalie Dormer.

Basically, if it can be sold, it can therefore have Anne's image and/or her signature 'B' necklace stamped all over it and then deployed to the masses for a suitable profit. On custom design websites – particularly Etsy – you can even have your own images of Anne emblazoned on tailormade t-shirts, coasters and the like. In fact, the business of Anne Boleyn 'cosplay' (dressing up as a historical or fictional character) is big business in some Boleyn-related locations; venues like the Tower of London and sometimes also Blickling Hall have employed Anne lookalikes to regale guests with the often gory particulars of Anne's life. Mostly, such enterprises are aimed at the more juvenile end of the market, but the cosplayer in question often slips in a saucy aside for the adults (with Anne, unfortunately, there is ample material readily available on that score, but one must take the rough with the smooth where such enduring fame is concerned). In fact, one is almost tempted to remark, albeit rather crassly, that getting beheaded might be a real 'advantage' for a sentimental heroine looking to secure her longevity. Certainly, there isn't a market for such merchandise for any of Henry VIII's other wives (not even poor, decapitated Catherine Howard), although Anne of Cleves does have her very own shop dedicated to flogging various memorabilia, in her hometown of Cleves in Germany. As though to prove that rather obtuse point in regard to the afterlives of Henry's other wives, it is actually only his great-niece Mary Queen of Scots who comes close to equalling Anne in being marketed so ferociously, with Scotland naturally providing most of the appropriate merchandise. This author once witnessed a machine operated by coin in which a toy axe swings down and lops the head from a small cardboard effigy of Mary. I have yet to discover anything quite as tasteless where Anne is concerned, but life is always full of surprises.

Eleanor Bavidge commented on the nature of commodification where historical figures are concerned, with particular emphasis on the marketing of Anne at the Tower of London. Her research was based on data actually gleaned from the Historic Royal Palaces website and is, therefore, worth quoting at some length:

> parts of the site promote this relationship with the past in a way that meets the expectations of key target audiences – overseas tourists and British school children. Williams notes that foreign tourists are particularly interested in instances of state crimes carried out against home citizens "because of their lack of ties and everyday immersion in the foreign society tourists are free to speculate ... about imagined dramas of hurt, accountability and retribution". When addressing its younger visitors, the Tower has adopted a similar approach to that of the popular *Horrible Histories* series (BBC), by focusing on unpleasant and gory aspects of the past. "Beat the Block" offers school-aged children the chance of historical game play in which they can "take the upward path that leads to freedom or the slippery slope to the scaffold. They are invited to vote on what happened to the two young princes and visit the site where (Anne) Boleyn was executed by the "clean stroke of an expert swordsman" and the death spot of Margaret Pole who was "less lucky" as a blundering executioner "hacked her head and shoulders to pieces". (Bavidge, 2013, pp327-328.)

Unfortunately for Margaret Pole, she was too old at the time of her death (aged sixty-seven) to apparently warrant so fervent a fanbase akin to that 'enjoyed' by Anne. Still, that doesn't quite account for the lack of enthusiasm where Catherine Howard is concerned...

These traditional images of famous – and fated – English monarchs are, as Bavidge explained, heavily geared towards tourists and as such ply classic images of English history which focus on the sexual aspects and/or the gory nature of the lives and deaths of the people in question. As Anne's image becomes increasingly sexualised by the media in order to sell her story, so the more macabre side of the tale is increasingly marketed by various tourist attractions in order to tempt the crowds seeking ever more grim fare. In this respect it is rather disheartening to discover that Anne and her ill-fated ilk are thus often treated as little more than fictional characters. That said, the practice does not entirely focus on people plucked from within the realms of Tudor royalty. For instance, in the nearby East End, the various victims of Jack the Ripper are often reimagined into comedy ciphers of good-time East End prostitutes by the various London tour guides who tout for business outside Tower Hill tube station, this whilst serious historians ('Ripperologists') battle to give some authentic representation of their lives and the social conditions in which they lived. However, it is an uphill struggle. Likewise for the serious Tudor historian; Anne Boleyn the six-fingered sexpot might not be at all accurate, but it certainly helps bring the punters in off the streets.

And it isn't just the 'big hitters' like Hever Castle and the Tower of London trading on their association with Anne Boleyn. Not far from Barking in East London – on the Barking Road, in fact – you'll find the Boleyn Tavern, plastered inside with wall-to-wall six wives portraits. Meanwhile, local football team West Ham's stadium was called 'The Boleyn Ground'. Apparently, it was built on the site of a building called Green Street House, often referred to as 'Boleyn Castle'. This is more 'urban myth' than vigorous reality, I'm afraid; legend says Henry VIII built it for Anne but there is scant architectural evidence to back this up. In reality, the house may have been built for one Richard Breame, a servant of the King. Either Breame or his descendants may have boasted that Henry courted Anne in Green Street House; it was demolished in 1955. And you'll find countless businesses and roads in the immediate area named for Anne or her counterparts – 'Parr Road' and 'Seymour Road', among others – as well as a wider Tudor vibe if you go for a good wander.

In the UK, children are taught about Anne's life from a relatively young age. For this author, it was a copy of the Ladybird Books edition on Henry VIII that served as a gateway into all things Tudor. Originally published in 1973, this slim but fact-filled little tome was – before *Horrible Histories* – many a child's introduction to England's most famous monarch. However, to the modern eye, much of the text smacks of the time in which it was published: 'Henry was determined to marry a young maid-of-honour named Anne Boleyn, the daughter of a wealthy London merchant. She had been well educated – partly in France – and was a good musician; but she was ambitious and unscrupulous. When she realised that she had attracted the attentions of Henry, she was determined to become Queen at any cost.' (Du Garde Peach, 1973, p24.)

Still, Jane Seymour fares almost as badly, being referred to simply as '...a rather silly young woman.' (Du Garde Peach, 1973, p32.)

The most recent History National Curriculum, which all schools were instructed to follow from September 2014, saw a shift in the way the Tudor period was taught to British schoolchildren. In the revised programme, the Tudor era was moved to what is classed 'KS3' or years 7-9, which covers ages eleven to fourteen. Prior to this change in the curriculum, the Tudor era was always taught in Year 4 classes – for children aged eight to nine – using the saga of Henry's six wives as one of the focal points (isn't it always?). The social and political changes of this period are myriad but remain for the most part – in the age ranges mentioned – mostly untouched. Nevertheless, ideas of 'Britishness' permeate throughout the curriculum, although these stresses are found in the timetables of almost any given country in regard to their own particular history.

All in all, it would seem that being taught about the Tudors is an important point for twenty-first-century schoolchildren, not only because of the major religious upheavals but also because of the 'bizarre' chronology of Henry VIII's marital life, along with the remarkable achievements of his daughters in such a painfully patriarchal age. The overall expectations at the end of these educational stages are that:

> *Most children will:* be able to place the Tudors within the context of Britain's history; make inferences and deductions from portraits; know about the work of a Tudor monarch; know in outline the story of Henry VIII's life; identify different ways in which people have represented and interpreted it; and so on and so forth. *Some children will not have made so much progress and will:* know that the Tudors were a long time ago; know that Henry VIII was an important king and that he had six wives; know about other events in his life; be able to make some deductions about the appearance of Henry VIII and his wives from their portraits. *Some children will have progressed further and will:* know the dates of the Tudor period and its key events; understand what sort of information can and cannot be deduced from portraits; know and understand aspects of the break with Rome and dissolution of the monasteries.

Schoolchildren are also invited to consider what Henry VIII was like as a person; what he did all day, etc, before asking why he divorced Catherine of Aragon (such conversation thus inevitably involving Anne Boleyn): 'Give the children a text with a simple description of Henry's problems, e.g., *the need for a son, Catherine's age, the need for money.* It should also include a few solutions. Ask the children to identify the problems. Help the children place the problems in order of importance and to suggest solutions and produce a grid with two columns: problems and solutions.'

Following on from this, the learning then moves specifically onto the topic of Anne Boleyn: 'Did marrying Anne Boleyn or Jane Seymour solve Henry's problems? Tell the story of Anne Boleyn. Ask the children to look at the list of Henry's problems and their grid with problems and solutions. Give them simple information about the marriage to Anne Boleyn and ask them to decide if the marriage solved any of Henry's problems. Ask them to add another column to their grids called: "Did the solution work?"'. Then, 'Tell the story of Jane Seymour and the birth of Edward. Explain that although the birth of Edward seemed to solve one of Henry's problems, on Jane's death Henry still had a problem.'

His. 8, meanwhile, deals mainly with the lives of the rich and the poor in Tudor times. His. 19 discusses the Tudor exploration of the world, with emphasis on the exploits of Francis Drake during Elizabethan times; how problematic these aspects of Elizabeth's legacy stand in regard to issues of slavery are – at this point – difficult to ascertain. Perhaps one day Anne's life might be considered 'problematic' in some way – one need only recall the antisemitic stance of Luther – and the subject will thus be gouged from the curriculum; times change and attitudes with them, after all. However, this author for one doubts it. Her story is universal, and almost a part of the national psyche. An England without the ghost of Anne Boleyn quietly praying in the background is almost unthinkable.

Finally, when it comes to A-level and the like, the emphasis is less on how Anne's life is taught as opposed to getting the student to present an argument which they can back with the facts and opinions of other historians.

It is for said students to interpret these facts and then present a coherent argument to the question posed on the exam paper. In some of these papers, at least, Anne has been rightly referred to as '...a queen who inspired a revolution'. You can't argue with that one.

18

Fan Boleyn

'Anne Boleyn has become a virtual celebrity on whom
people project their own preoccupations and fantasies'
(Weir in Carrick 2013, pIV)

'It got me thinking that the beauty of Anne Boleyn, the
thing that draws us in and won't let go, is her mystery and
the fact that she can be all things to all people.'
(Ridgway, 2012, p239)

'History itself had become the semi-mythic template of
emotional life and self-definition.'
(Lewis, 1998, p88)

The interest in Anne Boleyn has culminated – particularly in the last
decade or so – with a strong online presence. *The Anne Boleyn Files*
website is a particular favourite, although there are countless others.
This author particularly enjoys *The Tudor Files* on Facebook, as well
as *Anne Boleyn Obsessed*. On these and various other sites, the cause
of Anne's rehabilitation is championed – unsurprisingly – by a mainly
female fanbase. She does, however, also boast rather a large following
in the gay community; a colleague was, at the time of writing, preparing
a paper entitled *'Anne of the thousand gays'*, proposing to delve into
just such an affinity in greater, rigorously academic, detail. However, the
fact that much of the membership of these forums appears to be female
stems mainly from the fact that Anne's manipulated media image has
come to represent a myriad of different meanings for different women;
wronged woman, tragic woman, temptress woman, traitor woman,
religious revolutionary woman, sexually voracious woman, etc. All of
these personas reflect very strongly certain roles in which women are
either expected to conform to, or to refrain from conforming to.

Visit any of those groups concerning Anne and one will see that whilst the various aspects of her life are discussed in some detail, the main thrust taken up by the members seems to be the rehabilitation of Anne's memory, based around twenty-first-century 'sanitised' notions of Anne as a bona fide 'historical celebrity'. The less salubrious sides of her history – adultery, incest – are discussed only under the terms by which they must be disproved once and for all, underlined by the all-consuming caveat that such slanderous accusations were the result of an all-consuming patriarchy and must therefore be false. To this end, even female historians who dare to hint at a kernel of guilt are roundly lambasted. Often, the groups will employ what they ascribe as 'feminist thinking' to re-evaluate various aspects of Anne's life, and also as a way of reinventing her as a role model for their own lives. For instance, when Anne needs to be seen as the victim of the all-consuming Tudor patriarchy, well, she was then most definitely forced into her role as the King's concubine by her family. Conversely, when her fanbase needs her to be a sassy social climber, then it appears that she in fact instigated much of Henry's pursuit on her own initiative, although few if any imagine that she was actually doing so purely to further her own Reformist agenda.

The various groups often include drawings or artwork made by the fans; there were/are entire sections devoted to such fare on *The Anne Boleyn Files*, for instance. The subject of 'fan fiction' runs alongside this avenue of expression, wherein aficionados write their own stories featuring their heroes or heroines, with 'slash fiction' being the more sexualised version of this genre. There also exists an entire gamut of works where Anne escapes the Swordsman of Calais and goes on to wreak all sorts of vengeful havoc on Henry VIII and Jane Seymour, and that's just for starters. Meanwhile, some fans take selfies dressed up as Anne – 'cosplay', as previously mentioned under merchandising – whilst others might video an entire pilgrimage to Hever Castle or some similar location and then post it online in an episodic format; sometimes on Facebook but more often these days on Instagram or TikTok instead.

One of the many visible results of the 'feminist thinking' evinced by so many of these online fans is the description of Anne as a 'feminist icon'. Eric Ives went so far as to call for her virtual canonisation as a feminist icon: 'She was the most influential and important queen consort this country has ever had. Indeed, Anne deserves to be a feminist icon, a woman in a society which was, above all else, male-dominated, who broke through the glass ceiling by sheer character and initiative.' (Ives, 2004, pxv.) The trouble is, it can be problematic to describe Anne as a 'feminist icon' unless the term 'feminist' is very loosely interpreted as merely signifying, in this instance, a woman seeking purely personal power, which is one of the most quoted, but erroneous, depictions of Anne Boleyn there ever was. She was not seeking personal power, for starters; she was seeking religious reform for the entire country. In exploring feminist icons, Katharine Sarikakis issues an implicit warning not 'to glorify popular icons and treat them in isolation, as "unique" cases or cases that herald "new" ways of thinking about women and feminism.' (Sarikakis, 2011, p116.) Added to which, 'The sixteenth century had never heard of feminism, and though much has undoubtedly been learned from studying women of the period, "gender studies" is a modern invention and has become a growth industry. Like all constructs projected onto the past it can be enlightening but also misleading.' (Porter, 2010, p33.) Any real, organised movement for the advancement of women – or, more plainly put, what the modern reader would understand as feminism – simply did not exist during Anne's lifetime. However, Anne Laurence has observed that 'there were women who were conscious of those rights, but they were individuals, not part of any political movement.' (Laurence, 1994, p253.) Therefore, the idea of Anne Boleyn as some sort of feminist icon can be considered almost entirely the creation of her fanbase, and as a natural development of her initial transformation from wanton woman into wronged religious heroine. The real Anne Boleyn would find the notion of a 'feminist icon' both baffling and also faintly blasphemous.

Where they do exist, feminist icons are lauded as much, if not more so, for their achievements than for their looks, but Anne's appearance is in fact of paramount importance to her legend. Although she remains to a large extent the archetypal 'other woman', the fact that she is reported as not having been a conventional beauty indicates an 'accessibility' that makes her less of a threatening figure than an otherwise 'out and out' beauty would be. This makes the fact that she achieved what she did seem all the more, for want of a better word, 'admirable'; an uncontested beauty who clearly traded on her looks to become queen of England would seem a less appealing prospect for a feminist audience. In fact, forget the 'pretty duckies' altogether; Anne

Boleyn got where she was via her heady cauldron of wit, well-timed flattery, and, above all, her intense and burning zeal to spread the love and forgiveness of Jesus Christ.

Outside of cyberspace, Anne Boleyn fans still have ample opportunity to show their devotion, albeit in a more traditional manner. Besides the Anne Boleyn Festival held in 2012 at Blickling Hall (and those masques of previous years), various exhibitions and the like pop up with reassuring regularity, offering spaces for like-minded fans to meet up in the flesh and discuss the fate of their favourite historical heroine. As previously mentioned, in 2022, Hever Castle showcased 'Becoming Anne: Connections, Culture, Court', documenting Anne's rise from her relatively humble beginnings to her time at the court of Margaret of Austria, and then beyond; refreshingly, more therein is devoted to Anne alive than to the final grim months of her life. A later exhibition tried – albeit with tepid success – to seek the similarities between Anne and Catherine of Aragon; well, it made a change from pitting the two of them in opposition. Hever Castle and other locations also play host to authors wishing to furnish talks and flog tomes. Also, various authors – Alison Weir in particular – often make themselves available for large-scale but rather costly countrywide tours which cover various key locations and involve, for the participants, a night or two in these particular places/ palaces. In fact, there has never been a better time to be an Anne Boleyn fan. When facing her death, she said, 'And if any person will meddle of my cause, I require them to judge the best.' In that respect, one hopes Anne would approve of the efforts of historians and fans alike who choose to judge her with compassion.

19

Timeline, from 1501 (or thereabouts) to 2023

1501	Anne is born at Blickling Hall in Norfolk
1504/5	The family move to Hever Castle in Kent
1509	Henry VIII becomes King of England (22 April)
1513	Anne is sent to the court of Margaret of Austria
1515	Anne becomes a lady-in-waiting for Queen Claude of France
1521/1522	Anne returns to England; 'The Chateau Vert' (4 March)
1523	Anne is courted by – and then loses – Henry Percy
1526 (or thereabouts)	Henry VIII begins courting Anne
1528	Anne contracts the Sweating Sickness but survives (summer)
1530	Cardinal Wolsey dies (29 November)
1532	Anne is created Marquess of Pembroke (1 September); Henry and Anne secretly marry (14 November)
1533	Henry and Anne publicly marry (25 January); Anne is crowned Queen of England (1 June); Elizabeth is born (7 September)
1535	Bishop Fisher is beheaded (22 June); Thomas More is beheaded (6 July)

1536	Catherine of Aragon dies (7 January); Anne miscarries for the final time (29 January); John Skip preaches his controversial sermon against Cromwell (2 April); Mark Smeaton is arrested on Cromwell's orders and shortly confesses to adultery with Anne (30 April); Anne and several members of her court, including her brother, are arrested (2 May); George Boleyn and the others accused are beheaded while Anne's marriage to the King is annulled (17 May); Anne herself is beheaded (19 May)

1538	Elizabeth Boleyn dies (3 April)
1539	Thomas Boleyn dies (12 March)
1540	Hever Castle passes to Henry VIII's fourth wife, Anne of Cleves, as part of their divorce settlement
1542	George Boleyn's widow, 'The infamous Lady Rochford', is beheaded (13 February)
1543	Mary Boleyn dies (19 July)
1547	Henry VIII dies (28 January)
1558	Elizabeth ascends to the throne as Elizabeth I (17 November)
1603	Elizabeth dies; the Tudor era comes to a close (24 March)

1920	*Anna Boleyn* premieres
1933	*The Private Life of Henry VIII* premieres

1969	*Anne of the Thousand Days* premieres
1970	*The Six Wives of Henry VIII* premieres (TV)
1972	*Henry VIII and His Six Wives* premieres
1986	Eric Ives publishes *Anne Boleyn*
2001	*The Other Boleyn Girl* is published
2004	A revised version of Ives' work – now *The Life and Death of Anne Boleyn*, is published
2007	*The Tudors* premieres (TV)
2008	*The Other Boleyn Girl* premieres
2009	*Wolf Hall* is published
2012	*Bring Up the Bodies* is published
2015	*Wolf Hall* premieres on BBC Two (TV)
2017	*SIX* premieres at the Edinburgh Festival Fringe
2021	*Anne Boleyn* premieres on Channel 5, with the first black actress cast in the role (TV)

Bibliography

Ackroyd, Peter, 2012, *The History of England Volume II – Tudors*, London: Macmillan

Aslan, Reza, 2014, *Zealot – The Life and Times of Jesus of Nazareth*, London: The Westbourne Press

Bagley, J. J., 1962, *Henry VIII*, London: B. T. Batsford Ltd.

Baldwin Smith, Lacey, 1969, *The Elizabethan Epic*, London: Panther History

    2010, *Catherine Howard*, Gloucestershire: Amberley Publishing

Bavidge, Eleanor, 2013, The 'When' of Memory: Contemporary Memorials to Distant and Violent Pasts, *International Journal of Cultural Studies*, volume 16, issue 4, pp319-334.

Bellafante, Ginia, 2008, 'Nasty, but Not So Brutish and Short', *The New York Times*, 28 March 2008, https://www.nytimes.com/2008/03/28/arts/television/28tudo.html, para. 7 of 8

Bernard, G.W., 2011, *Anne Boleyn – Fatal Attractions*, London: Yale University Press

Bernstein, Alon & Scharf, Isaac, 2019, 'Mary Magdalene was not a prostitute but a devoted disciple who supported Jesus financially and spiritually, scholars say', *Independent*, 1st April 2019, https://www.independent.co.uk/news/world/middle-east/mary-magdalene-feminism-metoo-jesus-disciples-apostle-christianity-judaism-pope-francis-vatican-a8281731.html, para. 4 & 5 of 22

Bordo, Susan, 2013, *The Creation of Anne Boleyn*, New York: Houghton Mifflin Harcourt

Borman, Tracy, 2014, *Thomas Cromwell*, London: Hodder & Stoughton

    2017, *The Private Lives of the Tudors*, London: Hodder & Stoughton

    2019, *Henry VIII and the Men Who Made Him,* London: Hodder & Stoughton

    2023, *Anne Boleyn & Elizabeth I*, London: Hodder & Stoughton

Brenton, Howard, 2010, 'Anne Boleyn: Drama Queen', *Independent*, 23rd June 2010, http://www.independent.co.uk/arts-entertainment/theatre-dance/features/anne-boleyn-drama-queen-2007616.html, para. 2 of 14

Brenton, Howard, 2011, *Anne Boleyn*, London: Nick Hern Books

Brown, Mark, 2017, Students Take Hilary Mantel Novels as Fact, says Historian, *The Guardian*, 31st May 2017, https://www.theguardian.com/books/2017/may/31/students-take-hilary-mantels-tudor-novels-as-fact-hay-festival, para. 5 of 25

Bullough, Vern L., 2003, *Historical Overview Psychology and Human Sexuality*, volume 14, issue 2-3, pp17-33.

Bunbury, Selina, 1844, *The Star of the Court: or the Maid of Honour and Queen of England,* London: Grant and Griffith

Carrick, Joanna, 2013, *Fallen in Love – The Secret Heart of Anne Boleyn*, Ipswich: Red Rose Chain

Castor, H.M., 2005, *VIII*, Surrey: Templar Publishing

Collinson, Patrick, 2005, *The Reformation*, London: Phoenix

Cooper, John, 2012, *The Queen's Agent – Francis Walsingham at the Court of Elizabeth I*, London: Faber and Faber

Davies, C.S.L., 1976, *Peace, Print and Protestantism 1450 - 1558*, London: Hart-Davis, MacGibbon

Denny, Joanna, 2004, *Anne Boleyn*, London: Portrait
    2008, *Katherine Howard – A Tudor conspiracy*, London: Piatkus Books

Dickens, A.G., 1965, *The English Reformation*, London: B. T. Batsford Ltd

Dobson, Michael & Watson, Nicola J., 2004, *England's Elizabeth*, Oxford: Oxford University Press

Du Garde Peach, L., 1973, *Henry VIII*, Loughborough: Ladybird Books

Dunn, Jane, 2003, *Elizabeth & Mary*, London: Harper Perennial

Emmerson, Owen & Ridgway, Claire, 2021, *The Boleyns of Hever Castle*, UK: MadeGlobal Publishing
    & McCaffrey, Kate, 2022, *Becoming Anne – Connections, Culture, Court*, Exeter: Jigsaw Design and Publishing

Fletcher, Catherine, 2013, *The Divorce of Henry VIII – The Untold Story*, London: Vintage Books

Fox, Julia, 2008, *Jane Boleyn – The Infamous Lady Rochford*, London: Phoenix

Fraser, Antonia, 1993, *The Six Wives of Henry VIII*, London: Phoenix Press

Friedmann, P., 2013, *Anne Boleyn*, Gloucestershire: Amberley Publishing

George, Margaret, 1988, *The Autobiography of Henry VIII*, London: Pan Books

Golby, Joel, 2016, 'Six Wives with Lucy Worsley: why TV history shows are for the chop', *The Guardian*, 7 December 2016, https://www.theguardian.com/tv-and-radio/2016/dec/07/six-wives-with-lucy-worsley-henry-viii-history, para. 4 of 7

Grady, Constance, 2021, 'Six, the long-delayed pop musical about Henry VIII's six wives, is glorious nonsense', *Vox*, 4 October 2021, https://www.vox.com/culture/21171636/six-broadway-musical-review, para. 25 of 27

Gregory, Phillipa, 2001, *The Other Boleyn Girl*, London: Harper Collins Publishers

> 2007, *The Boleyn Inheritance*, London: Harper Collins Publishers

Grueninger, Natalie & Morris, Sarah, 2015, *In the footsteps of Anne Boleyn*, Gloucestershire: Amberley Publishing

> 2022 *The Final Year of Anne Boleyn*, Barnsley: Pen and Sword History

Guy, John, 1990, *Tudor England*, Oxford: Oxford University Press

> 2017, *Elizabeth – The Forgotten Years*, London: Penguin Books

Hackett, Helen, 1995, *Virgin Mother, Maiden Queen*, London: The Macmillan Press Ltd

Haigh, Christopher, 1993, *English Reformations - Religion, Politics, and Society under the Tudors*, Oxford: Oxford University Press

Hattersley, Roy, 2018, *The Catholics*, London: Vintage

Hibbert, Christopher, 1992, *The Virgin Queen – The Personal History of Elizabeth I*, London: Penguin Books

Hutchinson, Robert, 2006, *The Last Days of Henry VIII*, London: Phoenix

> 2008, *Thomas Cromwell*, London: Phoenix

Ives, Eric, 2004, *The Life and Death of Anne Boleyn*, Oxford: Blackwell Publishing

Jenkins, Elizabeth, 1965, *Elizabeth the Great*, London: Methuen & Co Ltd

Knecht, R.J., 1996, *Renaissance Warrior and Patron: The Reign of Francis I*, Cambridge: Cambridge University Press

Larson, Frances, 2014, *Severed – A History of Heads Lost and Heads Found*, London: Granta Publications

Laurence, Anne, 1994, *Women in England 1500 – 1760*, London: Phoenix Press

Legardye, Quinci, 2021, *Jodie Turner-Smith on Becoming Anne Boleyn* https://www.harpersbazaar.com/culture/film-tv/a38474875/jodie-turner-smith-anne-boleyn-interview/, para. 10 of 14

Lewis, Jayne Elizabeth, 1998, *Mary Queen of Scots – Romance and Nation*, London: Routledge

Licence, Amy, 2015, *The Six Wives & Many Mistresses of Henry VIII*, Gloucestershire: Amberley Publishing
    2016, *Catherine of Aragon*, Gloucestershire: Amberley Publishing
    2018, *Anne Boleyn*, Gloucestershire: Amberley Publishing

Lindsey, Karen, 1995, *Divorced, Beheaded, Survived – A Feminist Reinterpretation of the Wives of Henry VIII*, USA: Da Capo Press

Lipscomb, Suzannah, 2009, *1536 the Year that Changed Henry VIII*, Oxford: Lion

Loades, David, 2011, *The Boleyns*, Gloucestershire: Amberley Publishing
    2013, *Jane Seymour*, Gloucestershire: Amberley Publishing
    2014, *Thomas Cromwell*, Gloucestershire: Amberley Publishing
    2017, *The Seymours of Wolf Hall*, Gloucestershire: Amberley Publishing

Lofts, Norah, 1979, *Anne Boleyn*, London: Book Club Associates
    2006, *The King's Pleasure*, Gloucestershire: Torc
    The Concubine, Gloucestershire: Torc

Louise Bruce, Marie, 1972, *Anne Boleyn*, London: Collins

MacCulloch, Diarmaid, 2009, *A History of Christianity*, London: Allen Lane
    2019, *Thomas Cromwell*, London: Penguin Books

Mandell, Jonathan, 2021, 'Six review: Wronged queens in a Broadway musical of sonic wave feminism', *New York Theatre*, 7 October 2021, https://newyorktheater.me/2021/10/07/six-review-wronged-queens-in-a-broadway-musical-of-sonic-wave-feminism/, para. 9 of 10

Mantel, Hilary, 2009, *Wolf Hall*, London: Fourth Estate
    2012, *Bring Up the Bodies*, London: Fourth Estate
    2020, *The Mirror and the Light*, London: Fourth Estate

Marius, Richard, 1984, *Thomas More*, USA: Alfred A. Knopf, Inc.

Martel, Frederic, 2019, *In the Closet of the Vatican – Power, Homosexuality, Hypocrisy*, London: Bloomsbury Continuum

Matusiak, John, 2014, *Wolsey – The Life of King Henry VIII's Cardinal*, Gloucestershire: The History Press

Mayhew, Mickey, 2022, *House of Tudor – A Grisly History*, Barnsley: Pen and Sword History

Moorman, J.R.H., 1973, *A History Church in England*, London: Adam & Charles Black

Neale, J.E., 1960, *Queen Elizabeth I*, Middlesex: Penguin Books

Nolan, Hayley, 2019, *Anne Boleyn – 500 years of lies*, New York: Little A

Norton, Elizabeth, 2008, *Anne Boleyn*, Gloucestershire: Amberley Publishing

    2009, *Jane Seymour*, Gloucestershire: Amberley Publishing

    2013, *The Boleyn Women*, Gloucestershire: Amberley Publishing

Nussbaum, Emily, 2015, 'Queens Boulevard', *The New Yorker*, 27 April 2015, https://www.newyorker.com/magazine/2015/05/04/queens-boulevard, para. 3 of 11 [accessed 26 July 2022]

Paton, Maureen, 2008, 'Boho Boleyn girl: Actress Natalie Dormer', *Mail Online*, 7 November 2008, https://www.dailymail.co.uk/home/you/article-1081189/Boho-Boleyn-girl-Actress-Natalie-Dormer.html, para. 17 of 53

Patterson, Troy, 2007, 'Blazingly gratuitous sex - and other missteps in The Tudors', *Slate*, 30 March 2007, https://slate.com/culture/2007/03/the-tudors-reviewed.html, para. 6 of 6

Penn, Thomas, 2012, 'Booker Prize winner Hilary Mantel on Bring up the Bodies: the quicksilver queen', *The Telegraph*, 7 May 2012 http://www.telegraph.co.uk/culture/hay-festival/9243796/Booker-Prize-winner-Hilary-Mantel-on-Bring-up-the-Bodies-the-quicksilver-queen.html, para. 13 of 22

Plowden, Alison, 2010, *Danger to Elizabeth*, Gloucestershire: The History Press

    Two Queens in One Isle, Gloucestershire: The History Press

Porter, Linda, 2010, *Katherine the Queen*, London: Pan Books

Raeside, Julia, 2015, 'Claire Foy: Wolf Hall's perfectly complex Anne Boleyn', *The Guardian*, 26 February 2015 https://www.theguardian.com/tv-and-radio/2015/feb/26/claire-foy-wolf-hall-perfect-anne-boleyn, para. 3 of 7

Randell, Keith & Turvey, Roger, 2008, *Henry VIII to Mary I: Government and Religion, 1509 - 58*, London: Hodder Education

Rice, Anne, 1993, *Lasher*, New York: Ballantine Books

Ridgway, Claire, 2012, *The Anne Boleyn Collection*, London: MadeGlobal Publishing

Ridley, Jasper, 2002, *Elizabeth I*, London: Penguin Books

Robison, William B. (editor), 2016, *History, Fiction, and The Tudors – Sex, Politics, Power, and Artistic Licence in the Showtime Television series*, London: Palgrave Macmillan

Russo, Stephanie, 2020, *The Afterlife of Anne Boleyn - Representations of Anne Boleyn in Fiction and on the Screen (Queenship and Power)*, London: Palgrave Macmillan

Sarikakis, Katharine, 2011, Arriving at a crossroads, *Feminist media studies*, volume 11, issue 1, pp. 115-122.

Sergeant, Philip W., 1924, *The Life of Anne Boleyn*, New York: D. Appleton and Company

Soberton, Sylvia Barbara, 2022, *Ladies-in-Waiting: Women who served Anne Boleyn*, Slovenia: Golden Age Publishing

Somerset, Anne, 1997, *Elizabeth I*, London: Phoenix

Stanley, Alessandra, 2007, 'Renaissance Romping With Henry and His Ratpack', *The New York Times*, 30 March 2007, https://www.nytimes.com/2007/03/30/arts/television/30tudo.html, para. 5 of 19

Starkey, David, 2004, *Six Wives – the Queens of Henry VIII*, London: Vintage

Talbot, John Michael, 1998, *The Lessons of St. Francis – How to Bring Simplicity and Spirituality Into Your Daily Life,* London: Plume

Tremlett, Giles, 2010, *Catherine of Aragon*, London: Faber and Faber Limited

Turpyn, Richard, 1846, *The Chronicle of Calais in the Reigns of Henry VII. and Henry VIII. To the year 1540.* (edited by John Gough Nichols, F.S.A.), London: The Camden Society

van Krieken, Robert, 2012, *Celebrity Society*, Oxon: Routledge

Warnicke, Retha, 1989, *The Rise and Fall of Anne Boleyn*, Cambridge: Cambridge University Press
> 2000, *The Marrying of Anne of Cleves – Royal Protocol in Tudor England*, Cambridge: Cambridge University Press

Weir, Alison, 2007, *The Six Wives of Henry VIII*, London: Vintage Books
> 2008, *Henry VIII King and Court*, London: Jonathan Cape
> *Elizabeth the Queen*, London: Vintage Books

2009, *The Lady in the Tower – the Fall of Anne Boleyn*, London: Jonathan Cape

2011, *Mary Boleyn – 'The Great and Infamous Whore'*, London: Jonathan Cape

2016, *Six Tudor Queens – Katherine of Aragon – The True Queen*, London: Headline Review

2017, *Six Tudor Queens – Anne Boleyn – A King's Obsession*, London: Headline Review

2018, *Six Tudor Queens – Jane Seymour – The Haunted Queen*, London: Headline Review

White, Adam, 2021, 'Anne Boleyn Review: Jodie Turner-Smith is suitably arch in this very silly historical drama', *Independent*, 1 June 2021 https://www.independent.co.uk/arts-entertainment/tv/reviews/anne-boleyn-review-jodie-turner-smith-b1856923.html, para. 6 of 7

Williams, Holly, 2022, 'Six the Musical Review', *Time Out*, 30 May 2022 https://www.timeout.com/london/theatre/six-the-musical-review, para 4 of 10

Filmography

Anna Boleyn, d. Ernst Lubitsch (1920, Germany, 118 mins)

Anne Boleyn, d. Lynsey Miller (2021, UK, 45 mins (av.) per episode)

Anne of the Thousand Days, d. Charles Jarrott (1969, UK, 145 mins)

Elizabeth R, d. Roderick Graham & others (1971, UK, 85 mins per episode)

Elizabeth — The Golden Age, d. Shekhar Kapur (2007, UK, 114 mins)

Henry VIII, d. Will Barker (1911, UK, 40 mins)

Henry VIII, d. Pete Travis (2003, UK, 95 mins per episode)

Henry VIII and His Six Wives, d. Waris Hussein (1972, UK, 125 mins)

Henry VIII: the Mind of a Tyrant, d. David Sington (2009, UK, 50 mins per episode)

Horrible Histories, d. Steve Connelly, Simon Gibney, Ian Curtis (2009 – 2013; 2015 - present, UK, 30 mins per episode)

Six Wives with Lucy Worsley, d. Russell England (2016, UK, 58 mins per episode)

The Last Days of Anne Boleyn, d. Rob Coldstream (2013, UK, 60 mins)

The Other Boleyn Girl, d. Justin Chadwick (2008, UK, 115 mins)

Filmography

The Private Life of Henry VIII, d. Alexander Korda (1933, UK, 97 mins)

The Six Wives of Henry VIII, d. Naomi Capon & John Glenister (1970, UK, 85 mins per episode)

The Tudors, d. Ciaran Donnelly & others (2007 – 2010, USA, 55 mins per episode)

Wolf Hall, d. Peter Kosminsky (2015, UK, 60-65 mins per episode)

Index

A

A Man for all Seasons, 59, 154
Aless, Alexander, 97
Anna Bolena, 75, 152
Anna Boleyn, 152–154, 183
Anne Boleyn (TV Series), xi, 145, 167–169, 171
Anne of Cleves, 137, 153, 173, 183
Anne of the Thousand Days, 31, 144, 154–155, 184

B

Barker, William, 84
Barking, 82, 175
Barton, Elizabeth, 60–61
Bavidge, Eleanor, 174
Blanchett, Cate, 156
Blickling Hall, 1–5, 8–9, 11, 173, 181–182
Blount, Bessie, 22, 28, 34, 45
Bocking, Edward, 61
Boleyn, Anne, viii–xi, 1–8, 10–11, 13–14, 16–18, 20–22, 24–28, 30–32, 34, 36–38, 40, 42–44, 46, 48, 50, 52–58, 60–62, 64, 66–70, 72–75, 77–78, 80–82, 84–86, 88, 90–92, 94, 96, 98–104, 106–110, 112–116, 118, 120, 122, 124–126, 128–164, 166–168, 170–181, 184

Boleyn, Elizabeth, 5, 159, 183
Boleyn, Geoffrey, 3, 5, 9
Boleyn, George, 29, 37, 55, 63, 77, 89, 100, 122–124, 137, 152, 158, 169, 183
Boleyn, Lady, 103
Boleyn, Mary, 19, 27–28, 30–32, 34, 112, 118, 136, 148–149, 154, 157–160, 183
Boleyn, Thomas, 4–6, 9, 12–14, 17–19, 22, 24, 27–28, 32–33, 58, 81, 89, 103, 113–114, 135–136, 148, 159, 163–164, 171, 183
Boleyn, William, 5, 9
Bonham Carter, Helen, 156
Bordo, Susan, 21, 148, 155, 159, 163
Bourbon, Nicholas, 37
Bowman, Courtney, 171
Brandon, Charles, 14, 18, 27, 71, 113
Breame, Richard, 175
Breathnach, Tara, 161
Brenton, Howard, xi, 158
Brereton, William, 107, 124, 141, 165
Briem, Anita, 165
Bring up the Bodies, xi, 58, 68, 106, 149, 159, 184
Brooke, Elizabeth, 33

Bujold, Genevieve, 154–155, 163
Bunbury, Selina, 1, 143
Burton, Richard, 154–155
Butler, Lady Margaret, 5, 18, 35, 135, 148

C
Camden, William, 2
Campeggio, Cardinal, 46
Carew, Nicholas, 54, 68, 89
Carey, William, 28–29, 46, 112, 158
Casali, Gregorio, 65
Catherine of Aragon, ix, 5–6, 13, 19, 21–22, 24, 26, 28, 31–32, 42, 45–46, 48, 50, 53, 57, 59–61, 64, 66–67, 69–70, 73, 75, 77, 80, 85, 90–92, 96, 98–101, 103–109, 115, 118, 128, 133, 136, 139, 144, 150, 158, 160, 162, 164, 166, 170, 177, 181, 183
Cavill, Henry, 14
Chapuys, Eustace, 21
Charles V, Holy Roman Emperor, 12, 21, 46, 55, 91–94, 128, 132
Claude, Queen of France, 12, 15–18, 182
Cobham, Nan, 113
Coffin, Margaret, 103
Countess of Worcester, 72, 99, 104, 108
Cowrie, Laura, 152
Cranmer, Archbishop, 55–57, 67, 71–72, 91, 109, 118–119, 124
Cromwell, Thomas, 2, 4–6, 9, 11–14, 17–19, 21–22, 24, 26–28, 32–33, 37, 40, 49–51,
53, 55, 57–60, 66, 81–82, 89, 93, 103, 105, 108, 113–114, 119, 135–138, 148–149, 158–159, 163–164, 166, 171, 182–183
Czerny, Henry, 4

D
d'Angoulême, Margaret, 15–17, 40, 64, 153
da Vinci, Leonardo, 16
de Carle, Lancelot, 104
Denny, Joanna, 17, 147
Doctor Who, 159
Dormer, Natalie, x, 38, 157, 163–164, 166–167, 173
Doyle Kennedy, Maria, 164
Drake, Francis, 177
Dunning, Nick, 163

E
Elizabeth (Film), 156
Elizabeth I, x, 3, 63, 65, 67, 69, 71, 73, 75, 139, 141, 148, 165, 167, 183
Ellis, Margaret, 68
Eltham Palace, 65–66, 74–75
Erasmus, 19, 39–40, 56

F
Fish, Simon, 49–50
Fisher, Bishop, 40, 50–53, 60, 75, 81–82, 86, 105, 124, 182
Fitzroy, Henry, 22, 105, 107
Foole, Jane, 68
Foxe, John, 40
Foy, Claire, 62, 150, 159
Francis I, 15, 17, 29, 63–64

G

George, Margaret, 145
Greenwich Palace, 22, 73,
    97–100, 107
Gregory, Philippa, 149, 156, 167
Guildford, Henry, 67
Guy, John, 22, 56, 149

H

Hampton Court Palace, 14, 22,
    57, 135, 140
Heath, Nicholas, 84
Henry VIII, viii–x, 1–2, 4–6,
    8, 10, 13–26, 28–29, 31–37,
    41, 45–74, 77–83, 85–107,
    109, 111–119, 124–125,
    128–130, 132, 135–137,
    139–145, 147–148, 150,
    152–171, 173, 175–177, 179,
    182–184
Henry VIII and his Six Wives,
    155, 184
Herod Antipas, 81
Hever Castle, x, 2, 5, 8–11,
    27–28, 32, 35, 46, 131, 135,
    144, 151, 154, 172, 175, 179,
    181–183
Hill, Bernard, 4, 159
Hogan, Bosco, 81
Horrible Histories, 161,
    174–175
Howard, Catherine, 14, 111–112,
    137, 144, 153, 173–174
Howards, Thomas (Duke of
    Norfolk), 4, 18, 63–64, 72,
    79, 82, 87, 100, 104, 113,
    158–159
Hunter, Sophie, 161

I

I am Henry, 161
Ives, Eric, 17, 41, 98, 146, 167,
    179, 184

J

Jack the Ripper, 175
Jane Boleyn, 63, 77–78, 100,
    113, 115, 130, 137, 158,
    166, 183
Jesus Christ, 10, 36–37, 126,
    132, 181
Johansson, Scarlett, 157, 159

K

Keith, Fleur, 161
Kevin & Perry Go Large, 156
Kingston, Lady, 103
Kingston, William, 101, 103, 117,
    119, 124, 128

L

Latymer, William, 40
Laughton, Charles, 153
Lindsey, Karen, 147
Lofts, Nora, 149
Louis XII of France, 13, 15, 27
Louise of Savoy, 17, 153
Luke, Lady Eleanor, 77, 165
Luther, Martin, 21, 24–26, 39–43,
    49–50, 55–56, 58, 79–80, 83,
    94, 177

M

Magdalene, Mary, 43–44
Manson, Amy, 162
Mantel, Hilary, 48, 56, 62, 96,
    127, 148–150, 159–160

Margaret of Austria, 2, 12, 14, 100, 151, 181–182
Mary Queen of Scots, 54, 64, 152, 173
Mary Tudor, x, 2, 19, 33, 53–54, 66, 68, 103, 118, 130, 132, 139
McFly, 157
Mechelen, 12, 14–15, 18
More, Thomas, 19, 21, 24, 40, 50, 53, 57–60, 82, 114, 182
Morrissey, David, 158

N
Nisbet, Peggy, 172
Nolan, Hayley, 44, 88, 99, 159
Norris, Henry, 98, 100, 103, 106, 124, 141

O
O'Connell, Millie, 171
Oberon, Merle, 153
Orchard, Mrs, 103

P
Page, Richard, 108
Parr, Catherine, 30, 68, 141, 170
Paul (Apostle), 3–4, 40, 43–44, 61, 69–71, 81, 165
Percy, Henry, 31–32, 48, 63–64, 115, 182
Pontius Pilate, 81
Pope Gregory I, 43
Pope Leo X, 56
Pope Paul III, 81, 165
Pope Paul VI, 44
Porten, Henny, 152
Portman, Natalie, 156–157
Potter, Harry, 156

Princess Diana, 162, 166
Prisoner Cell Block H, 4
Purkoy, 78–79

Q
Queen Claude of France, 182

R
Raison, Miranda, 159
Rampling, Charlotte, 155
Redgrave, Vanessa, 154
Redman, Joyce, 154
Revell, Tristram, 42
Rice, Anne, 145
Rich, Richard, 81–82
Rouse, Richard, 51–52
Rylance, Mark, 158–159

S
Saint John the Baptist, 16, 81
Salle, 3, 43
Sanders, Nicholas, 140
Scott Thomas, Kristin, 158
Seymour, Jane, 36, 54, 68, 77, 79, 85–87, 89, 95–98, 113, 116, 130, 136, 138, 143, 147, 150, 152, 159, 165, 169, 176–177, 179
Shelton, Lady, 103
Shelton, Margaret ('Madge'), 77, 79, 103, 106–107
Six (Musical), 170
Skip, John, 42, 90, 96, 107, 117, 124, 183
Smeaton, Mark, 61, 76–77, 79, 81, 83, 85, 87, 89, 91, 93, 95, 97, 99, 101, 103–105, 107, 109, 111, 124, 141, 152, 160, 165, 183

Soberton, Sylvia Barbara, 151
Spencer, 162, 166
Stafford, William, 27, 29, 158
Stonor, Mrs, 103
Strickland, Agnes, 142–143
Symonnet, 13

T
Talbot, Mary, 31, 64
Tetezel, Johann, 83
The Concubine, 21, 104, 125, 144–145
The Other Boleyn Girl, xi, 5, 27, 29–30, 145, 147, 149, 156–158, 161, 184
The Simpsons, 157
The Six Wives of Henry VIII, 144, 155, 161, 184
The Swordsman of Calais, 37, 125–129, 133, 166, 179
The Tudors TV, 147, 149, 161, 173
The Virgin Mary, 36, 60, 70
Tower of London, x, 37, 42, 52, 59, 61, 69, 78, 81–82, 101, 104, 106, 113, 116, 125, 137, 147, 150, 154, 160, 166, 169, 172–175
Tudor, Margaret, 5
Tudor, Mary (Queen of France), 15, 27–28, 74, 139
Turner Smith, Jodie, xi, 145, 167–169, 171

Tutin, Dorothy, 155
Tyndale, William, 49–50, 59, 159

U
Ugly Betty, 159, 172

W
Wakefield, Charity, 159–160
Walsingham, Edmund, 101
Warham, Archbishop, 55, 60, 62
Warnicke, Retha, 74, 88, 111, 123, 146–147
Weir, Alison, x, 1, 21, 27–28, 32, 127, 131, 135, 143, 149–151, 158–159, 170, 172, 178, 181
Weir, Ashleigh, 170
West Ham, 175
Weston, Francis, 106–107, 114, 123, 141, 165
Whelan, Gemma, 161
Wingfield, Lady, 99, 112, 114
Wolf Hall, xi, 4, 48, 58, 62, 68, 82, 85, 96, 106, 149, 158–159, 184
Wolsey, Cardinal, 18, 23, 26, 31, 33, 46, 48–49, 51, 53, 56, 58, 63, 105, 152, 160, 182
Wyatt, Thomas, 33, 66, 105, 108, 119
Wycliffe, John, 25

Y
York Place, 23, 29, 48